Cyril of Scythopolis

LIVES OF
THE MONKS OF
PALESTINE

Errata

Page	line	Should be
xxvi	n. 32	'Spoudaili' ▸ 'Spoudaioi'
xxix	19	(170.21–171.5)
xlvii	¶11, 5	(180–181.14–17)
1	17	Naziansus ▸ Nazianzus
3–83	running heads (right)	*Introduction* ▸ *The Life of Euthymius*
15	4–5	barbarianis ▸ barbarians
45	48,15	*delete* Roubâ
60	64,5	ut ▸ out
81	82,31	asiduous ▸ assiduous
98	90,10	out it ▸ about it
113	104,18	be man ▸ by man
116	107,26	set off off ▸ set off
118	109.13	wealthy ▸ wealth
159	149,18	Euthyches ▸ Eutyches
160	150, 9	an ▸ and
178	13–16	*should read* distress exclusively, filling all its cisterns, on his being asked by its inmates and praying. On hearing this, the archbishop summoned blessed Sabas
197	188,14	inexperience ▸ inexperienced
199	190,6	hersy ▸ heresy
201	192, 14	Al ▸ All
202	193.	Your minds ▸ our minds
212	n. 39	Jerusalemvers ▸ Jerusalem vers
213	n. 42	Churchof ▸ Church of
215	n. 72	(see n. 41) ▸ (see n. 40)
		November 412 ▸ November 512
221	202,7	cannot; bear ▸ cannot bear
222	203,20	church ▸ the church
224	205, 8	suprised ▸ surprised
	205,10	wished ▸ wishes
	205,12	it was time ▸ it was at this time
232	212,25	*delete*: and enclosed him in
	213.10	*delete*: compelled by
236	217,15	form ▸ from
	217,18	form ▸ from
238	last 3 lines	*should read*: me. Do not exert yourself but rather wait, and, wherever you are staying . . .
243	n. 15	60,3 ▸ 64,3.
245	223,9–10	spending days and nights on them, when still young, was struck with amazement
247	224,10	*delete*: salem in the eighteenth year
248	225,9–10	*delete*: Consequently, in the for him
	23	*should read:* took a cell and became a solitary in the twenty-seventh year of his life
	bottom line	mode of ▸ mode of life.
252	229,22	nonnus ▸ Nonnus
253	230,4	totaldestruction ▸ total destruction
258	234,30	*delete*: his hundred-
260	n. 9	Gregoy ▸ Gregory
		Ad Eunomium ▸ *Adv. Eunomium (First Theological Oration)*
262	236, 4	Mogariassus ▸ Mogarissus
271	7	bay ▸ by
279	355,22	he said ▸ it said
281	notes 5–12	Renumber as notes 4–11. Delete present note 4

LIVES OF THE MONKS
OF PALESTINE

by

Cyril of Scythopolis

Translated by

R. M. Price

with an Introduction and Notes by

John Binns

Cistercian Publications
Kalamazoo, Michigan
1991

This translation is made from the Greek, edited by E. Schwartz, *Kyrillos von Skythopolis*, Texte und Untersuchungen 49:2. Leipzig 1939, with minor additions from the Georgian and Arabic versions.

The work of Cistercian Publications is made possible in part
by support from Western Michigan University to
The Institute of Cistercian Studies.

Available elsewhere (including Canada) from the publisher
Cistercian Publications
Distribution: St Joseph's Abbey
Spencer, Massachusetts 01562

Editorial Offices: Institute of Cistercian Studies
Western Michigan University
Kalamazoo, Michigan 49008

Library of Congress Cataloguing-in-Publication Data
Cyril, of Scythopolis, ca. 524-ca. 558
    Lives of the Monks of Palestine / by Cyril of Scythopolis ;
    translated by R.M. Price ; with an introduction and notes by John
    Binns.
          p.   cm. -- (Cistercian studies series ; no. 114)
    Includes bibliographical references.
    ISBN 0-87907-714-X. -- ISBN 0-87907-914-2 (pbk.)
    1. Christian saints--Palestine--Biography--Early works to 1800.
    2. Monks--Palestine--Biography--Early works to 1800. 3. Monasticism
    and religious orders--Palestine--History--Early church, ca. 30-600.
    4. Palestine--Church history. I. Price, R. M. (Richard M.)
    II. Binns, John, 1951-   . III. Title. IV. Series.
    BR1710.C912   1990
    271'.0092'25694--dc20
    [B]

Printed in the United States of America.

PREFACE

MY PERSONAL DISCOVERY of the writing of Cyril of Scythopolis took place six years ago when I was beginning a period of research into the history of the church in the century after the Council of Chalcedon. I was immediately captivated by the clarity and pace of his prose style, the vivid portrait of life in the monastic desert, and the placing of the events described in the perspective of the history of the Church and the Empire. I found it hard to understand why so little attention had been paid to the monastic life of Palestine, compared with that given to its neighbours Egypt and Syria. My research quickly came to concentrate on Cyril.

To have shared in the production of this volume which makes Cyril's Lives available in English for the first time has, then, been a very great pleasure. R. M. Price's faithful yet lively—at times almost racy—translation preserves the flavour of Cyril's set of biographies. It is made from the Greek text edited by Eduard Schwartz in 1939. Three sections found in Georgian or Arabic versions, but not in the Greek, are added at 222.17, 226.3 and 247.22 (in either the text or the notes). The modest quantity of literature about Cyril is set out in a separate section of the Bibliography. Invaluable is Derwas Chitty's classic study *The Desert a City*, which amplifies Cyril's narrative with evidence from other sources.

Having spent several years combining study at King's College, London, with ministry in a busy parish, I cannot let slip this opportunity of recording my gratitude to those who have generously encouraged me: Stuart Hall, who has supervised my work; Peter Selby, Bishop of Kingston, who arranged a period of study leave at a critical moment; the Community of the Sisters of the Church at Ham Common, Surrey, who provided truly monastic hospitality during that period; the clergy and people of the parishes of Mortlake and East Sheen and of Holy Trinity, Upper Tooting: and, of course, Sue and William, my wife and son, who cheerfully accepted even greater disruption to the home than usual. Needless to say, the Cistercian Publications have been supportive and patient throughout.

John Binns

TABLE OF CONTENTS

INTRODUCTION

1. PALESTINIAN MONASTICISM, FACTS AND TEXTS

BETWEEN THE DEEP VALLEY which contains the Jordan river and the Dead Sea, and the hill country of Judaea, in which Jerusalem and Bethlehem are situated, lies a narrow stretch of desert country about ten miles wide. It evokes memories of the great ascetics of the Bible, Elijah and John the Baptist; and many valleys, caves, and springs claim to be the sites of events in their lives.[1] The combination of the empty landscape and biblical associations presented a persuasive invitation to those seeking to live an ascetic life. Among those who responded was the saintly Narcissus, Bishop of Jerusalem, who became exhausted by the slander and intrigues in his diocese and lived for many years in a retreat in the desert.[2] His retirement took place in the early third Century and shows the existence of desert ascetics in the years before the monastic life became popular.

At the end of the third and during the fourth Centuries, the first monasteries appeared. Recognisable monastic communities evolved more or less simultaneously in different parts of Egypt, Syria, and Palestine. In Egypt, Anthony left his village for the desert in about 271. In Mesopotamia, James of Nisibis and Julian Saba had attracted their first followers well before the Council of Nicaea (325). According to tradition, the first monk in Palestine was Chariton, a confessor, who arrived in Jerusalem from Iconium in about 275 and founded monasteries at Pharan, in a valley northeast of Jerusalem; at Douka, on the summit of the ridge overlooking Jericho; and at

---

1. Elijah and John the Baptist were looked to as models of the ascetic life. See, among many examples, *Life of Antony* 7, and *First Greek Life of Pachomius* 2. The monasteries of Palestine still contain many memorials to this devotion to Elijah and John, including the cave where Elijah was led by ravens at Choziba. See J. Murphy-O'Connor, *The Holy Land,* 255.

2. See Eusebius, *Ecclesiastical History* 6.9.8.

Souka, near Thekoa. In addition to the account of his biographer (who admits to writing long after Chariton's death) there are other references to the existence of these three communities in the fourth century.[3] Another early Palestinian monk was Hilarion, who was born near Gaza, studied at Alexandria, lived a few months with St Antony, then returned to Gaza in 308 to live as a solitary, where eventually others joined him. According to Jerome, his biographer, there was nobody living the monastic life before him in Palestine or Syria, a claim which can have little basis in reality.[4] Another early monastery was that of Epiphanius at Eleutheropolis, which must have been in existence before 367, because that was when Epiphanius left it to become Bishop of Salamis in Cyprus.[5] The almost simultaneous and apparently unconnected manner in which the first monasteries developed has caused the old view that monasticism began in Egypt and spread northward to be abandoned. A variety of religious, social, and economic reasons for the origin of monastic life has been advanced.[6]

After 400, monasticism developed from these modest beginnings into a mass movement in which a huge quantity of both human and financial resources flowed into the desert monastic communities. There is clear literary and archaeological evidence for this. In the case of Palestine the material is conveniently summarised. S. Vailhé has compiled an alphabetical list of all the Palestinian monasteries mentioned in the literary sources, with a brief account of the

---

3. Pharan was flourishing when Euthymius arrived in 405 (see 14.9). Douka is mentioned by Palladius in the *Lausiac History* 48. Souka could be the monastery near Thekoa in John Cassian, *Conferences* 6.1.

4. Jerome, *Life of Hilarion* 14.24. Hilarion is also mentioned in Sozomen, *Ecclesiastical History* 3.14 and 5.10.

5. Sozomen, *Ecclesiastical History* 6.32.2-3.

6. Several works discuss the origins of monasticism. See, for example, A. Guillaumont, *Aux origines du monachisme chrétien*, 217, and P. Canivet, *Le monachisme syrien selon Théordet de Cyr*, 27.

history of each, and A. Ovadiah has summarised the archaeological findings made on the sites of Byzantine churches.[7] This table is compiled on the basis of their work and shows the periods in which monasteries were founded.

	Early	Mid	Late	Early	Mid	Late		(or later)
C4th	C5th	C5th	C5th	C6th	C6th	C6th	C7th	C8th
			[Literary Evidence (Vailhé)]					
6	4	9	1	14	2	0	0	1
		[Archaeological Evidence (Ovadiah)]						
2	2	4	5	6	8	12	2	4

Totals:	C4th	C5th	C6th	C7th	C8th
Vailhé	6	14	16	0	1
Ovadiah	2	11	26	2	4

The monasteries of Palestine were not only numerous: some were large. The monastery of Romanus near Thekoa for example, was home to over six hundred monks, and the fifth-century *Life of Hypatius* refers to a monastery of eight hundred monks near the Red Sea.[8] The impression received from all the evidence available to us is that the monastic movement was at the zenith of its size and influence between 450 and 600.

For this period, Cyril of Scythopolis is our main source. He begins his account in 405, when Euthymius arrived in Jerusalem, and finishes it in 558, when John the Hesychast died. His

7. These works are S. Vailhé, *Repertoire alphabétique des monastères de Palestine,* and A. Ovadiah, *A Corpus of the Byzantine Churches of Palestine.* Subsequent references in the notes refer to the number of the relevant monastery in the lists.

8. For Romanus' monastery, see John Rufus, *Plerophoria* 25, and, for the monastery near the Red Sea, *Life of Hypatius* 54.

stated intention is to describe the lives of two of the most celebrated of the Palestinian monks, and shorter notices of five others. In fact, he provides far more—a history of the Palestinian church during the period when it was at the height of its power and prestige.

In addition to Cyril's work mention should be made of the *Spiritual Meadow* of John Moschus, a collection of anecdotes from the monasteries of Palestine, Sinai, Egypt, and elsewhere which dates from the end of the sixth century, some thirty years after the period described by Cyril. In addition, a series of lives of the great monks exist. The *Life of Theodosius* by Theodore of Petra is especially valuable because it provides a fuller account of the saint described by Cyril in a short life. The *Life of Gerasimus* and the *Life of Chariton* are influenced by Cyril and have been sometimes attributed to him. There are also Lives of Peter the Iberian, a Monophysite, and George of Choziba.[9] These are the main writings which emerged from the desert of Judaea. Compared with the literature of Egypt, they are undistinguished, and none has been translated into English.

The history of recent work on Cyril is briefly told. An edition of the Greek text was published by Eduard Schwartz in 1939. This work, although not without defects, has become the standard text used by all modern commentators and historians.[10] The pagination of Schwartz's edition appears in the margin of this translation and all cross-references are made using these page and line numbers. This may seem cumbersome to readers of this volume, but it will enable the translation to be used alongside other modern works on Cyril. These

9. See the bibliography for full details.
10. Among the weaknesses of the text are the fact that Schwartz did not use the oldest known manuscript, the ninth-century Sinaiticus 494. For criticism of the text see P. Thomsen, 'Kyrillos von Scythopolis.' For correction of Schwartz's historical comments, see E. Stein 'Cyrille de Scythopolis: A propos de la nouvelle édition de ses oeuvres.'

include a series of articles pointing to additions to the Greek text
which appear in the early Georgian and Arabic versions; a series of
articles examining the relationship of Cyril with earlier ascetic
authors; and two more general works by French scholars, which
include a French translation.[11]

2. INFLUENCE OF THE GEOGRAPHY

The word 'desert', when used by the early monastic authors, is
not primarily a geographical term. It refers to the place to which
the monk retreats and so to his experience there. Two distinct
and, on the face of it, contradictory ideas are evoked by the
word. Firstly, the desert is a place of beauty and purity, to which
the holy man can withdraw to escape the risk of pollution and
corruption involved in city life. The wistfulness of the Old Testament prophets for the days of the Exodus when religion was
pure and living was upright continued to influence the Church.
Origen describes how John the Baptist 'fleeing the tumult of the
towns, went away into the desert where the air is purer, the sky
is more open and God is closer.'[12] In the same vein, Cyril gives
a lyrical description of the natural beauties of the site of
Euthymius' monastery (23.24-24.7). The monks' love for their
desert home has often been noted.[13] At the same time the desert
is a sterile place, where life is threatened by wild beasts and by
devils. The monk goes into the desert not only to enjoy peace
but to battle with devils and struggle to live in an inhospitable
environment. This fear of the desert was rooted in the popular
imagination of the villagers.[14]

The geographical nature of the desert varied considerably,

11. See the relevant section of the bibliography.
12. Origen, *Homilies on Luke 11*.
13. For example, *The Life of Antony 50*.
14. For an account of the connotations of the word 'desert', see A.
Guillaumont, *Aux origines du monachisme chrétien*, 73-82.

and this in turn affected the way of life followed by the monks. Peter Brown has pointed to the difference between the Egyptian and Syrian desert. In Egypt there was an absolute contrast between the settled agricultural life of the Nile valley and the arid desert which extended on either side. Rainfall in Egypt is twenty millimetres *per annum*, and monastic life necessitated a settled struggle for existence in the marginal areas between cultivated land and the true desert. In Syria, by contrast, desert and settled land intermingled. Rainfall was more plentiful, and the monk could range freely through the mountainous hinterland living off plants and reserves of water trapped in holes in the rock. 'To go in to the desert in Syria was to wander into the ever-present fringe...it was not to disappear into another unimaginable world. The desert was a standing challenge on the edge of the village.'[15]

In Palestine the characteristics of the Desert near Jerusalem conditioned the style of life which the monks followed.

A journey from Jerusalem to Jericho is a breathtaking experience. The distance is under fifteen miles and there is a dramatic drop from mountains eight hundred feet above sea-level to the shores of the Dead Sea, the lowest land on the earth's surface, four hundred feet below sea level. The landscape undergoes several changes. Around Jerusalem, the hills are fertile and productive, as a result of a heavy winter rainfall (over six hundred millimetres *per annum*). There are olive groves, date palms and cereal crops. Within two miles, agriculture ceases, and the trees die out. The soil is similar to that of the Asian steppe, and allows shrubs and rough plants to grow. It is hilly and dry, and today is inhabited by a strange combination of Bedouin tribesmen and Israeli settlers claiming the West Bank by building brash modern settlements, one of the largest of which covers the site of Euthymius'

---

15. P. Brown, 'Rise and Function of the Holy Man in Late Antiquity', 83.

monastery.[16] It is grazing, rather than farming, land. Near the Dead Sea, the vegetation becomes sparser, the land becomes even drier and habitation declines. The landscape is flat, empty, and sandy. Within a few miles the traveller passes down from the Mediterranean coast through Asian Steppe to African desert.

Not surprisingly this extreme contrast in the environment in which the monks lived led to distinctly different patterns of monastic life.

The area around Bethlehem and Jerusalem favoured the development of large agricultural units. In this well-populated area, the monks gathered together in enclosed and well-equipped monasteries. The monastery excavated at Khirbet Siyar El-Ghanam, a couple of miles east of Bethlehem, on a traditional site of the Shepherds' Fields, contained a network of water cisterns, olive and wine presses, a bakery, and grain-silos as well as a church and living quarters built around a central court. It seems likely that this is the monastery of Marcianus, archimandrite of the monks of Palestine, who offered support, in the form of donkeys laden with provisions, to Sabas and his monks during building work on Castellium.[17] Marcianus was moved to do this because of his awareness that life in his own monastery was more comfortable and better provided for than that in Sabas' community (112.1-9). The large cenobium of Theodosius lay on the edge of this area. The strip of land is about five miles wide. In it, the large cenobium drawing subsistence from agriculture was a natural form of life.

The next strip of land to the east, also about five miles wide, saw the development of a different form of monastic life, the laura. The first monks naturally gravitated towards the deep wadis

16. A brief description of the site is given in J. Murphy-O'Connor, *The Holy Land*, 216-8.

17. See also Ovadiah 97, and Chitty, 'The Monastery of Euthymius'. The excavations are described in V. Corbo, *Gli Scavi di Kh. Siyar el-Ghanam (Campo dei Pastori) e i monasteri dei dintorni*. Corbo does not agree that this was Marcianus' monastery, preferring a location in the hills to the east of Bethlehem at Khirbet Giohdham (pp. 162-3). See also Ovadiah 126 A-B.

where water, shelter, and vegetation were most likely to be found. Many of these steep cliffs are filled with caves, and here the monks settled. They lived off the plants which grew in the neighbourhood, the gifts of food brought by the shepherds who grazed their flocks in the area, and on proceeds from the sale of their handicrafts in the villages to the west. The process by which a laura grew is described vividly by Cyril on several occasions (e.g. 15.10-16.9, 98.16-102). The discovery of a suitable cave, the contact with local shepherds, the growth of the monastery and the eventual construction of central buildings to serve the scattered monks are the stages of development of Euthymius' and Sabas' communities. An agricultural way of life encourages monks to gather together so that the estate can be efficiently organised; but the laurite life encourages dispersion. The monks spread out along the ravine seeking a suitable place to settle within reach of the water at the bottom. The precipitous cliffs made access to the caves difficult, and this added further discouragement to regular contact between monks. The use of the word laura, to describe a scattered settlement of monks loosely grouped around a centre containing a church and communal buildings, seems to have originated in Palestine. The meaning of the word in this context is illustrated by Chariton's foundation, the Old Laura or Souka, a few miles south-east of Bethlehem. This is located in a deep ravine full of limestone caverns, which still bears its founder's name: the Wadi Khureitun. The name *Souka*, or in Syriac *Shouqa*, is equivalent to the Arabic *suq*, which means 'market' or 'bazaar', and *laura* is intended as a translation of this word. The Arabic *suq*, encountered in towns throughout the Middle East today, is a narrow winding street with houses and shops leading off it. It is not dissimilar to the path which runs along the side of the ravine and from which access can be gained to the caves.[18] It suggests that the pressure which led the monks

18. See D.J. Chitty, *The Desert a City*, 14-16.

to develop these settlements was economic. The monks gathered together at the centre of the community at the weekend.
This gathering was for worship and for a shared meal, but also
so as to exchange the mats, baskets, and other handicrafts,
which they had produced during the previous week, for food
and for raw materials. To a peasant compelled to leave his
home through economic pressure, the laura offered not only a
place to lead a life of prayer but also a society in which he
could work and earn a living.[19]

The great monasteries of the desert seem to have originated in
this way: the three foundations of Chariton (including Pharan
which provided a prototype for the Euthymian foundations), the
monasteries of Theoctistus and Euthymius, and the Great and
New Lauras of Sabas. Once these were established, it became
clear that there was a need for a more organised form of monastic
life, particularly for the less experienced monks who were not
able to cope with the solitude and independence of the laurite way
of life. So both Theoctistus' and Euthymius' monasteries developed into cenobia and Sabas established cenobia alongside the
lauras. These cenobia remained dependent on the great lauras in
this central area of the desert. When the dual appointment of
Sabas and Theodosius as archimandrites was made, with the former presiding over monks in lauras and the latter over the
cenobites, it is probable that this referred to a responsibility over a
certain area as well as over a specific form of institution
(114.23-115.26). Theodosius presided over the most prestigious
of the great cenobia in the agricultural belt east of Bethlehem, and
Sabas over the lauras of the central area of grazing land, where the
laurite life predominated. It is hard to imagine a cenobium
founded by Sabas in the midst of his area of influence, as for example the cenobium he established a little to the north of the
Great Laura, relating more closely to the Theodosius than to the
founder (113.6, 221.8-10).

19. The economics of the monasteries is discussed in the important work of
E. Patlagean, *Pauvreté Economique et Pauvreté Sociale à Byzance* , 300-338.

The next belt of land to the east led down to the shores of the Dead Sea. This was inhabited only by experienced ascetics and usually only at certain times of the year. This was the 'utter desert' or *panerêmos*. Such rain as there was fell between the months of November and February, and ensured a minimum of plant-life and water supply for Euthymius, Sabas, and their favoured associates when they left their monasteries for a period of greater solitude during Lent. They left the monastery after the feast of the Theophany, at the height of the rainy season, and returned for Palm Sunday, when the heat and dryness were making the desert uninhabitable even for the experienced desert-dweller. The only all-the-year-round settlement in this section of the desert of which we know was Cyriacus' hermitage at Sousakim (228.23-30).

Cyril's writings describe the monasteries of the central strip of desert. He is the historian of the lauras, and offers only incidental information about the cenobia grouped in the immediate neighbourhood of Jerusalem and Bethlehem. His picture of the monastic life of Palestine is vivid, but not exhaustive. The main source for the cenobitic life is Theodore of Petra's *Life of Theodosius*, which provides a valuable, if long-winded, account of the development of Theodosius' cenobium, on the hills between Bethlehem and Sabas' Great Laura.

The loose structure of the laura encouraged diversity within the community. The constituent parts of the laura were the cells or *kellia*. Sometimes these cells appear to have housed single monks (26.15) and sometimes groups of monks, as when a new monastery was formed by the building of three cells (24.19, 26.15, 105.8). Leading monks gained a reputation for sanctity and leadership, and a small community would gather around them. If this group continued to grow, it could form the basis of a new monastery. The careers of Martyrius and Elias are an example of this process. They were recognised by Euthymius as outstanding leaders and quickly became close to him. They later departed from his laura because the cells 'were extremely cramped and uncomfortable'—a reference to the fact that they were inadequate to accommodate the growing circle of disciples rather than that they were insufficiently luxurious (51.15). Both founded new monasteries, and both became Patriarchs of Jerusalem. This quasi-organic tendency within the laurite pattern of monastic life to split, transplant and colonise accounts for the influence of Euthymius over the subsequent history of Palestinian monasticism.

A similar pattern can be observed in Sabas' monasteries. Cyril lists a total of seven monasteries founded by Sabas: three lauras and four cenobia. In the narratives which describe the foundations, the leadership and initiative of the saint are strongly emphasised. But, since each monastic group consisted of monks from the Great Laura and was led by a monk appointed by Sabas, it is clear that within the Great Laura groups were continually emerging which had a need to be allowed to establish themselves as separate communities. Usually this process happened under the direction of Sabas. Through it his influence extended and he became the dominant figure in the Palestinian Church.

3. CONFLICT IN THE MONASTERIES

The natural tendency in the laurite life towards flexibility, diversity, and creativity was at the same time a source of conflict, division, and failure. Diversity easily became division.

It is surely not accidental that the first episode in the life of the Great Laura, after it was established through the discovery of the church and water supply, was a rebellion of a group of monks trying to challenge Sabas' authority. They sent a deputation of monks to the Patriarch complaining that Sabas was uneducated or 'rustic', and so unfit to lead the community (103.17-104.1). The complaint seems to have been sim-

mering for some time, as the objectors waited until Patriarch
Martyrius had died and a new Patriarch, who did not know
Sabas, had succeeded him. The result of their complaint was
to confirm Sabas in his position of superior, but this did not
stop the opposition. Cyril describes how Sabas withdrew from
the laura on two occasions because of the conflict, and how
eventually his opponents retired to a deserted laura near
Thekoa, which was established on a proper footing through
the patronage of Sabas. Later this group evolved a distinctive
doctrinal identity through allegiance to certain Origenist
opinions. The conflict was not finally resolved until after
Sabas' death (118.21-125.25).

A less serious conflict also developed over the attempt of
the monk Jacob to establish a separate laura within the area of
the Great Laura. This separatist movement was easily dealt
with by Sabas, who established a laura under properly appointed stewards (129.3-130.21).

The problem in both cases was one of authority, or the lack
of it. Sabas is presented by Cyril above all as a founder of
monasteries. His life's work is summarised thus:

> Sabas... by the favour of God the Father, the as-
> sistance of Christ and the inspiration of the Holy
> Spirit, colonized the desert with a huge number
> of monks and founded in it seven celebrated
> monasteries (158.15-18).

His relationship with these monasteries did not extend to concern for the continuing care and guidance of each community.
With the exception of his first monastery, the Great Laura,
Cyril gives no indication that Sabas visited any of his
monasteries after they had been founded. Faced with a threat
to his position from the 'intellectual' party, he preferred to
leave the monks and retire to a remote spot from which he
could not be recalled, rather than to seek to resolve the
problem. It is hard to avoid the conclusion that Sabas was out

of touch with the routine events of the daily life of his monasteries. His was not the authority of the superior or *hegumenos*.

Nor was it the authority of the teacher. The criticism made of him by the intellectuals was that he was 'rustic', or *agroikos*. In fourth-century Egypt this word was complimentary. It referred to the simplicity and humility of the true ascetic as opposed to the intellectual brilliance of the secular scholar. As monastic society became more settled, it came to refer to an inability to exercise authority.[20]

Sabas was the son of a soldier, and, according to Cyril, his education was limited to 'the psalter and the observance of the cenobitic rule' (88.1-2). There is no reference at any point in his Life to any of his ascetic teaching and he is not described as giving instruction or discourses to his monks. When Cyril describes the achievements of Euthymius he refers to his ascetic life and his ability to lead others in the same way, but when he extols Sabas, it is because of his energy in founding new monasteries.[21]

These weaknesses stand out with greater clarity when Sabas' foundations are compared with those of Pachomius. Pachomius' monasteries were established in rural rather than desert areas. A wall kept the monks apart from the secular world and this helped the development of a centralised and cohesive organisation. An elaborate structure for maintaining authority was established with 'housemasters' and 'seconds' appointed to care for the monks. Pachomius emphasised the

20. Compare the Chalcedonian historian Theophanes' description of the Monophysite leader Dioscorus as 'completely uneducated and rustic' (*Chronographia*, ed. de Boor 97).

21. Both lives follow a similar pattern, interweaving the themes of the history of the monasteries, anecdotes about monks, and doctrinal conflict. After the theme of doctrinal conflict is introduced in 32.7-33.21 and 118.22-125.6, each life contains a section describing the virtues of the saint (34.1-39.17 and 125.27-129.2). In the case of Euthymius, the section describes his ascetic achievements; in the case of Sabas, the foundation of monasteries.

importance of teaching, and required housemasters to give three periods of instruction each week, and seconds to give two periods. He preferred novices to be free from physical labour so that they could concentrate on learning, and had an enviable reputation as a teacher and interpreter of the Bible. His monasteries had clearly defined boundaries, a recognised leader, and regular teaching.[22]

The genius of Sabas lay in his ability to establish an environment in which the monastic life could take root and grow. He was less successful in directing the growth once it was under way.

4. THE HOLY CITY

Jerusalem was the great fact which dominated the lives of the monks. From its site at the summit of the range of hills which divides the Jordan valley from the Mediterranean plain, it looks down over the monasteries. The monk who set out on the walk to Jerusalem would be conscious that his journey was an ascent to a holy place on a mountain. Once arrived, he was vividly aware that he stood in the place where Jesus died and rose again. The monks wrote to the Emperor Justinian that they as 'inhabitants of Jerusalem touch as if with their hands the truth each day through the Holy Places' (154.15-17). The growth of the monasteries of Palestine depended on the growth of Jerusalem as a goal and centre of pilgrimage.

The Jerusalem of Jesus had long since disappeared. The Temple he had known was destroyed in AD 70; and a statue of Jupiter was erected over the hill of Calvary by the emperor Hadrian in 135. Helena, the mother of the newly-converted

22. See among many relevant sections, *First Greek Life of Pachomius* 28, 54, 56, 74, 131.

Christian Emperor Constantine, arrived in Palestine, 'finding that which was once Jerusalem desolate as a preserve for autumn fruits'.[23]

This sad situation did not last long. Excavation revealed the place of the crucifixion and the resurrection, and a ditch containing three crosses. In September 335, the great basilica of the Holy Sepulchre, built at the rock of Golgotha, was consecrated. From this time onward Jerusalem was established as a centre of pilgrimage. The festival of the Dedication or Encaenia, which commemorated this event, was celebrated with great solemnity on 14 September, and many bishops and monks came from all parts of Palestine and from areas further afield.[24]

The holy places attracted visitors from all parts of the Empire. Some pilgrims were wealthy, as were the group of noble Roman ladies over whom Jerome presided from his monastery at Bethlehem and the enthusiastic travellers, Egeria and Poemenia, who covered huge distances in opulent style, including Egypt and Mesopotamia on their itineraries as well as the Holy Places of Palestine.[25]

But a far greater, although less well-documented, group came from a humbler background. Nomadic ways of life were deeply ingrained in Syrian society and, for many, continual movement was a normal way of life. Roads connected Jerusalem with Syria and the East; and bands of poor pilgrims often found their way to Jerusalem. These visitors were not always welcome. The celebrated ascetic Barsaumas, who was born near Samosata, made four visits to Jerusalem, accompa-

23. Socrates, *Ecclesiastical History* 1.17.

24. It was the Feast of Dedication which brought Sabas back to Jerusalem from Nicopolis and so led to his return to the Great Laura (121.14-20). For a description of the festival see the *Travels of Egeria* 48-49 and Sozomen, *Ecclesiastical History* 2.26.

25. The stories of these wealthy pilgrims is told in E.D. Hunt, *Holy Land Pilgrimage in the Later Roman Empire AD 312-460*.

nied by a wild band of men from the mountains. Barsaumas, with his long hair and iron tunic, worn for ascetic reasons, struck terror into the hearts of Jews and other local inhabitants. His band left a trail of destruction behind them.[26] The visitors who settled as monks in the lauras of the Judaean Desert would have been more likely to come from the circles in which Barsaumas moved than from the villas and estates of Rome which produced Paula and Eustochium and the other ladies of Jerome's circle.

Behind the growing popularity of pilgrimage lay political and economic pressures. The great age of pilgrimage was also that of barbarian invasion.. Jerusalem provided a secure haven for those fleeing invading forces in the West. Melania, who arrived in Palestine in 373, had sold off her estates in Spain and fled with only 'a small sum of money, snatched from the jaws of the lion'; it was, however, sufficient to found monasteries on the Mount of Olives as well as paying for other building and charitable work.[27]

Jerome tells us that after Rome fell to Alaric in 410 the volume of pilgrim traffic increased dramatically.[28] In the case of Eudocia, who dominated Jerusalem society during the lifetime of Euthymius, it was court intrigue and rivalry in the imperial circle at Constantinople which led her to settle in Jerusalem. Her vast wealth financed a building programme which was intended to set up Jerusalem as a rival to Constantinople in its size, affluence, and influence. Her political ambition was channeled into the development of the Holy City.[29]

The increasing building activity was a sign of Palestine's growing prosperity. From the spate of construction under

26. Barsaumas' visits to Palestine are described in F. Nau, 'Deux épisodes de l'histoire juive sous Théodose II'.

27. *Life of Melania* 37.

28. Jerome, *Commentary on Ezekiel* 3 prologue, 7 prologue.

29. A chapter is devoted to Eudocia in E.D. Hunt, *Holy Land Pilgrimage*, 218-248.

Constantine, when the great basilicas at Golgotha, the Mount of Olives, and Bethlehem were built, the volume of new building increased until it reached a peak during the reign of Justinian. Hospitals and other charitable institutions were built as well as churches. At a time when other parts of the Empire were in decline, Palestine could offer employment in the building trade and charitable relief for the poor and sick. Not surprisingly, the population increased and with it the demand for agricultural and other goods.[30]

Within this booming society, the monasteries thrived. They benefited from gifts of money and opportunities to erect new buildings, and they contributed by providing a welcome for visiting pilgrims and relief for the poor and sick.

The importance of Jerusalem in Palestinian life meant that monasteries needed easy access to the capital. The founders chose their sites carefully. Euthymius settled on a small hill on the plain of Sahel overlooking the main Jerusalem-Jericho highway.[31] Cyril tells us that Euthymius chose the place because he loved it. Presumably a further reason for his decision was that he wanted to be within reach of the Holy Places, and to be in contact with the pilgrims who came to the City (23.24-24.10, 27.5-28.5). The Great Laura of Sabas is further from Jerusalem, but its position in the Kidron valley, which leads directly to the city walls, ensured that the journey would not be difficult. The road along the valley appears to have been well-used as a means of reaching the monastery, since Cyril refers to it as 'the road of the Great Laura' (168.8). The other monasteries founded by or dependent upon Euthymius and Sabas could all be reached in a comfortable day's journey by a traveller from Jerusalem.

As the monasteries expanded, a high priority was given to procuring premises in the main pilgrimage centres. The first sub-

30. See M. Avi-Yonah, 'The Economics of Byzantine Palestine'.
31. The Roman road ran about half a mile to the north of the modern Jerusalem-Jericho road at this point. Its route is traced by R. Beauvéry, 'La route romaine de Jérusalem à Jericho'.

stantial bequest received by Sabas, after he had founded his laura, was spent on buying a guesthouse in Jericho and building a guesthouse in the monastery (109.12-13). Two years later he bought two guesthouses in Jerusalem, one for monks of the laura and one for monks from abroad (116.8-25). These were situated near the Tower of David on Mount Sion, which developed into the monastic quarter of the city, with hermit's cells, monasteries, and the guesthouses of the larger monasteries of the desert. There were also communities of monks attached to the main churches. These could be large: the monastery of the 'Spoudaioi' attached to the church of the Resurrection seems to have housed over two hundred monks.[32]

The monks were not passive spectators but were fully involved in all aspects of church life. Cyril describes the progressive strengthening of the relationship between the monasteries and the Jerusalem patriarchate. This arose naturally out of the concern of the monks for the holy places preserved and presided over by the Bishop. The attitudes of Euthymius and Sabas form the beginning and end of the process, and show the development of a distinctive style of monastic life peculiar to Palestine.

5. THE MONKS AND THE SEE OF JERUSALEM

Cyril presents the ascetic life of Euthymius as following the example set by Egyptian monks, especially Arsenius. Like them, he made consistent efforts to avoid contact with the life of the cities and to protect his solitude. His early wanderings

---

32. Our knowledge of the topography of late Byzantine Jerusalem is based on the account of the Persian conquest of the city in 614, written by a priest of the Great Laura, Strategius. He lists the numbers of dead bodies found at each place after the massacre by the Persians. He tells us that two hundred twelve were buried in the monastery of the 'Spoudaili'. See J.T. Milik, 'La Topographie de Jêrusalem vers la Fin de l'Epoque Byzantine', 157 and 187.

were motivated by a vain attempt to escape notoriety and the crowds of visitors attracted by his reputation (21.20-25, 23.18-20). After venerating the holy places when he first arrived in Palestine in 405/6, he left the city to live at the laura of Pharan. There is no indication that he again set foot inside Jerusalem. His hunger for solitude is the explanation given for his refusal to meet the Patriarch Anastasius which, he feared, would stimulate a greater flow of traffic to his monastery. Later, when they met at the funeral of Theoctistus, the conversation was respectful but recognised the difference of the environments to which the monk and the bishop belong (52.9-18, 54.17-55.12). Euthymius, throughout his life, had little contact with the Jerusalem church. In fact, his advice to delegates to the Councils of Ephesus and Chalcedon—to follow the lead given by Cyril of Alexandria and Acacius of Melitene rather than Juvenal of Jerusalem—suggests that his contact with the church of his home town was closer than with that of the nearby city, although the aggressive and ambitious personality of Juvenal could also have led Euthymius to distrust his integrity in matters of belief (33.44-45).[33]

In one important respect Euthymius accepted a relationship with the church. In contrast to many Egyptian ascetics who preferred flight or even self-mutilation to ecclesiastical office, Euthymius accepted the appointment of many of his monks to prominent posts in the church. Two Patriarchs, Martyrius and Elias, spent time in the monastery (50.26-51.21). Monks were appointed to the bishoprics of Jamnia, the Encampments, Medaba, and Scythopolis, and to senior positions in the Jerusalem churches (33.28-31, 53.3, 55.22-3). In addition to these appointments, there are several examples of his

33. Juvenal made a dramatic change of sides at Chalcedon. He switched his support from Dioscorus to the imperial party and helped to frame the Chalcedonian definition. John Rufus, *Plerophoria*, shows the hatred of the Monophysites for Juvenal. His career is followed by E. Honigmann, 'Juvenal of Jerusalem'.

monks going to found monasteries in other parts of the desert. An ascetic and monastic style of Christian living infiltrated all levels of the Palestinian church.[34]

Cyril claimed that 'the whole desert has been colonised by his [Euthymius'] spiritual progeny.' He would not have been exaggerating if he had attributed a modest transformation of the church in Palestine to the influence of the saint (29.4-5).

The extent of the transformation is revealed in the life and ministry of Euthymius' most prominent disciple, Sabas. In contrast to the retiring Euthymius, Sabas maintained a close contact with Jerusalem. He was a regular visitor to the city and, throughout his life, was ready to associate with the patriarch. When faced with a complaint about Sabas from rebellious monks, Patriarch Sallustius found little difficulty in thinking up an excuse which brought Sabas to Jerusalem within twenty-four hours (104.13-14). Sabas often turned to the patriarch for support and assistance, for example, when he was in need of funds for building work at a new monastery or when he had a candidate for ordination (123.20-22, 207.50).

The working relationship between the monk and the patriarch was sealed when Sabas and Theodosius were appointed archimandrites. In normal contemporary usage, an archimandrite was a leader of monks. The abbot of Sabas' first monastery, Flavianae, is described as an archimandrite, and his responsibilities do not appear to have extended beyond the monastery (90.11). In Jerusalem, however, the title came to be restricted to a leading monk who exercised authority over the monks of the diocese. The position was recognised both by the body of the monks and by the patriarch (115.14-20). It is probable that the post of archimandrite was

---

34. Cyril's home town of Scythopolis is a good example of how monasticism influenced the church. Euthymius' disciple, Cosmas, was bishop for thirty years; Sabas impressed the townsfolk during his stay in the neighbourhood and made subsequent visits (56.1-3, 119.15-20, 162.19-20). Cyril's memories of his childhood show how the church was dominated by monks.

equivalent to that of chorepiscop or rural bishop. In the *Life of Euthymius*, Passarion is described as being both chorepiscop and archimandrite, but after his death there is only one reference to a chorepiscop in the Jerusalem diocese— Anastasius who later became patriarch (47.21-2, 48.12). While the post of chorepiscop was falling into disuse, that of archimandrite was developing. The *Life of Sabas* shows Theodosius and Sabas exercising an increasingly prominent role in the diocese of Jerusalem. They acted on behalf of the bishop, ensuring the good order of the monasteries and promoting the peace and prosperity of the Holy City.

In describing the relationship between Sabas and successive patriarchs, Cyril is in no doubt where the true authority lies. After a five-year famine and drought, the patriarch used his power to employ workmen to dig for water. His efforts were unsuccessful, and it was only after he asked Sabas to pray for God's mercy that rain fell and the water supply was restored (167.25-169.24). This episode is followed by the cure of the patriarch's sister through the prayers of Sabas (170.21-170.5). In these narratives, Cyril contrasts the limited authority of the patriarch with the God-given power which is released through the prayers of the saint. Sabas' influence was also effective in the volatile political climate after the Emperor Anastasius deposed the patriarch Elias. Sabas and Theodosius, symbolically placed at each side of the new patriarch, John, ensured both that the Chalcedonian faith was affirmed and that the new patriarch's position was secured through the support of the huge body of assembled monks, numbering, we are told, ten thousand. On this occasion, it was the acclamation of the monks which was decisive, indicating the importance of the monastic body in the diocese of Jerusalem and, as a result, the authority of the archimandrites (151.10-152.2).

Sabas' activities were not limited to Jerusalem. He was sent on two diplomatic missions to the Imperial Court at Constantinople. Both Anastasius, who otherwise exhibited hostility towards the Jerusalem church, and the more sympathetic Justinian acknowledged the sanctity of the old man and fulfilled his requests with alacrity. Sabas also travelled around Palestine on behalf of the patriarch on two occasions, ensuring his acceptance of imperial proclamations and the fair distribution of financial resources (162.19-23, 179.26-180.2). The extension of Sabas' ministry into the diplomatic sphere is a further indication of the growing integration of the monasteries of the Judaean Desert into the life of the church.

6. MIRACLE AND HISTORY

The two lives of Euthymius and Sabas are conceived as a unity. They emerged together from Cyril's process of research and, in the vision which preceded the actual task of writing, both saints appeared to Cyril to bestow on him the grace required to write the two lives (83.4-23). The opening sentence of the *Life of John the Hesychast* makes it clear that the five shorter lives comprise a distinct literary endeavour. Cyril writes, 'I place Abba John the Hesychast *first* in this work' (201.4). His desire to write these lives emerged out of his researches into the exploits of Euthymius and Sabas, and they form a natural supplement. The two longer lives of Euthymius and Sabas are the expression of his intention to chronicle the development of the monastic life of Palestine.

The history is understood in a theological framework. It is part of God's purpose for his creation. Cyril's prologue to the *Life of Euthymius* begins with statements, drawn from the theological writing of Cyril's time, about the incarnation of Christ (6.22-7.123). This good news of salvation is entrusted successively to the apostles, the martyrs, and then the ascetics, among whom is Euthymius. The saints whose lives Cyril describes are placed in an historical succession which reaches back to Christ. The elaborate dating of the deaths of

Euthymius and Sabas derive from the Christian chronographical tradition, which had the intention of claiming that the Christian faith was no novelty but has its roots in the past and provided a fulfilment of that same past (59-60.14, 183.5-184.2). The clearest expression of Cyril's conviction of the significance of the monasteries of Palestine in the history of the church and of the world comes in his account of the vision promising a son to the mother of Euthymius who would bring *'euthymia'* or 'confidence' to the churches. His birth coincided with the end of a succession of Arian and pagan emperors and the accession of Theodosius I (9.20-10.4). This happy chance is seen by Cyril as the start of a new era in which the monks are bringers of piety, peace, and orthodoxy to the world.

Cyril's history is an account not of secular events but of the action of God in calling out his chosen ones and working his purpose through them. The lives of the saints are a response to the divine initiative, and the signs of God's power are present throughout. The miracle stories, therefore, are not a series of remarkable events which form a superstitious accretion to the pure and reliable historical episodes. They are essential to Cyril's purpose, and show that he is writing a true history, because it is God's history. Miracle and history are for Cyril indistinguishable.[35]

A variety of words were available to Cyril to refer to his miracle stories. The New Testament writers favour *dunamis* (power) or *sêmeion* (sign), and to these two words monastic writers added a third: *thauma* (wonder or marvel).[36] Cyril almost invariably chooses the word *thauma*, or its verbal

35. The acceptance of the category of the miraculous into historical writing was characteristic of the age. See, for example, Averil Cameron, *Procopius and the Sixth Century*, 24-32, and E. Patlagean, *Pauvreté Economique et Pauvreté Sociale,* 19-23.

36. For the vocabulary of miracles, see C.F.D. Moule, *Miracles,* 235-238, and B. Ward, *Lives of the Desert Fathers* 39.

derivative *thaumatourgeo*. This choice of vocabulary reflects
the admiration and amazement which were evoked in him as
he travelled around the desert collecting his evidence. The
word *sêmeion* comes only once, and describes the providential death of the Origenist leader, Nonnus, which led to the
fragmentation and defeat of the Origenist party (195.26). It
describes the direct intervention of God in human affairs,
while the word *thauma*, or marvel, refers to the action of God
through an intermediary, and is amazing because it shows
powers at work which go beyond what would be considered
as normal for a mortal man.

There is a uniqueness about miracles. Each shows the power of God working in a special set of circumstances. Yet is is
helpful to classify miracle stories into groups to gain an idea
of how the author and his contemporaries understood God to
work. In her introduction to the *Historia Monachorum*,
Benedicta Ward uses five categories: clairvoyance, dreams
and visions, healing, nature miracles, and judgments.[37] These
are helpful in assessing Cyril's miracles.

Altogether Cyril records ninety-four stories which, in my
view, should be considered to fall into these categories. This
is a large figure. My own count produced sixty-two stories in
the *Historia Monachorum*, and only twelve in the *Life of Antony*. The high figure for Cyril shows the importance of the
theme of God's action for Cyril's understanding of the events
he is recording.

The most important group, using Sister Benedicta's
categories, is that of nature miracles—which accounts for over
a third of all Cyril's miracle stories. These miracles show the
saint influencing the natural world around him. Water is
miraculously provided either by the holy man praying for rain
in time of drought or discovering a spring of water at the time

----

37. Sister Benedicta says she is working with four categories but in fact
uses five: Ward, *Lives of the Desert Fathers*, 40-45.

or the place when it was most needed (e.g. 56.29-57.11, 38.1-39.11); or food arrives when the storehouses are empty, either through an inexplicable act of divine power filling an empty cupboard or through the fortuitous arrival of a donor bringing a supply of provisions to the monastery (27.16-23, 211.1-4). Several stories concern wild animals becoming tame in the presence of the saint (117.12-18). These animals are usually lions, which were common in the Judaean Desert.[38]

The nature miracles have a common theme of survival. They are not necessarily supernatural, and, in fact, some of the stories describe everyday events, such as the arrival of a visitor with a gift of food for the monastery.[39] They describe the difficulties of survival in a terrain in which water and food are scarce, and wild animals a continual threat. The monk is vividly aware that his existence is precarious and his environment hostile. For the provision of everyday needs he is dependent on God's grace. The survival and multiplication of monasteries in the desert is the result of the guiding power of God.

A closely-related category is that of healings and exorcisms. Devils were present everywhere in Cyril's world. The forces of evil could inhabit a human being or a desert mountain-top with equal ease, and the processes by which they were banished were similar. Wherever he encountered demonic powers, the saint first resisted the temptation to flee, then prayed ardently, signing with the cross or sprinkling holy oil. The devils would then depart with much shouting and commotion (e.g. 110.7-18). The fight with devils is perceived

38. In Palestinian literature, the saint tames lions. Compare, also, John Moschus, *Spiritual Meadow* 2.18. In Egypt, the equivalent stories concern crocodiles (*Life of Antony* 15), hyenas (*Lausiac History* 18) or asps (*Lausiac History* 2.18).

39. A similar event reported in the *Life of Antony* does not purport to be miraculous. The visitor arrives with food because Antony has arranged it (*Life of Antony* 8).

as part of the fight to survive in the desert, since devils and wild beasts were both aspects of the hostility of the environment in which the monk had to survive. Since the habitat of devils was so varied and far-reaching, the monk's conflict with evil extended beyond the desert to other areas of life, especially the ministry to visitors to the monastery who were sick or possessed and the maintenance of an order within the community (36.13-37.29, 75.15-27). Struggle with the powers of evil was an activity expected of the holy man. As Peter Brown has written, 'the Christian missionaries advanced principally by revealing the bankruptcy of men's invisible enemies, the demons, through exorcisms and miracles of healing'.[40]

The categories of clairvoyance and of dreams and visions can be considered together. These miracles show the fathers perceiving the purposes of God within events going on around them. Clairvoyance is a spiritual gift which is received only after long practice of the ascetical life (99.6-7). It enabled the saint to perceive the inner realities behind outward appearances. So Euthymius became aware of the true state of soul of members of his community, and could also see into the future, knowing who would advance to high office in the church and when the deaths of himself and of others would take place (45.28-46.3, 33.22-28, 35.3-25, 57.12-14, 58.22-23). Sabas found the same gift useful on his diplomatic missions, prophesying the untimely end of those who presumed to oppose him, and the military successes of Justinian who had resisted the major heresies (146.11-18, 163.8-13, 175.9-176.2). The application of this miraculous power both to the conduct of everyday life in the monastery and to involvement in the conduct of the Empire point to a recurring theme of Cyril's view of history. There is an intimate connection between the building up of monastic life in Palestine and the well-being of the Church and Empire—and the saints have responsibility in both areas.

40. P. Brown, *The World of Late Antiquity*, 55.

7. THE HOLY MAN AS MEDIATOR

The holy man was somebody through whom the power of God was active. This power was not only active but also available, and exercised for the benefit of those who came seeking the saint's help, whether a deputation from a city in desperate straits through drought or an individual afflicted by illness (38.1-39.17, 136.8-19). Recent studies, especially the often-quoted and important essay by Peter Brown, 'The Rise and Function of the Holy Man in Late Antiquity', have examined the relation of the saint to the society around him, and shown how he used his power to resolve conflicts, mediate on behalf of villages with an overbearing secular authority, and remove the tensions and destructiveness attributed to demonic forces. He was a mediator between ordinary people and the huge forces which threatened their security in the realms of both the material and the spiritual.[41]

The attention of Brown's article is focused on Syria, where the holy man often developed a relationship with a local community. For Palestine, the picture must be modified. The relationship between the village and the ascetic is more important to the village than to the ascetic. Local people often provide the holy man with food or swamp him with requests for assistance but this interest is not allowed to develop (16.7-9, 22.11-17). Too much anxious support has the effect of driving Euthymius away, and Sabas' priority is always the welfare of the monastery rather than the village. The Palestinian holy man does not seem at home in the village. He belongs in the monastery, in the city, or even in the imperial court, and it is in these areas that his power is exercised.

Once again, it is the presence of Jerusalem which determines how the power of the holy men should be exercised. In

41. Peter Brown's article, along with the work of the French scholar Evelyne Patlagean, examined the social environment within which the holy man lived.

his article, Peter Brown enquires about the locus of spiritual power:

> Much of the contrasting developments of Western
> Europe and Byzantium in the Middle Ages can be
> summed up as a prolonged debate on the precise
> *locus* of spiritual power. In Byzantium, the *locus* of
> spiritual power wavered as paradoxically as did the
> fluid society in which it was exercised'.[42]

For Cyril there is no doubt where spiritual power is to be found. The holy places contained the power of God in a unique way. The account given by a Piacenza pilgrim shows this power being par-celled up and taken home in the form of oil or earth:

> In the place where the Lord's body was laid... has
> been placed a bronze lamp... we took a blessing
> from it. Earth is brought up to the tomb and put in-
> side, and those who go in take some as a blessing.
> They offer oil to be blessed in little flasks. When the
> mouth of one of those little flasks touches the wood
> of the cross, the oil instantly bubbles over, and un-
> less it is closed very quickly, it all spills out.[43]

This overwhelming concentration of holiness dominates the lives of the Palestinian monks. Exorcisms and miracles take place through the signing with the cross or through the application of oil from the Sepulchre (110.11, 136.16-17, 164.18, 20.22-3, 171.4-5). The power of the holy man is dependent on the divine power pre-sent in the Holy Places.

After the deaths of Euthymius and Sabas, their tombs became focusses of holiness in a way similar to, but on the smaller scale

---

42. P. Brown, 'Rise and Function of the Holy Man in Late Antiquity', 95.
43. Antoninus Placentinus 18,10. This document describes a journey made in the sixth century and somore or less contemporary with Cyril.

than, the Holy Places of Jerusalem.[44] Cures are effected through physical contact with objects imbued with the saint's holiness. The sick person could be laid on the tomb or anointed with oil from the lamp which burned there (75.24-25, 76.10, 68.14-18, 76.2). On one occasion the sufferer even drank the oil from the lamp (76.20-21). The veneration of the tombs of holy men and their relics was a growing practice throughout the christian world, and the Palestinian environment was especially favourable to this development—thanks to the large number of biblical characters whose relics could be confidently expected to be contained within Palestinian soil.[45] Cyril's personal experience of miracles at the tomb of Euthymius convinced him of the continuing efficacy of the saint's intercession before God and led him to embark on his literary career.

The sense of God's presence in Jerusalem led to the growth of the monasteries as an institution, the integration of the monks into the Jerusalem church, and their involvement in the political life of the Empire. Involvement in the life of Jerusalem and the aspirations of its church took the holy man out of the fluid and uncertain society of the mountains and villages of the countryside and into a more formal and urban environment. Sabas was a mediator, but, instead of protecting the interests of the individual against his oppressor, he protected the interests of a church against the Emperor. In the Palestinian saint, personal and institutional power blend. He was the driving force behind the advance of the church.

44. A valuable study of the growth of interest in the tombs of the saints and their relics is P. Brown, *The Cult of the Saints*.

45. The historian Sozomen describes the discovery of the bones of Habakkuk and Micah, and notes the importance in Palestinian Church of holding a yearly festival to honour the relics of the saints (*Ecclesiastical History* 3.14 and 7.29).

8. THE LIFE OF CYRIL OF SCYTHOPOLIS

We do not know when Cyril was born. Since, however, he tells us that he was a young boy when Sabas visited Scythopolis in 531-2 and selected him to be his follower, and was approaching manhood when he made his monastic profession and left home for Jerusalem in 543, we would not go far wrong if we assumed 525 to have been the approximate date of his birth.

We have more information about where he was born. The city of Scythopolis was the capital of Palestine II, a province which had been created as a result of administrative changes in the Empire in 399. It is a city whose origins lie deep in antiquity. Excavations carried out on the city mound between 1921 and 1933 show that the site was occupied at least as early as 3500 B.C. It was known as Beth-Shan in the Old Testament (Joshua 17:1, Judges 1:27, 1 Samuel 30:18-12, 1 Kings 4:12) but around 200 BC was re-named Scythopolis. The reason for this association of the Galilean town with the the Scythians, a warlike tribe from the South of Russia, are obscure and no satisfactory explanation has been advanced for this curious choice of name.[46]

The Scythopolis known by Cyril lay in the fertile valley of the river Harod. It was, and still is, irrigated by the thirty natural springs which ensured that a variety of crops could be grown in spite of an erratic rainfall. The area was known especially for its date palms, which probably drew Egyptian Origenist monks. The date palms would have offered raw material for their trade of basket and rope making.[47] It was also a commercial centre which produced the finest linen in the Byzantine empire. A price edict of Diocletian, promulgated in

46. For a summary of the different explanations of the name Scythopolis, see M. Avi-Yonah, 'Scythopolis', 123-7.

47. For further historical details see Rowe, *Beth-Shan Topography and History, passim*, and Sozomen, *Ecclesiastical History* 8.13.

301, refers to Scythopolitan 'tunics without stripes, dalmatics for men and women, short and light mantles, short cloaks with hoods for women, kerchiefs and shirts,' all of the best quality and superior to those produced in any other city.[48]

It was a city of monks. Monastic influence was ensured by the association of the area with John the Baptist. Aenon near Salim, the traditional site of John's baptising, lay eight miles to the south, and an alternative site, Sapsaphas, was not far away. Both these places are shown on the Madaba Mosaic Map, which was laid down about the time when Cyril was born.[49] A contemporary visitor describes the area as populated by hermits, and refers to Scythopolis as 'the place where St John performs many miracles'.[50] The reputation of the city may have attracted the haemorrhoid woman who was lying on a bed in the street near the apse of St John and who was cured by Sabas on his visit to the city (163.23-164.10). Cyril tells us of other monasteries in the city, that called Enthemenaith and those dedicated to the martyr Basil, the martyr Procopius, and the apostle Thomas (126.14, 180.6-8, 180.17). Archeological discoveries confirm this picture of a city of monasteries, and the remains of five monasteries active in the sixth century have been excavated in the city of Scythopolis and its environs. The dominance of monks in Scythopolis is emphasised by the contrast with Caesarea, where only one Byzantine monastic building has been discovered.[51]

Cyril's writing contains several autobiographical passages (71.10-72.7, 82.12-89.25, 180.9-181.18, 216.8-217.29). These

48. The quality of these goods is recorded in Diocletian's Edict of Maximum Prices 26-28. See S. Lauffer, *Diokletians Preisedikt*, Texte und Kommentare (Berlin, 1971).

49. The Medaba Mosaic Map, set into the floor of a church in Madaba in Arabia, depicts Palestine at the time of the Emperor Justinian. For a description of the map, see M.Avi-Yonah, *The Madaba Mosaic Map*.

50. This is the Piacenza pilgrim who visited Palestine in the sixth century (Antoninus Placentinus 89).

51. See Ovadiah 21,23,24,25,160.

sections provide us with all the information we have about the life of Cyril. They describe a boy who was brought up in an ecclesiastical environment with a father who worked in the bishop's residence and a mother who was known for her piety. He was singled out for special attention by Sabas when he visited Scythopolis and was educated in the bishop's house. As soon as possible, he became a monk and went to Jerusalem. There the noted ascetic, John the Hesychast, who was a friend of the family, advised him to enter the monastery of Euthymius which, to judge from Cyril's reluctance to follow this advice, had probably fallen away from its former glory. After a short stay near Jericho, brought to an end by a spell of illness, he entered the monastery of Euthymius, where he spent the next ten years. He was among the group of monks who reclaimed the New Laura for orthodoxy after the expulsion of the Origenists, but he stayed there for only two years. The last time we hear of him, he is at the Great Laura, where he went in 557. It is assumed that, since he did not start writing until after his arrival at the New Laura in 555, and since he succeeded in producing seven biographies—albeit of uneven length—in the following two years, only an unnaturally early death, probably in 558, could have put an end to his prolific literary activity. The titles to his Lives show that he was a priest.

9. THE NATURE AND PURPOSE OF HIS WORK

Cyril's whole life was spent in Palestine. So far as we know, he never travelled outside the Roman provinces of Palestine I and II. The great journey of his life took him from his childhood home in Scythopolis to Jerusalem and the desert surrounding it—a distance of about fifty miles. Once arrived, he embraced whole-heartedly the way of life of the desert monks and showed no desire for anything else. In his writing he is describing his own world, the only world he had ever experienced. He writes as an insider.

This makes his lives different from most early monastic literature, which is almost entirely the work of outsiders. The authors were sometimes visitors and their writing took the form of a travel diary. An important work is the *Historia Monachorum in Aegypto*. This was written by one of a group of seven monks from a monastery on the Mount of Olives in Jerusalem who made a visit to the monks of Egypt in 394-5. The author describes the journey they took and the old men they visited. The impact of the experience on the writer is apparent from the tone of amazement and admiration which runs through the work. He wanted to share the lessons learned and the inspiration received with a wider audience. Other examples of this approach are the *Lausiac History* of Palladius, written by a Galatian who spent several years in Egypt before becoming Bishop of Helenopolis in Bithynia; the *Institutes* and *Conferences* of John Cassian, a monk from Bethlehem who later settled in Gaul; and the *Spiritual Meadow* of John Moschus, which records his travels in Palestine, Egypt, Sinai, Antioch, Cyprus, and Rome.[52]

Other contributions to the literature about the monks come from the pens of sympathetic bishops. Antony's biographer, Athanasius, was bishop in Alexandria, among the richest and most influential of the sees of the early christian world and had experience of doctrinal controversy at the Councils of Nicaea and Constantinople; he had tasted exile on three occasions. His *Life of Antony* reveals his admiration for the holy monk who spent his whole adult life in seclusion in the desert of Egypt. The motives of Theodoret in writing his *History of the Monks of Syria* are similar. The embattled bishop, caught up in christological controversy, looks longingly at the ascetics of the mountains of his native Syria, a group of men with whom he had once had close links but from which the demands of his position in the church had distanced him.

An emphasis on instruction as a motive for writing betrays the standpoint of the outsider. Athanasius writes in the introduction to the *Life of Antony:*

---

52. Full details of these works are noted in the bibliography.

> Since you have asked me about the career of the
> blessed Antony... so that you might also lead
> yourselves in imitation of him, I received your
> directive with ready goodwill. For simply to re-
> member Antony is a great profit and assistance
> for me also.[53]

This statement of intention is echoed in the other works
mentioned above. The anonymous monk from the Mount of
Olives wrote in the *Historia Monachorum:*

> Since I have derived much benefit from these
> monks, I have undertaken this work to provide a
> paradigm and a testimony for the perfect, and to
> edify and benefit those who are only beginners
> in the ascetic life.[54]

Cyril's stated motive for writing is different. He hoped of
course, that people would follow the same ascetic path trod-
den by Euthymius and Sabas: their deeds are 'a common
benefit, image, and model for those who wish to take
thought for their salvation' (8.16). But there is no clear
statement that he is writing to instruct the reader in the way
of virtue, and few passages of ascetic teaching. The *Life of
Euthymius* contains some short extracts from the saint's
spiritual teaching in which Cyril draws extensively on his
literary sources (16.25-18.11, 30.10-32.5, 58.2-20). John the
Hesychast is depicted offering guidance and encouragement
to visitors who 'lay before him' their temptations and afflic-
tions (216.19, 217.26, 218.15). With these exceptions,
Cyril's monks offer little spiritual guidance and teaching.

Cyril's subject is the life of the Palestinian monasteries
and the achievements of the great monks. He describes the

---

53. *Life of Antony*, Introduction.
54. *Lives of the Desert Fathers*, Prologue 12.

ascetic struggles and miraculous powers of the saints with the clarity and simplicity of one who is familiar with what he is writing about, rather than the open-mouthed amazement of the tourist. Cyril's writing is admired for its accuracy, especially in historical, chronological, and topographical detail. His claim is justified when he states: 'I have noted precise details of time and place, of persons and names, so as to achieve close investigation of the truth in these matters' (86.22-3). He wants to report the events and to prevent them being lost in the 'abyss of long time and oblivion' (86.3). The readers, he hopes, will be struck with admiration for the holiness and authority of the saints, and will then, like the procession of sick, possessed, and troubled who came in supplication to the tombs of the holy men, be led to trust in the efficacy of their power to heal and to intercede in the heavenly court. Cyril wants people to pray to—or through—the saints rather than to imitate them.

10. DOCTRINAL DISPUTES

Cyril's monastic career took place in a society divided by doctrinal controversy. He arrived in Jerusalem in 543, and could not have avoided being drawn into the painful events which he describes vividly in the closing pages of the Life of Sabas. It was a time when monks of the Great Laura could not walk the streets of the capital in safety (193.21-7). He was not an impartial observer but took a keen interest in the issues under discussion. His mother was anxious lest her son be seduced by the attraction of theological speculation and firmly instructed him to be guided by the advice of John the Hesychast. Her concern was clearly well-founded, for Cyril shows himself sympathetic to the teachings of the Origenist group and has to have the error of this way of thinking firmly demonstrated by Cyriacus (229.24-230.22). This conversation points to a process by which he became a firm supporter of the 'orthodox' and took part in the final victory by participating in the settlement of the New Laura after the Council of Constantinople.

Cyril's holy men played an important part in the struggle for orthodoxy. The opposition of Euthymius to the Monophysites and of Sabas to the Origenists follow a similar pattern. First, the enemy is identified (41.19-42.15, 103.12-17). Then the saint, rather than risk defilement by consorting with heretics, retires to a remote spot (44.15-45.4, 118.29-121.2). His absence is brief and before long he is back in his monastery (45.5-6, 121.14-122.18). The correctness of his faith is recognised and his authority acknowledged by, among others, representatives of the imperial family (47.26-49.2, 141.24-144.28). The final downfall of the heresy takes place after the saint's death, a sign of the effectiveness of his intercession in the courts of heaven rather than any weakness in his ministry on earth (66.18-67.20, 198.7-200.16). The struggles of Cyril's other subjects for orthodoxy are referred to but not described (221.18-22, 229.7-230.22, 235.14, 238.25). The prophecy made about Euthymius, that he would restore *euthymia* or confidence to the churches, could apply equally to any of the saints described by Cyril (9.6-9).

The two heresies of Monophysitism and Origenism were very different phenomena. Monophysitism was a widespread and popular movement of opposition to the christological definitions of the Council of Chalcedon. The instructions given by Euthymius to a delegate to the Council of Ephesus in 431, to uphold the teaching of Cyril of Alexandria and Acacius of Melitene, was typical of the doctrinal views of the bulk of the Byzantine Church (33.3-6). The teaching of Cyril, which was rigidly adhered to by the Monophysites, was seen as authoritative. But the doctrinal statements of Chalcedon were influenced by the theological positions and language of the Western Church, expressed in the Tome of Leo as well as by the more familiar writings of Cyril. The result was a statement about the two natures in Christ couched in novel terms

which seemed to many to be a return to the Nestorianism successfully demolished at Ephesus in 431. The monks, especially, received the news of the Council of Chalcedon with shock and
amazement.[55]

The reaction to the Council was immediate and violent in both
Egypt and Palestine (41.19-42.9, 50.20-51.1). But whereas in Egypt
the anti-Chalcedonian feeling hardened and led eventually to the
establishing of a separate monophysite hierarchy, in Palestine the
uprising was swiftly quelled and Chalcedonian orthodoxy eventually triumphed. Several reasons for this different historical development have been suggested, among them nationalistic forces.[56] In
Egypt the strength of the monophysite movement lay in the
Coptic-speaking communities in which loyalty to the memory of
Cyril of Alexandria and Dioscorus blended with social and economic grievances to form an intractable popular separatist church.
Similar characteristics are found in the Monophysite parts of Syria,
except, of course, that the language was Syriac. In Palestine the
christian community was Greek. The written rule attributed to
Sabas shows signs of discrimination against Syriac speakers with
its refusal to allow a superior to be chosen from among this group.
The writings of Cyril and Theodore of Petra make no mention of
the Syriac language being used in the monasteries. The monasteries
were more open to influence from outside than those in Egypt, and
the Chalcedonian faith slowly gained ground.[57]

55. John Rufus' *Plerophoria* is a Palestinian Monophysite source which
describes vividly the repugnance of the monks towards Chalcedon and their
hatred of Juvenal.

56. The nationalist view of Monophysitism is argued by Hardy, *Christian
Egypt, Church and People*. A criticism of this thesis is in Jones, 'Were the
ancient heresies nationalist or social movements in disguise?' Jones' evidence
for Palestine is limited and does not derive from the area around Jerusalem.

57. The list of Euthymius' first monks shows their international character
(25.13-26.14), but the fullest evidence comes from the inscriptions in the
monastery burial chambers of Choziba, presented by Schneider, 'Das Kloster
der Theotokos zu Choziba'. The Rule of Sabas is summarised in Kurtz, 'Tupos
kai paradosis'. Some of the doctrinal statements of this period are presented in
A. Grillmeier, *Christ in the Christian Tradition*, vol. 2/1, especially pages

But even in Palestine the debate was protracted. Cyril has exaggerated the importance of Euthymius' contribution. The doctrinal views attributed to the saint are, in fact, those of a century later and are taken from the writings of the Emperor Justinian (39.18-41.3). Monophysite historians give a very different account of the events, suggesting that the decisions of Chalcedon were not accepted in Palestine until the accession of the Emperor Justin I in 518 (162.10-18).[58] It is intriguing to speculate why Euthymius did not support Theodosius after the Council of Chalcedon. Was he really persuaded of the orthodoxy of the council's definition or was he repelled by the violence and illegitimacy of Theodosius' uprising?

The second doctrinal debate described by Cyril is that with the Origenists. Origenist speculation, with its basis in the study of the Bible and its interest in the fate of the soul after it has left this world, exercised a powerful attraction over the more intellectual monks. The history of monasticism shows Origenists sometime living in harmony with other monks, sometimes in uneasy tension, and sometimes in open conflict. Conflict had been especially bitter in Egypt following Theophilus of Alexandria's condemnation of Origenism in 400.[59] Cyril describes the existence in the Great Laura of a group of intellectual monks who complained of Sabas' lack of education and its development into an organised party boasting influential spokesmen at the imperial court and unified by an acceptance of Evagrian doctrinal opinions.[60]

The zenith of the group's influence came during the reaction to Justinian's Edict against Origenism promulgated in 543. In

----

98-105, 200-201, 250-252, 279-281.

58. The dependence of Cyril of Justinian is shown in Schwartz, 362. For further background on the history of the Monophysite heresy, see Frend, *The Rise of the Monophysite Movement*.

59. Palladius, *Lausiac History* 10.6, 11.4, gives an account of several respected Origenist monks in Egypt. The conflict over Origenism is described by Sozomen, *Ecclesiastical History* 8.11-22, and Socrates, *Ecclesiastical History* 6.7-13.

60. See *Life of Sabas*, note 133.

the years following, it was able to secure the appointment of its favoured candidates to the important posts of superior of the Great Laura and, finally, Patriarch of Jerusalem. Its downfall came at the Council of Constantinople in 553, and two years later the Origenists were expelled from their stronghold in the New Laura.

Cyril wrote in the flush of victory when he was inhabiting the New Laura, a member of the vanguard of the triumphant army. A theme of his work is the vocation of the monastic leaders to establish the orthodox faith in the church. Involvement and interest in the doctrinal controversy of the sixth century led to his Lives becoming an apologetic statement of the faith which has come to be called neo-Chalcedonian.[61]

11. CYRIL'S MENTORS AND SOURCES

Cyril was educated—enough, but not too much. He refers briefly to his upbringing and education. In response to the commission laid on him by Sabas, the Metropolitan of Scythopolis took an interest in the lad and often asked after him (141.14-12). Cyril's teacher was his father, who held an important administrative post in the bishop's house and so would have achieved a high standard of education. He was well qualified to act as a teacher for his son. Cyril emerged with a detailed knowledge of the Bible, which he refers to continually throughout his writings, and of the lives of the saints which were popular in the Palestine of his day. He acquired some knowledge of rhetoric, and is capable of elegant writing in approved classical style, as when, for example, he includes the polished description of the beauties of the site of

61. Neo-Chalcedonianism is the name given to the theology of the second Council of Constantinople (553). It harmonised the theology of Chalcedon with the thought of Cyril of Alexandria. See, for example, C. Moeller, 'Le Chalcédonisme et le Néo-Chalcédonisme en Orient de 451 à la fin du VIe siècle'.

Euthymius' monastery (64.21-65.8). He does not, however, appear to have any familiarity with classical non-christian writing. No non-christian author is referred to by name or quoted by Cyril at any point in the lives. Cyril claims, apparently correctly, that he is 'employing a style which is artless and without knowledge of secular culture' (6.17-18).

This is a clear statement of his educational background. In comparison with the cultured city of Caesarea with its centres of pagan, Jewish and Christian learning, Scythopolitan society must have seemed provincial and unsophisticated. Cyril's basic and biblically-inspired education enabled him to write in a clear, direct and unfussy style, which has been much appreciated by his readers. 'He did not learn rhetoric— fortunately', commented E. Schwartz.[62]

Cyril's understanding of the ascetic life emerges, like so much else in his writing, from his own experience. His early vocation to the monastic life, in his case spoken through the mouth of the holy man Sabas, and an education designed to lead him towards the exemplary fulfilment of this calling, contributed to his idea of the appropriate way for a monk's life to develop. Descriptions of his own family background and childhood closely resemble those of the family background and childhood of Euthymius.[63] Euthymius was born nearly two centuries before Cyril wrote, and he filled in gaps in his knowledge with details from his own life.

The lives of Euthymius and Sabas develop in a manner similar to that of Cyril. Like Cyril, Euthymius and Sabas both seem called to the ascetic life from their birth. Like him, they both receive an appropriate education. Like him they start the monastic life in their home town and then travel to Jerusalem to make a deeper discovery of the ascetic experience. There is

---

62. E. Schwartz, *Kyrillos von Skythopolis*, 462. But Cyril's modest comment cited here could be interpreted as a rhetorical technique and so a sign of education.

63. Compare 10.6-8 and 10.15 with 180.4-6, and 10.19-21 with 181.17-18.

no notion of a sudden conversion as was the case in the Life of Pachomius.[64] Monastic life starts at birth and grows steadily.

Cyril was obedient and accepted the authority of senior monks without question. The awe-inspiring words of Sabas— 'From now on this boy is my disciple and a son of the fathers of the Desert'—were never forgotten (180.11-12). The authoritative intervention of the saint into the life of the young boy determined his future vocation. In its development he relied heavily on the guidance and direction of others. In particular, he refers to his dependence on two older men. The first was George of Beella who lived in a monastery near Scythopolis. Cyril had known him as he grew up, made his monastic renunciation before him, remained in contact with him for the rest of his life, sought information from him about Sabas' visits to Scythopolis for the projected biography, and followed his guidance over the question of whether he should settle in the New Laura (71.11-16, 164.25–28, 181.2-14). The Lives were written in response to George's insistence that Cyril set down clearly the evidence he had collected, and they were dedicated to him. Cyril's second main guide was John the Hesychast. John was also a friend of the family, and directed the early stages of Cyril's monastic career. Cyril's description of his relationship with John in the *Life of John the Hesychast* shows that he regularly visited the old man and confided closely in him, seeking his blessing for his subsequent movement around the desert. Cyril records an attempt to break away from the authority of those set over him when he ignored John's direction to settle in Euthymius' monastery. This independent action ended in a period of illness from which he was healed only after he returned to a more obedient attitude. It was his deeply-rooted conviction of the importance of obedience that led Cyril to collect and then record the events in the lives of the great saints. He describes a visit

64. *First Greek Life of Pachomius 5.*

he made to Cyriacus, in which the old man gave him both clear instructions about the orthodox interpretation of the christian faith and also a valuable collection of information about the lives of Euthymius and Sabas. His enquiries extended to others of the old monks of the desert, and before long he had accumulated much evidence which he 'recorded mixed together on various sheets in disorganised and jumbled narratives' (83.5-7). Sabas, whose appearance in a fleshly body at Scythopolis had made such a strong impression on Cyril, appeared again, this time in the company of Euthymius and in a more spiritual glorified state, and at an opportune moment encouraged Cyril to start on his work of writing the Lives. Cyril's monastic life, his collection of information, and his final work of authorship should be seen as an expression of the obedience which his dependent relationships with others had encouraged.

Careful research rather than literary creativity is the hallmark of Cyril's writings.[65]The process by which his Lives emerged included a series of interviews with the monks who had known Euthymius and Sabas (82.30-83.7). These oral sources enabled Cyril to produce the vivid narratives which describe the struggles of the saints in setting up monasteries in hostile and threatening environments and in witnessing to the orthodox faith. In the other sections of his writing—especially those parts which present the ascetic teaching of the saints and the introductory prologues—he had had to look elsewhere for source material.

He found it in the monastic literature available to him. He admits to quoting from only one author, Gregory of Naziansus,[66] but the instructional and introductional sections of his writing are carefully constructed and draw on a large number of standard Christian works. Athanasius' *Life of Antony* has, not surprisingly, provided the largest amount of material. A recent study discovered twenty-six passages in which Cyril has borrowed ideas or

65. That 'we have little impression of originality in Cyril's personal religion' is the view of D. Chitty, *The Desert a City*, 131.

66. See 12.2 and 229.27.

phrases from Athanasius.[67]Other works used by Cyril are Theodoret's *History of the Monks of Syria,* the *Apophthegmata Patrum,* Palladius' *Lausiac History,* the *Life of Pachomius,* and Basil of Ancyra's *Life and Miracles of Thekla.* To demonstrate fully the extent of Cyril's use of these authors, it would be necessary to set out the Greek text in parallel with the texts of the work concerned. Since Bernard Flusin has collected together the findings of several studies describing the dependence of Cyril on various authors and has added further evidence of his own, it is unnecessary to repeat the exercise here. The main borrowings appear in the annotation to the text and the interested reader is advised to consult Flusin's study for further analysis.[68]

The distinctive features of the writing of Cyril of Scythopolis are the simple, clear, and readable style of writing, the careful recording of places, dates, and events, and the placing of the narrative in a broad historical context. He combines two styles of writing which had previously been separate: the historical and the hagiographical. His work has been seen as inaugurating a new style of literature in which the saints' lives become history rather than pious legend.[69]

12. CONCLUSION

Cyril's writing stops in 558, as a result, it is assumed, of his death. At that moment the struggles of Euthymius and Sabas appeared to have been successful. The monasteries were thriving. The

67. G. Garitte,'Reminiscences de la Vie d'Antoine dans Cyrille de Scythopolis', 83-86.

68. B. Flusin, *Miracle et histoire dans l'oeuvre de Cyrille de Scythopolis,* 43-86.

69. E. Stein describes these two styles of hagiographical writing, claiming that Cyril is a pioneer of the historical approach to hagiography associated with the Bollandists. See E. Stein, *Histoire du Bas-Empire,* II, 699. E. Schwartz concludes: 'Damit gab er der Asketenvita eine neue Form' (E. Schwartz, *Kyrillos von Skythopolis,* 355.

heresies had been beaten back. The Emperor was an upholder of orthodoxy. The tombs of the saints provided ample proof, in the form of miraculous healings and exorcisms, that the saints were powerful advocates in the heavenly court. The church was united under an orthodox Emperor and Jerusalem was its heart.

This situation was not to last. In 615, the invading Persian army marched into Jerusalem, and for three days massacred the inhabitants. A contemporary source gives the number of victims as 33,000 or 67,000, depending on which text is accepted.[70] In 629, peace was made between Rome and Persia, and two years later the Emperor Heraclius restored the True Cross to Jerusalem. But this respite was brief. The next enemies to threaten the Holy City were the Arabs, and in 638 Patriarch Sophronius surrendered the city to the Sultan Omar. That date marks the end of Byzantine Jerusalem. It also marks the end of Cyril's vision of a church centered on Jerusalem and presided over by a God-loving Emperor advised by holy monks.

But the Great Laura of Sabas survived. Today it is the only monastery of the Palestinian desert to have been occupied continuously since its foundation. Among its monks have been many influential theologians and hymn writers, including St Andrew of Crete, whose *Great Canon* forms an essential part of Orthodox Lenten worship, and St John of Damascus.[71]

The Palestinian monasteries described by Cyril have mostly vanished. But they have left behind them a living monastic tradition which has had an enormous influence on the Eastern Church.

70. The figures are given in Strategius, *The Capture of Jerusalem*. This text survives in a Greek and a Georgian version which offer the alternative figures.

71. For the later history of Mar Saba, see G. Heydock, *Die Heilige Sabas und seine Reliquien*, and D. Chitty, *The Desert a City*, 179-81.

LIFE OF OUR FATHER SAINT EUTHYMIUS

DEDICATION

TO THE MOST HONORABLE and truly virtuous spiritual father Abba George,[1] priest and superior, who leads the solitary life in a manner pleasing to God in the place near Scythopolis called Beella, Cyril sends greetings in the Lord.

May faith be the guide in the account of the well-named Euthymius—faith that 'gives substance to things hoped for,'[a] by which we are justified and 'in which we stand and make our boast in the hope of the glory of God,'[b] for 'without faith it is impossible to be well-pleasing,' since (as Scripture continues) 'one who approaches God must believe that he exists and that he is always a rewarder of those who seek him.'[c][2] He who attempts to hear or say anything without faith labors in vain, unable to procure himself any benefit; but he who has attained a faith powerful in everything is able to do whatever he wishes, especially if he keeps this faith unwavering and does not yield to unbelief but is always vigorous and strengthened in his faith, not hesitating or doubting. 'He who doubts is like a billow of the sea, driven by the wind and tossed'[d]— and so on.

I for my part place unwavering faith as the origin, root, and foundation of the account of holy Euthymius, so that those who in future read it may attain this faith and disbelieve none of it, but through faith incline their minds to assent. May you yourself, most honor-

5,5

5,10

5,15

5,20

a. Heb 11:1.
b. Rom 5:2.
c. Heb 11:6.
d. Jam 1:6.

1

able father, fortified by the power of the Holy Spirit, be strengthened in firmness of faith. For it is relying onfaith that I have commenced this labor, emulating the love of labor of the bee, that gathers from many flowers the ingredients for making honey.[3] Applying

6,5 zealous prayer, I have gathered up from truthful saints, the most aged in this desert, stories that had been lost through time; flitting hither and thither, collecting and gathering them together, I have recovered them from some abyss, as it were, of long time and oblivion, in certain trust that I shall receive from God the rewarder

6,10 the reward for restoring to memory things worthy to be remembered and providing a fine model for those who read such a painstaking endeavor as this. Even if I fall short of the deserts of the venerable father I am prais-ing, I have none the less judged it right rather to fall short of his deserts, while moved by good will, than to give up the whole attempt in ill will and thereby dis-

6,15 obey Your Fatherhood; in addition I am afraid of the terrible rebuke of the wicked and slothful servant who hid his talent in the ground.[e] This is why I have been so bold, employing a style that is artless and without knowledge of secular culture, as to begin with the help of God the following account, while he inspires

6,20 my speech at the intercession of holy Euthymius, who has provided the subject of the account.

1. PREFACE TO THE LIFE, OR PROLOGUE[4]

The only-begotten Son and Word of God, who is coeternal with the Father, similarly without beginning and of the same substance, deigned, in his ineffable

7. love of men, according to the Father's good pleasure

---

e. Cf. Mt 25:25-26.

and the will of the Holy Spirit, to become flesh and man for our salvation by the immaculate Mary, Mother of God, and to be born of her, as neither only God nor

7,5 mere man, but rather as God incarnate, hypostatically uniting the manhood to himself, neither undergoing confusion or change nor altered in nature: he remained what he was when he became what he was not, the difference between the natures that came together being evidently preserved, as they concurred in inseparable union into one *prosôpon* and *hypostasis*.[5] Hence in each

7,10 of the essences there is one and the same Christ, the Son of the living God, acknowledged to be both undivided and unconfused. Therefore, though impassible God, he did not refuse to become man capable of suffering and, though immortal, he consented to be subject to the laws of death, so that by such tender condescension towards us and voluntary self-emptying he

7,15 might bestow on us ascent to himself. Accordingly, when he sent out his disciples for the salvation of our race, he said, 'Go and teach all nations, baptizing them in the name of the Father and of the Son and of the Holy Spirit.'[a] On receiving this teaching, they

7,20 sped through the whole world to proclaim piety by both word and deed, teaching by word and confirming the word by their deeds and lives. They experienced every discomfort, being persecuted, afflicted, stripped bare, deprived even of necessities; finally they were courageous even in death, as in all things excellent

7,25 imitators of the Master. This is why the knowledge of God has risen upon the world; this is why the human race has been illuminated and set free from the tyranny of the devil; this is why the grace of salvation has dawned upon men without hope, benefiting all in many and diverse ways; this is why from all nations

a. Mt 28:19.

8.   flocks of holy martyrs have sprung up, in emulation of
            whose contests so many, after the persecutions, have
            shone like stars in the monastic life. These men have
            made their lives impresses of the Apostles' virtues,
            since they fit the scriptural saying, 'They went about in
8,5   skins of sheep and goats, destitute, afflicted, ill-treated,
            wandering in deserts and mountains and caves and
            apertures of the earth.'[b] This unimpeachable life was
            also shared by our great father Euthymius; dedicated to
            God from infancy and emulator of the life of the saints,
8,10   he became both pleasing to God and esteemed by men.
            Commanded to record the life in the flesh of this holy
            father, I obey your command without any delay,
            honorable father George; for you command what is
            pleasant and beneficial and also worthy of your Holi-
            ness. For it is indeed right to depict in word deeds that
8,15   have been lost with time and are known to few, and not
            to let them grow dim in the depths of oblivion but to
            offer them as a common benefit, image and model for
            those hereafter who wish to take thought for their sal-
            vation. So now accordingly, after invoking the Son and
            Word of God, and placing him at the head of the pre-
            sent account, I shall begin my account of Euthymius.

                  2. EUTHYMIUS' FATHERLAND, HIS PARENTS'
                          VISION AND HIS BIRTH

8,20   Euthymius, citizen of heaven,[6] had parents called
            Paul and Dionysia. They were not undistinguished but
            of most noble birth and adorned with every godly
            virtue, while as fatherland and home they had
            Melitene, the famous metropolis of Armenia. Blessed
            Dionysia, after cohabiting with her husband for many

            _____
            b. Heb 11:37-38.

years, had not given birth, being sterile.[7] Being as a
9.   result much disheartened, the two of them continued
for a long time to entreat God earnestly to give them a
child. Going to the shrine near the city there of the glorious and victorious martyr Polyeuctus,[8] they per-
severed for many days in prayer, as the account of the
9,5   ancient monks that has come down to me has made
known; and one night, as they were praying alone, a
divine vision appeared to them and said, 'Be confident,
be confident; for behold, God has granted you a child
who will bear the name of confidence (*euthymia*), since
at his birth he who grants you him will give confidence
to his churches.' Noting the hour of the vision, they
9,10   returned home. From the time of his conception they
recognized that the vision had proved true, and from
the moment of his birth they called the child
Euthymius and promised to offer him to God. He was
born, as tradition relates, in the month of August in the
fourth consulship of Gratian. That the vision is true, let
9,15   our readers acknowledge: for though the holy churches
[AD 377]   had been disheartened for around forty years, the
champions of the orthodox faith expelled, the Arians
in control from the time of Constantius, and persecution pressing down on the faithful in the time both of
the usurper Julian and of his successor as emperor
9,20   in the East, Valens, as soon as Euthymius, the appropriately named, was born, all the distress of the
holy churches was transformed into confidence. For
before the completion of the fifth month in his sixth
[AD 378]   consulship, Valens, the enemy of God, set off under
arms against the barbarians ravaging Thrace and,
crushed in battle a short time afterwards, paid a penalty
10.   worthy of his enmity towards God: in a village near
Adrianople in Thrace, vanquished by force of arms and
in flight, he was burnt by the barbarians in pursuit, together with the village harboring him, before the completion of the first year after Euthymius' birth.

3. HE IS BAPTIZED AND BECOMES A LECTOR

10,5   After the inception of his third year,[9] his father
[AD 379] Paul came to the end of his life. Blessed Dionysia had
a highly educated brother called Eudoxius, who had
authority in the episcopal palace there as the bishop's
assessor.[10] Making him her adviser and intermediary,
10,10   she presented the child to the great Otreius, who at that
time was ruling the most holy church of Melitene and
who distinguished himself at the holy council of
Constantinople;[11] she thereby fulfilled her promise, by
offering him as an acceptable sacrifice to God just as
the celebrated Anna had done with Samuel. The holy
10,15   bishop the great Otreius, on seeing the child and hearing from the *scholasticus*[12] Eudoxius about the vision
that had appeared to the parents, and that before his
birth his mother had promised him to God, without
anxiety about the future, and that the conception itself
had been the work of prayer, said in amazement, 'The
10,20   Spirit of God has truly rested upon this child.' Accepting the child, he baptized him, gave him the tonsure,
and made him lector in his church;[13] taking him into
the bishop's palace and virtually adopting him, he be-
11.   gan to bring him up. Blessed Dionysia, since devoted
to God and to the things of God, he ordained deaconess
of holy Church. No sooner had Euthymius been
thereby enrolled in the list of the clergy than
Theodosius the Great received the scepter of the
Roman empire. Through one event God granted the
11,5   Roman state and his holy churches a divine gift full of
all confidence (*euthymia*), and effected that at this time
the reality occurred in accordance with the name; for it
was necessary that the vision which had appeared to
his parents concerning him should be fulfilled.

4. HOW AND BY WHOM HE WAS EDUCATED

11,10

11,15

11,20

12.

12,5

12,10

A short time afterwards, observing that the boy had passed infancy and ought now to apply himself to studies, the bishop entrusted him to teachers of sacred letters. There were at that time among the lectors two youths respected for their birth and self-control, outstanding in every intellectual gift, and carefully educated in secular culture[14] as well as in Sacred Scripture; their names were Acacius and Synodius. After many ascetic labors they received, each in his turn, the office of archbishop of the most holy church of Melitene;[15] both of them lived a life that accorded with the office of archbishop, and the descendents of their flock recount many wonderful things about them, truly worthy of the priestly office. It was these men who received Euthymius from the hands of the bishop and taught him perfect piety. In a short time Euthymius had surpassed a great many of his contemporaries in the soul's love of God and love of learning; for he showed a keenness beyond his age, with the result that Acacius was amazed at his inspired mental grasp. So it was that this holy youth was educated in the bishop's palace during his earliest years, and received the best and purest moulding, that which, as Gregory the Theologian says,[16] the godly David aptly calls that 'of the day' in contrast to that 'of the night'. As he studied the divine Scriptures, he yearned to be an emulator of the godly and virtuous men contained in them, and was pained when chatterboxes separated or distracted him from the divine sayings. In imitation of the habits of his teacher Acacius, he showed not the slightest interest in dainty fare nor longed for empty glory, nor did his mouth grow tired of praising God, but with undistracted heart and unwavering mind he performed at the appointed times with fear and compunction the divine liturgy of the Church's rule, reflecting that one must

worship God in fear and trembling, and not make the
church a theatrical stage with laughter and backbiting,

12,15   but that each man should go to church reverently, as
about to encounter through prayer his God and king.
The time in between he spent at home in prayer, psalmody and reading the divine sayings all day and all
night, knowing that 'he who rehearses the law of the
Lord day and night will be like a tree planted by the

12,20   effluence of waters, which will give its fruit in its
season'.[a] And he gave to God the fruit appropriate to
each season: in time of anger he brought to God the
fruits of love and patience, in time of gluttony his fruit
was self-control, and again, when thoughts came to

12,25   him of some bodily pleasure, it was chastity that blos-
13.   somed in him. He had as his comrades and familiars
not the undisciplined but the self-controlled, whose
company was the most beneficial for one devoted to
piety. And so through daily athletic contest[17] he built
up self-control as regards the tongue and the belly, per-

13,5   fect freedom from possessiveness, true humility, and
sanctification of the body. Especially attentive to chastity, he kept the luster of his virginity unextinguished,
adorned with the balm of pity and compassion.

5. HE BECOMES A PRIEST
AND OVERSEER OF MONKS

By undergoing this training for a long time Euthy-
13,10   mius attained perfection in the virtues. Divine
Providence, by making him wise in this way and well-
known through many intermediaries, established his
fame right from the start. Reared and educated in the
way described, and after proceeding through the whole
sequence of the ecclesiastical grades, he was ordained

a. Ps 1:3.

13,15   by the then bishop,[18] despite his reluctance, priest of the most holy church of Melitene and entrusted with the care and charge of the monasteries near the city. He received this charge because he had loved monasticism from boyhood and in his desire for solitude had spent most of his time at the monasteries of St Polyeuctus

13,20   and of the Thirty-three Holy Martyrs. During the holy season of Lent he would retire to a mountain that was then uninhabited but has now received the buildings of a wonderful monastery near the city, called by the surrounding population the monastery of the Ascension; he would cling to this desert place from the day of the

13,25   holy Theophanies till the Paschal festival, imitating the philosophy of Elijah and John.[19] This is why he was entrusted, as I have said, with the care and direction of the monks there. Considering the charge an obstacle to virtue, as a hater of glory and lover of God Euthymius

14.   left the city and went as a fugitive to Jerusalem,[20] out of a desire to inhabit its desert.

6. COMING TO JERUSALEM HE STAYS AT PHARAN

     Our great father Euthymius, led by the Holy Spirit,

AD 405/6   came to Jerusalem in the twenty-ninth year of his life.

14,5   After he had venerated the holy Cross, the church of the holy Resurrection[21] and the other venerable places, and also visited the inspired fathers in the desert, studying the virtue and way of life of each one and impressing it upon his own soul, he came to the laura of

14,10   Pharan, lying six miles from the holy city.[22] In his love of solitude he stayed in a hermit's cell outside the laura, possessing absolutely nothing of the goods of this age. He learnt to make cords in order not to be a burden on anyone but rather to give to those in want a share in the fruit of his labors. Freeing himself from

14,15   every earthly care he had as his one sole aim how to please God through prayer and fasting. In his concern for every virtue he cut off the thorns of the passions at the root, like a good cultivator, 'clearing away thoughts and every high thing raised up against the knowledge of God,'[a] and fulfilling the prophetic saying that runs,

14,20 'Break up your fallow ground and do not scatter seed on thorns.'[b]

7. HOW HE WAS SPIRITUALLY ATTACHED TO THEOCTISTUS

He had as neighbor an inspired man called Theoctistus. He came to love him and grew so united to him in spiritual affection that the two became indistinguishable in both thought and conduct and displayed, as it were, one soul in two bodies.[23] Announcing each

14,25 to the other his godly aim, they set off each year after the octave of the holy Theophanies to the desert of

15. Coutila,[24] sundered from all human intercourse and yearning to consort with God in solitude through prayer; they remained there till Palm Sunday, continuously subduing and enslaving the body while applying spiritual nourishment to the soul. The great Euthymius

15,5 carried off the prize for singleness of character, meekness of behavior and humility of heart. On account of this he received the grace of the Holy Spirit, in accordance with the divine saying, 'Upon whom shall I look but on a man meek and quiet, who fears my words?'[a] Thence too his familiar access[25] to God increased each day.

a. 2 Cor 10:5.
b. Jer 4:3.
a. Is 66:2.

8. HOW HE CAME TO THE GORGE
AND FOUNDED A MONASTERY

15,10
[AD 411]

After spending five years at Pharan, he set off with blessed Theoctistus at their usual time for Coutila. As they passed through the desert they came to a terrifying gorge, extremely steep and impassable. On seeing the

15,15

place and going round the cliffs above it they found, as if guided by God, a huge and marvellous cave in the northern cliff of the gorge. Not without danger they made the steep ascent and just managed to climb up to it. Overjoyed as if the cave had been prepared for them by God, they made it their home, feeding on the plants that happened to grow there. The cave had earlier been

15,20

a lair of wild animals; but tamed by the holy hymns and ceaseless prayers of these pious men, it was sanctified by becoming a church of God.[26] When it pleased God to make them known, he contrived that some herdsmen of Lazarium[27] should lead their flocks to this very gorge. The fathers' appearing to them above in the cave so frightened them that in terror they

16.

took to flight. The fathers, perceiving their panic, called to them with gentle and kindly voice, saying, 'Do not fear, brethren: we are men like yourselves,[28] but inhabit this place because of our sins.' At this the goatherds recovered confidence, and climbed up to

16,5

them in the cave. On finding that the fathers had none of the goods of this age, they went off to their farm, to recount their amazement to their own people. From that time the people of Lazarium ministered to them. In addition, the fathers of Pharan, discovering after search where they were, came to them frequently to make a visitation.

16,10

The first to renounce the world[29] to join them were two brothers called Marinus and Luke. Educated in monasticism by the great Euthymius and made into athletes of the ascetic life, they later attained distinc-

tion in the region of the village of Metopa, where they
founded monasteries;[30] it was they who taught monas-
16,15   tic perfection to Abba Theodosius who became a great
cenobitic superior of this desert and an archimandrite
of cenobia. In a short time, as Euthymius' fame spread,
many flocked to him and, hearkening to the word of
God, desired to live with him. But Euthymius, as a
16,20   hater of glory and lover of God, was eager to attain the
first of the beatitudes as well as the rest[a] and, as if possessing the status of a stranger, entrusted each of those
who renounced this life to the blessed Theoctistus, after exhorting him in every way to take on this charge.
He, not knowing disobedience, accepted this charge
and carried out everything in accordance with the
wishes of the great Euthymius.

9. THE TEACHING OF EUTHYMIUS[31]

Originally they planned to make the place not a
cenobium but a laura on the model of Pharan. But
17.   when they saw that no one could get to the church by
night, because, as I said above, the place was impassable, they gradually transformed it into a cenobium,
with the cave for a church. Living the solitary life in
this cave, the great Euthymius was a doctor of souls,
17,5   treating and encouraging each one, and none of the
brethren drew back from confessing his thoughts to
him. He, with his plentiful experience, taught them to
resist every single alien thought, saying, 'Brethren,
strive for what brought you out here, and do not neglect your own salvation. You must at all times stay
17,10   sober and awake. As Scripture says, "Keep awake, and
pray not to enter into temptation."[a] Above all recognize

a. Mt 5:3.
a. Mt 26:41.

this: those who renounce this life must not have a wish of their own but in first place acquire humility and obedience. They must always await and ponder the

17,15 hour of death and the dread day of judgment, fear the threat of eternal fire and desire the glory of the kingdom of heaven.' Again he used to say, 'In addition to keeping watch on the thoughts within, monks, especially young ones, ought to practise bodily labor, remembering the words of the Apostle, "We labor day

17,20 and night so as not to be a burden on anyone",[b] and, "These hands ministered to me and to those with me".[c] While those in the world endure labor and hardship in order to support wives and children from their work, pay the first-fruits to God, do good according to their power and in addition be charged taxes, it is absurd if

17,25 we are not even to meet the needs of the body from manual labor but to stay idle and immobile, reaping the fruit of the toil of others, especially when the Apostle

18. orders the idle not even to eat.'[d] This was the teaching with which our father Euthymius enlightened the community. He also gave instructions that no one was to talk in church during the time of office, nor in the refectory while the brethren were eating. He was also displeased whenever he saw a brother in the cenobium,

18,5 especially a young one, trying to surpass the community in abstinence. 'Correct abstinence,' he said, 'is to take only just enough at meal-times, while guarding the heart and making secret warfare against hidden passions; the weapons of the monk are meditation, dis-

18,10 cernment, self-control, and godly obedience.' This and similar teaching inspired and stimulated the brethren to bear fruit worthy of their calling.

b. 1 Thess 2:9.
c. Ac 20:34.
d. 2 Thess 3:10.

10. TEREBÔN

Concerning Terebôn the Elder all the senior fathers
gave me a unanimous report, but a more detailed one
was recounted to me by his descendant and namesake,
the celebrated Saracen chieftain of this region. Now
18,15   Terebôn the Elder, the grandfather of the Younger,
when he was very young and still a boy, was struck by
a demon and paralysed all down his right side from
head to foot. His father, who was called Aspébetus,
spent huge sums, but to no avail. Now Aspébetus,
18,20   though a pagan and a Persian subject, became an ally
of the Romans in the following way. At the beginning of the persecution that occurred at this time in
Persia, towards the end of the reign of Isigerdes, king
19.   of Persia,[33] the *magi*,[34] in their desire to capture all the
Christians, set the chiefs of the Saracens under them to
guard the roads everywhere, to prevent any of the
Christians in Persia from fleeing to the Romans.
Aspébetus, who was then a tribal chief, witnessing the
cruelty and inhumanity shown the Christians by the
magi of the cities and taking pity on them, did not
hinder any of the Christians from flight but on the contrary even assisted them, moved by sympathy, even
though he had inherited from his forebears the practice
19,5   of paganism. Denounced to king Isigerdes, he took his
half-paralysed son (I mean Terebôn) and all his family
and wealth, and fled to the Romans. They were received by Anatolius, then commander-in-chief in the
East, who bound them in treaty to the Romans and
entrusted Aspébetus with the office of chieftain of the
Saracens in Arabia who were in alliance with Rome.
19,10   When accordingly they encamped in Arabia, the boy
saw a vision in a dream, which he announced to his
father. Without any delay he took the child together
with a host of barbarians and many bodyguards and,
spurred by faith, made his way to the place indicated in

the dream, where dwelt the pious men Euthymius and
Theoctistus. Most of the brethren were terrified at the
sight of the barbarians; but the blessed Theoctistus,
seeing his disciples' panic, climbed down to the bar-
barianis and said to them, 'What are you looking for?'
They replied, 'We are looking for Euthymius the servant of God.' Abba Theoctistus said to them, 'Till
Saturday he will not see anyone, for he practises
solitude.' Aspébetus took Theoctistus by the arm and
showed him the boy in pain. At his father's bidding the
boy said, 'I received this affliction in Persia some time
ago. I have passed through all medical science and
magic arts, and these have not helped me in any way
but have rather increased the disorder. On reaching this
state and reflecting on my condition in godly compunction, I said to myself one night, when tormented by this
disorder, "Terebôn, where now is the vanity of life and
all medical skill? Where are the fantasies of our
magicians and the power of our rites? Where are the
invocations and invented myths of the astronomers and
astrologers? Where are the incantations and the
sophistries of sorcerers? For see, none of these have
effect, unless God gives his assent." On these reflections, [he said] I turned to prayer and besought God
with tears, saying, "O God, great and terrible, creator
of heaven and earth with all their panoply, if you take
pity on my sickness and rescue me from this dire disorder, I will become a Christian, renouncing all lawlessness and pagan worship." On making this resolution in
my mind, I suddenly fell asleep and saw a grizzled man
with a great beard, who said to me, "What are you suffering from?" When I had indicated my disorder, he
said to me, "Are you going to fulfil the pledge you
have made to God? If so, he will cure you." I replied,
"I will fufil the promise I have made to God if I am
freed from this disorder." At this he said to me, "I am
Euthymius, who resides in the eastern desert twelve

19,15

19,20

19,25

20.

20,5

20,10

20,15
miles from Jerusalem in the gorge to the south of the
Jericho road. If you wish to be healed, come to me
without delay, and God will cure you through me." On
getting up, I recounted the matter to my father and,
behold, putting everything else in second place, we
have come to him, and beg you not to keep hidden the
doctor revealed to me by God.' On hearing this, the
20,20
blessed Theoctistus reported the matter to the great
Euthymius in his solitude. Euthymius, judging it
preposterous to oppose visions from God, came down
to them. By praying fervently and sealing Terebôn with
the sign of the cross, he restored him to health. The
barbarians, astounded at so total a transformation and
20,25
so extraordinary a miracle, found faith in Christ; and
casting themselves on the ground they all begged to
receive the seal in Christ. The miracle-working
Euthymius, perceiving that their faith in Christ came
from the soul, ordered a small font to be constructed in
21.
the corner of the cave—the one preserved even now—
and after catechizing them baptized them all in the
name of the Father and of the Son and of the Holy
Spirit. Aspébetus he renamed Peter; him he baptized
first of all and after him one Maris, his brother-in-law,
21,5
both men of exceptional intelligence and adorned with
conspicuous wealth, and then likewise Terebôn and the
rest. He kept them by him for forty days, enlightening
and strengthening them with the word of God, and then
let them depart no longer Agarenians and Ishmaelites
but now descendants of Sarah and heirs of the promise,
21,10
transferred through baptism from slavery to freedom.
Maris, the uncle of Terebôn, did not leave the
monastery again, but renounced the world and remained there throughout his lifetime; he was greatly
pleasing to God, and gave all his wealth, which was
considerable, for the building and extension of the
21,15
monastery. As the miracle that had occurred was
noised abroad everywhere, many afflicted by various

disorders came to the great Euthymius, and were all healed. And so in a short space of time he achieved fame in this place, with the result that his name spread through all Palestine and the surrounding provinces.

11. ARRIVAL AT MARDA

21,20   Our father Euthymius, seeing many importune him for a cure and remembering the former peace he had enjoyed when a solitary ascetic, became extremely vexed and impatient at being importuned, and praised, by many. Despite being named after confidence (*euthymia*), he was in great despondency (*athymia*),

21,25 and sought to depart secretly and flee to Roubâ.[35] On discovering this, the blessed Theoctistus assembled the brethren and got them to beg him on bended knee not to leave them. Wishing to gratify them, he promised not to depart then and there. But a few days later, taking with him a youngish brother called Domitian, of

22. Melitene by birth and of virtuous character, he left the cenobium and went down to Roubâ. Then, journeying through the desert to the south by the Dead Sea, he came to a high mountain, separated from the others,

22,5 called Marda.[36] Finding in it a well of water that had collapsed, he restored it and then remained there, feeding on the plants he found and on *malôa*.[37] After first building a church there, the one preserved till the present day, and erecting an altar in it, he left there and came to the desert of Ziph, out of a wish to see the

22,10 caves where David took refuge from the face of Saul.[a]

---

a. Cf. 1 Sam 23:14.

12. THE MONASTERY OF CAPARBARICHA
AND THE PEOPLE OF ZIPH

In this region he founded a monastery. The cause of
the foundation of this monastery is said to have been as
follows. A son of a certain headman of the village of
Aristobulias had an evil spirit and would in his shrieks

22,15   invoke the holy Euthymius by name. The father of the
boy, hearing of Euthymius' being in the region between his village and Caparbaricha, made search and
came to him. As soon as the youth saw the saint, he
was thrown into convulsions and the demon came out
of him, at which he was cured. When the miracle was
noised abroad, people came to him from Aristobulias

22,20   and the villages round about and built him a monastery; some brethren gathered and remained with him,
while God satisfied their bodily needs. Some of the
people of Ziph who had formerly adopted the heresy

23.   called after 'mania' renounced the impure heresy as a
result of his inspired teaching: declaring anathema on
Manes, its begetter,[38] they were instructed in the
catholic and apostolic faith and baptized.

13. HIS CHARISM WITH WILD ANIMALS

In addition to the other charisms possessed by the
23,5   godly Euthymius, he also received this one from God—
the grace of living with carnivorous and poisonous animals without being harmed by them. This should be
doubted by no one initiated into holy Scripture, who
has precise knowledge that when God dwells in a man
and rests upon him all beings are subject to him, as
they were to Adam before he transgressed God's com-
23,10   mandment. Not only the wild animals but the very elements are subject to such a man: to my statement bear

witness those who divided the sea,[a] curbed the Jordan,[b] made the sun stand still,[c] turned fire into dew[d] and performed innumerable other prodigies. Accordingly the very God who worked these miracles subjected to 23,15 the inspired Euthymius also not only the visible but also the spiritual monsters, I mean the spiritual powers of wickedness; for such are the charisms bestowed by God.

14. ARRIVAL AT THE SITE OF THE MONASTERY

The great Euthymius, finding himself again importuned by many (for the place was near the villages), 23,20 said to his disciple Domitian, 'Come, my child: let us pay a visit to the holy Theoctistus and the brethren.' So leaving the monastery of Caparbaricha he came to the holy spot where now, with the help of God, has been founded his holy monastery, at a distance of about three miles from the thrice-blessed Theoctistus. He fell 24. in love with this spot because it lies on level ground and is at the same time solitary and airy, being at that time especially deserted and impassable, before so many monasteries were founded in the desert to the south; now it is passable, since the whole desert has been 24,5 colonized by his spiritual progeny. In this spot he settled with his disciple in profound solitude in a small cave where now is the tomb of his honored remains. The blessed Theoctistus, on learning that the great Euthymius had arrived, came in haste to greet him and begged him to return to his monastery. But because of his love for 24,10 the solitude of the place he did not consent, except that on Sundays they celebrated the liturgy together.

a. Ex 14.
b. Jos 3.
c. Jos 10:12-13.
d. Dan (LXX) 3:50.

15. THE TENTS AND THE SARACENS

Aspébetus, also called Peter, on hearing that the great
Euthymius had eventually returned, came to him with a
great number of Saracens, men, women and children,
and begged him to preach to them the word of salvation. The holy elder catechized them all and received

24,15   them into the lower monastery, where he baptized
them. After remaining with them for the whole week,
he then ascended with them to his own cave. Peter
brought along skilled workmen and constructed the
great cistern with two openings that has been preserved
in the garden till now; nearby he built a bakehouse and
for the holy elder constructed three cells and an oratory

24,20   or church in the middle of the cells. Moreover, these
men who had formerly been wolves of Arabia but had
then joined the rational flock of Christ begged to remain near him. Out of his devotion to the solitary life
Euthymius did not agree to this because of the disturbance involved, for he keenly loved solitude. But taking them to an appropriate spot he said to them, 'If you

24,25   want to be very near me, settle here.' This spot lies
between the two monasteries. Marking out a church for
them and tents round it, he told them to build the
church and settle there.[39] He frequently made visita-
tions to them, until he assigned them a priest and dea-

25.   cons. Those who had already been baptized came and
settled there, and others too who arrived gradually
were baptized by him. Since in consequence they became extremely numerous and spread out to form various encampments, our great father Euthymius wrote to

25,5   Juvenal patriarch of Jerusalem requesting the ordination of a bishop and, when he consented, sent him
Peter the father of Terebôn, as most capable of drawing
souls to salvation. So it was that Peter was the first to
be ordained in Palestine bishop of the Encampments.
One could witness a multitude of Saracen barbarians

25,10   coming to the great Euthymius, receiving baptism and
being taught to worship the one who is God over all.
So much for the Saracens.

16. HE BEGINS TO ACCEPT DISCIPLES
AND MAKE THE PLACE A LAURA

     The great Euthymius himself did not want to make
his place a cenobitic house or even a laura; when peo-
25,15   ple came to him wishing to renounce the world, he
would send them to the blessed Theoctistus in the
monastery below, as he did with those who wished to
make some offering.[40] But when God chose to make
this place inhabited, he sent first of all three brothers in
the flesh, who were of Cappadocian origin and Syrian
25,20   rearing, and preeminent in all spiritual knowledge—
Cosmas, Chrysippus, and Gabrielius. When these men
begged to remain with him, he would not accept them;
three things prevented him—his love of solitude, their
youth, and the fact that Gabrielius was a eunuch from
birth. That night, however, he had a vision of someone
25,25   saying to him, 'Accept these brothers, since God has
sent them, and stop repelling those wishing to be saved.'
At this the saint accepted them, and said to Cosmas, the
26.   eldest of them, 'See, I have acted as God has commanded me. But take care not to let your youngest
brother come near my cell, for because of the warfare
of the enemy it is not right for a feminine face to be
found in a laura. As for you, I do not think you will
stay here long, since you are destined to become in
26,5   time shepherd of the church of Scythopolis.' After
these recruits he accepted one Domnus, of Antiochene
origin and the nephew of John archbishop of Antioch.
In this same period he also accepted three other brothers from Melitene, cousins of that Synodius who together with Acacius had reared the great Euthymius—

26,10 Stephen, Andrew, and Gaianus. Three others likewise
he accepted from Raithou—John the priest, Thalassius,
and Anatolius. He also accepted one Cyriôn, who originated from Tiberias and was a priest of the revered
chapel of the holy martyr Basil at Scythopolis. On ac-

26,15 cepting these eleven,[41] he got bishop Peter to build
them small cells and embellish the church in every
way, thereby making the place a laura on the model of
Pharan. Archbishop Juvenal came down to the laura,
accompanied by the sainted Passariôn, then rural
bishop and archimandrite of the monks,[42] and by the

26,20 inspired Hesychius, priest and teacher of the church,
and consecrated the church of the laura on 7 May of

[AD 428] the eleventh indiction[43] in the fifty-second year of the
life of the great Euthymius. When the laura had been
consecrated and had as priests John and Cyriôn, the

26,25 archbishop ordained Domitian and Domnus deacons.
The great Euthymius rejoiced in spirit, especially at
seeing together with the patriarch the Abraham-like

27.   Passariôn and the theologian Hesychius, who were
celebrated luminaries, resplendent in the whole world.
The sainted Passariôn, however, passed away before
seven months had elapsed.

17. HIS HOSPITALITY AND BLESSING[44]

27,5   When our father Euthymius had begun to make his
place a laura and the twelve brethren with him were in
great straits as regards the necessities of life, and
Domitian had been appointed steward for the first year,
it happened that a crowd of Armenians, around four
hundred in number, on their way from the holy city to

27,10 the Jordan, deviated off the road to the right and arrived at the laura, as if by pre-arrangement—an occurrence, in my opinion, contrived by Providence to reveal his virtue and God-given grace.[45] On seeing them,

the elder summoned Domitian and said, 'Serve these people with something to eat'. He replied, 'The cellar,

27,15 venerable father, does not contain enough to feed ten persons. How, then, can I give bread to such a multitude?' The godly Euthymius, filled with prophetic grace, said, 'Proceed as I have told you, for the words of the Holy Spirit are, "They shall eat and have something left over."'[a] Going accordingly to the small cell

27,20 called by some the pantry, where a few loaves were lying, Domitian was unable to open the door, for God's blessing had filled the cell right to the top. So calling some of the men, he took the door off its hinges, and out poured the loaves from the cell. The same blessing occurred likewise with the wine and the oil. All ate and

27,25 were satisfied, and for three months they were unable to reattach the door of the cell. Just as God through the prophet's voice made the jar of meal and the cruse of oil well up for the hospitable widow,[b] so in the same way he granted to this godly elder a supply of blessings equal to his zeal for hospitality. Domitian in his amazement threw himself at his teacher's feet, begging to

28. receive forgiveness for having felt something natural to human beings. The elder made him rise and said, 'My child, "he who sows with blessings will also reap with blessings."[c] Let us "not neglect to show hospitality, for thereby (as the Apostle says) some have entertained

28,5 angels unawares."[d] Be confident that if you and those after you receive with faith and treat worthily all the strangers and brethren who visit you, the Lord will never fail this place from now on till eternity. For God is well-pleased with such an offering.'

a. 2 Kgs 4:44.
b. 1 Kgs 17:14.
c. 2 Co 9:6.
d. Heb 13:2.

18. AUXENTIUS

28,10   From the time of the miracle just related the laura
began to be blessed in both income and expenditure
and in other ways too. As, with God's help, the
brethren multiplied and reached fifty, and cells were
built for them and the liturgy performed in the church,
the steward was compelled to obtain certain necessities; his acquisitions included mules for the service of
28,15   the fathers. There was in the laura an Asian by race, by
name Auxentius. When he was asked by the steward to
take on the office of muleteer, being judged a practical
man and made for the office, he would not consent.[46]
On being refused, the steward got the priests John and
28,20   Cyriôn to urge Auxentius to accept the office; but not
even their request could persuade him. When Saturday
came round, the steward reported the case of Auxentius
to the great man. Euthymius summoned him and said
to him, 'Listen to me, my child, and accept this office.'
But he replied, 'I cannot, venerable father. There are
28,25   three things that stop me discharging it: firstly lack of
acquaintance with the country and ignorance of the
29.   local language, secondly fear of fornication, and thirdly
fear that such distraction and excitement would prevent
me sitting in my cell and enjoying tranquillity.' The
great Euthymius said, 'We will beg God not to let any
of this harm you. For God is not so unjust as to forget
29,5   your obedience,[a] especially since he knows that it is
out of fear of him that you minister to his servants
according to his commandment and the strength he
has given you. Listen to the Lord as he says, "I did
not come to be served but to serve,"[b] and, "I accomplish not my own will but the will of the Father who

a. Heb 6:10.
b. Mt 20:28.

29,10

29,15

29,20

29,25

sent me."'ᶜ Despite all these words Auxentius remained stubborn and disobedient. Then the most gentle Euthymius became irate and said, 'I have given you, my child, the advice I believe to be to your benefit. Since you persist in your refusal, you will now witness the reward for disobedience.' Immediately Auxentius was seized with demonic trembling and fell to the ground. The fathers present interceded for him with the great man, and the elder said to them, 'Now before your eyes is fulfilled the divine word that says, "Every wicked man stirs up rebellion, but the Lord will send him a pitiless angel."'ᵈ On being further importuned by the fathers, the compassionate elder took him by the hand and raised him up, and sealing him with the sign of the cross restored him to health. Then Auxentius prostrated himself to beg both forgiveness for the past and prayers for safety in the future. The saint said to him, 'The reward for obedience is great, since God wants obedience rather than sacrifice,ᵉ while disobedience causes death.' And after praying for him, he blessed him. Consequently Auxentius accepted the office with joy and alacrity.

19. MARÔN AND CLEMATIUS

30.

Abba Cyriacus the anchorite, who was conspicuous for godly virtues in the laura of Old Souka and preeminent in monastic virtues in the same laura for almost seventy years, and who had made his renunciation in his youth in the community of the great Euthymius and associated for a long time with his successors, gained accurate knowledge of the whole manner and style of

c. Cf. Jn 5:30.
d. Pr 17:11.
e. Cf. 1 Sam 15:22.

30,5   life of the great Euthymius, and transmitted to me most
         of the stories contained in this account.[47] The stories he
         told me include the following.[48] Two brethren of the
         laura, called Marôn and Clematius, having made their
         preparations in concord, had the discordant intention of
         leaving the laura by night without the saint's permis-
         sion. Their plan was revealed to him in his solitude: he
30,10   saw the devil casting reins over them and drawing
         them into a fatal snare. He summoned them immedi-
         ately and gave them much detailed admonition on per-
         severance, exhorting them as follows: 'Everywhere we
         need protection by God's help, wherever we are. For
         Adam broke the commandment of God in Paradise,
30,15   while Job kept it while sitting on a dung-heap.'[a] He
         included in his admonition the following: 'We ought
         not to admit evil thoughts that insinuate into us a feel-
         ing of resentment or loathing towards the place where
         we are and towards our companions, or implant accidie
30,20   or suggest moving to other places, but we must at all
         times be on our guard and oppose the mind to the wiles
         of the demons, for fear that our rule be subverted by
         change of place. For just as a plant that is constantly
         rebedded cannot bear fruit, so a monk does not bear
         fruit if he moves from place to place. So if someone
30,25   resolves to do some good in the place where he is, and
         is not able to, he should not suppose that he could ac-
         complish it elsewhere. For it is not the place that is in
         question but the character of the intention. As proof of
         my words, hear the story told me by some Egyptian
         elders. A brother who belonged to a cenobium in Egypt
31.   was constantly moved to anger. In his despair he left
         the cenobium and settled in a place on his own, reason-
         ing that through not having contact with anyone but
         being a solitary the passion of anger would leave him.
         One day when he filled his jar with water and put it on

         a. Job 2:8.

31,5   the ground it toppled over; filled a second and a third
time, it toppled over again. The brother, tricked by the
devil, lost his temper with the jar and grabbed hold of it
and smashed it.' At these words, Clematius, as a result
of satanic temptation, burst into laughter. Perceiving
this, the elder said to him fiercely, 'You have been

31,10   tricked by the devil, brother. You have reacted in a
foolish and boorish manner. You were invited to
weep, and you laugh. Have you not heard the Lord
calling those who laugh wretched and those who weep
blessed?[b] So recognize that is is folly for a monk to
speak or react unsuitably or to talk insolently. The
fathers have defined that insolence[49] is dangerous and

31,15   a source of all the passions.' After saying this, the saint
dismissed Clematius and withdrew to the inner part of
his cell. At once Clematius fell to the ground, seized
with trembling and shuddering. Domitian, who admired both the appropriate mildness and the due

31,20   severity of the holy father, assembled some of the
venerable fathers and led them in with Marôn to intercede for Clematius. Yielding to the intercession of the
fathers, the great man came out, raised up the outstretched man, and by the sign of the cross ended his
convulsions and stopped the chattering of his teeth. On
restoring him to health, he applied a remedy to his soul

31,25   as well by saying, 'Attend to yourself carefully in future and do not despise godly words and the teaching
of the fathers. Be all eyes, as we have read of the cher-

32.   ubim.[c] So ought a monk to be, watching himself from
all angles; he ought for his own protection to keep the
eye of his soul awake, as journeying always in the midst
of snares.' When he had rebuked and counseled him
with this teaching, and strengthened and instilled fear

32,5   in the rest by this example, he dismissed them in peace.

b. Cf. Lk 6:21,25.
c. Cf. Rev 4:8.

20. THE COUNCIL OF EPHESUS

In the fifty-fourth year of the life of the great
Euthymius occurred the first ecumenical council of
[AD 431]   Ephesus.[50] At this time the Synodius mentioned
above, a venerable man and priest of the holy church
32,10   of Melitene, having come to venerate the holy places,
visited the laura out of a desire to greet the great
Euthymius and also because he had three cousins in the
laura, Stephen, Andrew, and Gaianus. After greeting
the elder, he told him about the impious heresy of Nestorius, who by the permission of God had obtained for
32,15   a short time the see of Constantinople and shaken the
world with his evil doctrines; he informed him too of
the zeal and orthodoxy of Archbishop Cyril of
Alexandria and Bishop Acacius of Melitene,[51] and that
there was to be an ecumenical council at Ephesus to
deal with Nestorius. The saint was delighted to hear
32,20   about Acacius, who had in a sense reared him in his
early years. After saying goodbye, the blessed
Synodius took from the laura his cousin Stephen, went
up to the holy city, and persuaded the archbishop to
ordain him, at which the archbishop made Stephen
himself and Cosmas the Cappadocian deacons of the
holy church of the Resurrection.

While the bishops were assembling for the council
33.   and the Palestinians were about to set off with their
archbishop, the great Euthymius told Peter bishop of
the Saracens, who was on his way to the council, to
follow in every way Archbishop Cyril of Alexandria
33,5   and Bishop Acacius of Melitene, as being orthodox and
opponents of impiety. Accordingly, when the council
had assembled at Ephesus and deposed the impious
Nestorius, Bishop Peter of the Saracens came to the
laura and gave the great Euthymius a detailed account
33,10   of everything that had happened at the council. On
learning of the conduct of the eastern bishops,

Euthymius was extremely distressed about Archbishop John of Antioch, who, though orthodox, had been led astray by the supporters of Nestorius. The deacon Domnus, distressed in mind by his own uncle, asked to be allowed to go to Antioch to correct his uncle. The
33,15   great Euthymius, however, would not agree to let him go, saying, 'You must not set off, my child, for it is not to your advantage. Your uncle does not need your presence. Even if he has for a short time been led astray by the wicked, God in recognition of his rectitude will not let him perish, but will soon show him
33,20   to belong to the party of the saved.[52] As for you, my child, if you remain in the place to which you were called and do not yield to the thoughts drawing you from the desert, you will be able to make progress and receive glory in God's sight. But if you disobey me, you will inherit your uncle's see only to be stripped of it by wicked men, after earlier being led astray by them
33,25   against your will.' These were the words of Saint Euthymius. But Domnus, disobeying the injunction of the holy father, departed to Antioch without his leave and experienced everything that had been predicted.[53] Later, however, he returned to the elder and expressed his contrition. Archbishop Juvenal ordained Stephen of Melitene bishop of Jamnia; Cosmas the Cappadocian he ordained priest and made guardian of the Cross.

21. HIS MODE OF LIFE; HOLY ARSENIUS

34.   The successors of the great Euthymius, who lived with him for a considerable time, used to recount the following to Abba Cyriacus, who repeated it to me: 'We never caught him eating or conversing with anyone, without grave necessity, except on Saturday
34,5   and Sunday. We never knew him to sleep on his side, but sometimes he would snatch a little sleep when

seated and at other times, grasping with both hands a
rope hanging from a corner of the ceiling of his cell, he
would take a little sleep out of physical necessity, perhaps repeating the saying of the great Arsenius, "Come

34,10   here, you bad servant."' They also affirmed the following, that stories about the great Arsenius himself, who
had reared and educated the emperors Arcadius and
Honorius in the manner of a father and for this reason
was called their father by the holy fathers, and who at
this time was resplendent with virtues in the Egyptian

34,15   desert,[54] were heard with joy by the great Euthymius,
when the venerable fathers who came to him at various
times from Egypt recounted details of Arsenius' life.
On hearing them, he would exert himself to the full to
imitate the man's virtues, his recollection, reserve and
humility, his simplicity in dress, abstemiousness in

34,20   food and endurance in all things, his self-cultivation
according to his saying, 'Arsenius, remember what you
came out here for.' He also emulated his compunction,
tears and all-night vigils, his love of solitude and hatred of glory and of success, his ardor and vigor in
prayer, his compassion and powers of discernment.

34,25   Since he exerted himself to the full to imitate his life, he
was deemed worthy of enjoying the same gifts of grace
that he possessed— participation in the all-holy Spirit,
illumination by the divine light and the charism of second
sight. As for his abundant charisms of healing and against
impure spirits, they have as their witness the manifesta-
tions we see even today welling up from his tomb.

22. PROPHECY CONCERNING ANASTASIUS

35.   Concerning his charism of second sight and how
he began to emit its rays and was revealed as a
clear beacon, I shall now proceed to speak. One
Anastasius, a cleric of the holy Resurrection, guar-

dian of the sacred vessels, and rural bishop, who
had shared as a friend in the ascetic contests of the
sainted Passariôn, longed to see the holy Euthymius.
Confiding this longing to Fidus bishop of Joppa and to
Cosmas guardian of the Cross, he went to see him, taking in addition to them Fidus grandson of bishop Fidus,
then a young lector at the holy Resurrection, who
recounted the episode to Abba Cyriacus, who in turn
transmitted it to me. As they were on their way and
approaching the laura, their visit was revealed to the
saint, who called Chrysippus, as steward of the laura,
and said to him, 'Get ready, for behold, the patriarch is
arriving with your brother.' When they arrived, the
great Euthymius was carried away by the eyes of the
mind and addressed Anastasius as patriarch of
Jerusalem. Those present were amazed, and Chrysippus approached the elder privately to say, 'Revered
father, the patriarch is not here: this is Anastasius the
sacristan. Observe that he is wearing colored garments,
which it is impossible for the patriarch of Jerusalem to
wear.' The elder, in his turn, was amazed and
dumbfounded, and replied, 'Believe me, my child: until you spoke, I saw him wearing white garments.'[55]
Then he said in the hearing of all, 'Truly, I have not
made a mistake, but what God has foreknown and
preordained he will certainly accomplish, "for he does
not repent of his gifts".'[a]

35,5

35,10

35,15

35,20

35,25

23. THE BARREN WOMAN GIVES BIRTH

Terebôn the Saracen, despite taking a wife from his
own tribe and living with her for a long time, had no
child, since she was barren. Taking her to the miracle-
working Euthymius, he begged him, 'I know and am

a. Rom 11:29.

convinced, venerable father, that God listens to your prayers, for "he does the will of those who fear him."[a]

36. Since so great a time has passed without my receiving the favor of a child, since she is barren, I now ask you, venerable father, to entreat God in his love for men to grant us a child.' Recognizing their faith, the elder

36,5 sealed them three times with the sign of the cross, also touching the woman's womb, and said to them, 'Depart rejoicing in the Lord; for behold, in his love for men he bestows on you three male sons.' Trusting the word of the holy elder, they returned home with joy. The barren woman conceived and bore their first

36,10 born, Peter, the father of the Terebôn who gave me this account, which tallies with that of the elders. After Peter he begot two other sons, in accordance with the prophecy of the inspired father.

24. AEMILIANUS

There was a brother in the laura, a Roman by birth, Aemilianus by name, who one night, as Sunday was

36,15 dawning, was severely tormented by the demon of fornication and fiercely troubled in his mind by impure thoughts. At the hour of the night office, when the holy Euthymius came to the church, he joined him in a dark corner. The elder, sniffing a demonic stench and guessing there to be some activity by demons, breathed upon

36,20 him, saying, 'God will confound you, you impure spirit.' Immediately the brother fell to the ground, foaming in demonic frenzy. Ordering light to be brought, the saint said to the assembled fathers, 'Look how this brother, despite enjoying a good reputation and living in purity of body from youth till now, has

36,25 been mastered by the devil through being slightly led

a. Ps 145(144):19.

astray by the pleasure of the flesh. This is why I always say to you, let us be on our guard against every impure thought. For those who are tempted by bodily pleasures without physical intercourse still commit fornication in their thoughts. So let each of us keep a careful watch on his thoughts, and "work out his own salvation in fear and trembling."[a] Listen to an edifying and true story that some Egyptian elders I met told me about a

37.   man thought holy by all but who in the secret stirrings of his heart angered God because, I think, of assent to impure thoughts. Their story went as follows.[56] A man with second sight, on entering this man's city, found

37,5   him gravely ill and all the citizens affirming with tears, "If this saint dies, we have no further hope of salvation; for we are all protected through his intercession." On hearing this, the man with second sight hurried off to get a blessing from the supposed saint. When he drew

37,10 near, he saw many candles all ready and great crowds of clerics and laymen, including the bishop himself, waiting to conduct the funeral. Going in to him, he found him still breathing, and saw with the eye of his mind the devil of hell with a fiery fork inserting the

37,15 fork into his heart and with many tortures pulling at his soul; and he heard a voice from heaven saying, "Just as his soul did not give me rest for a single day, so you too are not to stop pulling at his soul and torturing it." I have recounted this to make us at all times ready for combat and prepared for the departure of the soul from the body, lest, seduced by love of pleasure, we be un-

37,20 bearably tormented at the time of departure. This brother whom you see has been allowed by God to be mastered by the devil in order to teach you and many others self-control. But let us entreat God, who has applied corrective not capital punishment, to free his

37,25 creature from the plot of the impure and pleasure-

a. Phil 2:12.

loving spirit.' When the inspired father had prayed accordingly, the demon came out, shrieking, 'I am the spirit of fornication,'[57] and filling the whole place with a stench as of burning sulphur. And from then on Aemilianus was freed from impure thoughts and became a vessel of election.

25. THE DROUGHT

38.

In this same year a drought oppressed the earth, and everyone lamented at seeing fulfilled the saying of Moses, 'The sky over your head will be brass and the earth under you iron.'[a] The blessed Theoctistus and the

38,5 fathers of the laura of the great Euthymius were reduced to straits by the lack of water in the cisterns and pressed the great Euthymius to entreat God on this matter. He refused, saying, 'Through this correction God wants to teach us self-control.' In this situation an immense crowd gathered from the holy city and the

38,10 surrounding villages on the octave of the holy Theophanies, especially since they had heard that the great Euthymius, according to his custom, was about to set off for the utter desert. On their arrival, they cried aloud the *Kyrie eleison*, as they carried the crosses of the nearby villages. Hearing their cries and learning that the present drought was the cause, the elder came

38,15 out and said to them, 'What are you seeking from a man who is a sinner? I, my children, because of the quantity of my offenses cannot pray over this with confidence of being heard. God, who fashioned us, is good and benevolent, and "his pity extends over all his works."[b] But our sins stand between us and him.[c] We

a. Dt 28:23.
b. Ps 145(144):9.
c. Cf. Is 59:2.

38,20   have obscured his image and defiled his temple by being slaves to a variety of lusts and pleasures. We live in cupidity and envy, and are ourselves abominable through hating each other. This is why in his anger he has brought this correction upon us, so that, disciplined by it and bettered through repentance, we may app-

38,25   roach him in fear and he accordingly may hear us. This is the meaning of the saying, "The Lord is near to all who call upon him in truth."[d] On hearing this, they all cried out in unison, 'You yourself, venerable father, must entreat God for us, for we have faith that the Lord listens to your prayer; for "he does the will of those

39.   who fear him."[e] Won over by these and similar pleas, the great Euthymius took the fathers who were present and, telling the people to address earnest entreaty to God, went into his oratory without making any promises. Casting himself on his face, he begged God

39,5   with tears to have mercy on his creation and to visit the land with mercy and pity and water it abundantly. As he was praying, there suddenly blew up a south wind, the sky was filled with clouds, heavy rain descended and there arose a great storm. At this the saint stood up and ended his prayer; coming out, he said to them, 'Be-

39,10   hold, God has heard your prayer and granted your request. He is going to bless this year above other years. So attend carefully to yourselves and by good works glorify God, who has shown his mercy to us all.' With these words he dismissed them. The rain continued to pour down torentially, with the result that he was un-

39,15   able for many days to go down to the utter desert. This year was blessed above other years in accordance with the words of the inspired father.[58]

d. Ps 145(144):18.
e. Ps 145(144):19.

26. ON DOCTRINES[59]

Abba John, bishop and solitary, and Abba Thallelaeus
the priest, who at the present time pursue the spiritual
combat in the laura of blessed Sabas, have told me that
both blessed Sabas and many other elders were full of
admiration for the burning zeal for the doctrines of the
Church displayed by the great Euthymius, even though
he was constitutionally endowed with great gentleness
and moderation of spirit. They would assert that he
rejected every heresy opposed to the correct account of
the faith, and that he detested with a perfect hatred the
following six heresies especially: he loathed the
Manichaean abomination; and when those of Origen's
persuasion, numerous at that time especially in the region round Casesarea, came to him with a show of
piety, he combated courageously their myth of a
preexistence of minds, he completely refuted, and with
ridicule, the consequent monstrosity of a general restoration, and he pilloried the godless and impious doctrines that these tenets give birth to. As for the Arian
assertion of distinctions and the Sabellian denial of
them, he rejected both equally: he abominated their
diametrically opposed wickedness and impiety of equal
gravity, since he had been taught by the Holy Spirit to
revere the unity in trinity and trinity in unity—a unity
in godhood, essence and nature, not in *hypostasis* as
according to Sabellius, and a trinity not of natures or
essences as according to Arius but of *hypostases* or
specific properties or persons, conjoined in respect
of essence but distinguished in the *hypostases*.[60] For
he glorified one sole indivisible Godhead, inseparable
in essence, unconfused in the *hypostases*, acknowledged in Father, Son and Holy Spirit. In addition, as
regards the mystery of Christ he rejected equally the
division of Nestorius and the confusion of Eutyches,
piously confessing that God the Word, one of the holy

39,20

39,25

40.

40,5

40,10

40,15   and consubstantial Trinity, became in the last days incarnate of the Holy Spirit and the immaculate Mary
mother of God, becoming man and being born of her
ineffably, even he who is our Lord Jesus Christ,
glorified with the Father and the Holy Spirit. He acknowledged his single, composite *hypostasis*, out of
two natures of godhood and manhood. He accepted in

40,20   christological confession neither one single nature after
the union according to the insane Eutyches nor 'in two
hypostases' according to the Judaizing Nestorius, since
he recognized accurately the difference between nature
and *hypostasis*, that nature and essence signify the

40,25   generic and common, while *hypostasis* and person indicate the individual. Therefore the saint himself believed the ineffable union in the virgin's womb to have
occurred hypostatically; for the animate flesh taken
from the virgin came into existence in the *hypostasis* of
God the Word, not in virtue of a preexistent soul nor of
flesh fashioned beforehand. It is not the case, as ac-

41.   cording to these erring mythologies, that Christ is one
and God the Word another, but he is one and the same
only-begotten Son of God, Jesus Christ our Lord, even
though the difference between the natures that concurred is not ignored.

27. THE COUNCIL OF CHALCEDON

[AD 451]   In the seventy-fifth year of the life of the great
41,5   Euthymius took place the Council of Chalcedon, at
which almost all the bishops of the world assembled
because of the innovations by Dioscorus of
Alexandria[61] at Ephesus two years previously; they
expelled Dioscorus himself and the other heretics from
the sacred lists and issued a definition of the faith. Pre-

41,10   sent at the council were two disciples of the great
Euthymius—Stephen bishop of Jamnia and John bishop

of the Saracens (Peter had already passed away, and
his successor Auxolaus had died under censure for having supported Dioscorus at Ephesus). These disciples,
bringing the definition of the faith issued and pro-

41,15 claimed by the council, came post-haste to the great
Euthymius, in fear lest they be censured as Auxolaus
had been when he returned from the 'robber council'.[62]
After receiving them and reading the definition of the
faith, our father Euthymius, as a true examiner of correct thought, welcomed the profession of faith it contained.

41,20 When the news had circulated, as people reported
that the great Euthymius had accepted the definition of
the faith proclaimed at Chalcedon, all the monks were
about to accept it, had they not been prevented by one
Theodosius, in appearance a monk but in reality a
precursor of Antichrist.[63] Coming to Palestine, this
man beguiled the empress Eudocia, who was here at
that time, and seduced all the monastic population, in-
veighing against the Council of Chalcedon as having

42. subverted the true faith and approved the doctrine of
Nestorius. After effecting his murderous intent in this
way, he seized in barbarous fashion the patriarchal
throne of Jerusalem and, making war on the holy
canons, ordained many bishops, while the true bishops

42,5 were still at the council. Perpetrating many brutal acts
of war, he achieved total control for twenty months.
While at that time almost all the urban population and
the monks of the desert followed his apostasy, of the
whole desert only the great Euthymius refused to be of

42,10 his communion. Theodosius was clever enough to send
for him because of his great reputation; since the great
Euthymius refused to come to the holy city,
Theodosius sent to him two monastic archimandrites to
invite him to join his party—Elpidius, the disciple and
successor of the great Passariôn, and Gerontius, who

42,15 had succeeded blessed Melania. When these men arrived and began their plea, the great Euthymius said, 'Far be it from me to share in the murderous crimes of Theodosius or be seduced by his heresy.' Elpidius and Gerontius replied, 'But ought we to share the doctrines of Nestorius, which have been approved by the council

42,20   now assembled at Chalcedon by means of the expression "*in* two natures"? Where have we read in holy Scripture, or which of the holy fathers has taught us, that Christ is to be acknowledged in two natures, as the council has affirmed?' The great Euthymius said in answer, 'I have not read in detail everything that this

42,25   council has examined and enacted, but as regards the definition it has issued I cannot in any respect accuse it of heresy. It commends the faith of the three hundred and eighteen holy fathers who assembled at Nicaea, and professes observing it and keeping it unshakable

43.   and inviolate; it teaches following the one hundred and fifty fathers at Constantinople and those who assembled at Ephesus against the impious Nestorius; it calls Bishop Cyril of Alexandria its ally and inscribes him as

43,5   teacher of the true faith; it proclaims the holy Virgin mother of God, and professes that of her was born according to the flesh the only-begotten Son and Word of God, and ascribes to him two generations, one from the Father, timeless and bodiless, and the other from the virgin mother, in time and in an animate body; it professes that the one Christ is to be acknowledged in

43,10   two natures in accordance with the concepts of godhood and manhood. Consequently, it applies the expressions "without confusion, without change, without division, without separation" both because of those who have the effrontery to divide or separate the ineffable and irreversible hypostatic union that took place in the womb and because of those who say that the Word of God became flesh by transformation and

43,15   make the flesh of the Only-begotten of one substance with the godhood, and further because of those who do not profess the hypostatic union of the Word with the flesh but concoct the impious monstrosity of a commixture, confusion, and blending of essences, and who say that the nature of the godhood and that of the flesh have been made one nature, with the consequence that, according to their account, neither can Christ's passibility be preserved because of the impassibility of his godhood nor, conversely, can his impassibility because of the passibility of his manhood. It was, accordingly, for this purpose of a correct understanding that the council inserted the expression "in two" into its definition, not as if dividing Christ into individual parts but professing the same Christ in each one and each one in the same Christ. Consequently, we too, when we hear the council affirming Christ in two natures, do not suppose that it is introducing division or cleavage into the one composite *hypostasis* of Christ, but acknowledge that it signifies the difference of the natures, in accordance with the words of the sainted Archbishop Cyril of Alexandria, "not as if the difference of the natures is destroyed by the union".'

When the saint had said all this, Elpidius admitted and confessed that the great Euthymius had spoken throughout in accordance with truth and piety, even if he did not immediately break off association with Theodosius; Gerontius, however, remained unconvinced, and so it was in disagreement that on taking their leave they returned to him who had sent them. Theodosius, who had obtained total control of Palestine, did his best to extinguish with plausible words this remaining living spark of piety, quite unique in the desert, but he was cheated of his hopes; like an arrow striking a more powerful object he was repelled, and like a fierce billow of the sea he broke against this great bulwark and champion of the true faith, and dissolved. Nevertheless, he did not give up his enticements, but sent others at various times to try and win him over. Noting Theodosius' utter shamelessness, the great Euthymius told the fathers not to share in his apostasy and so departed to the utter desert; on hearing of this, many of the anchorites adopted the same

44,20 policy. At that time there was a great anchorite of Lycian origin, called Gerasimus, who after succeeding in the monastic life in his own homeland and display-ing many combats against the spirits of wickedness had recently left his homeland and was practising the

44,25 anchoritic life in the desert by the Jordan.[64] He with the other anchorites had been seduced by the false teaching of Theodosius; but on hearing from almost all the anchorites of the resplendent grace of the great Euthymius he went to him at Roubâ, and after staying with him for a considerable time was persuaded to as-sent to the definition issued by the Council of Chal-

45. cedon and break off his association with Theodosius, as did other anchorites also, Peter surnamed Gournites, Mark, Joullôn and Silvanus. The great Euthymius re-mained there until Theodosius had been ousted.

28. THE VISION THAT APPEARED AT THE OBLATION

45,5 The great and inspired Euthymius returned from Roubâ to the laura after two years. One holy Sunday he was offering the bloodless sacrifice to God, while

45,10 Domitian was standing to the right of the altar and holding the liturgical fan.[65] As he was performing the anaphora, Terebôn the Saracen, who was standing near the altar with his hands resting on the sanctuary rails,[66] suddenly beheld fire descend from heaven, which spread out over the altar rather like a veil and con-cealed the great Euthymius and the blessed Domitian, remaining there from the start of the doxology of the

45,15 Trisagion till its completion. No one saw this miracle save those within the fire and Terebôn and also

Chrysippus' brother Gabrielius, a eunuch from birth, who after twenty-five years had now for the first time advanced forward into the church, as was related to me by Abba Cyriacus the anchorite, who received an accurate account of this from Terebôn and Gabrielius.[67]

45,20 Overcome by awe, Terebôn fled to the back, and resolved from then on no longer to lean on the sanctuary rails as, brashly and presumptuously, he had been wont to do at the time of the holy oblation, but instead he stood in awe and reverence at the back near the door of

45,25 the church at the time of the *synaxis*, in accordance with the commandment that orders the sons of Israel to be pious and not contemptuous.[a]

29. HOW HE BEHELD THINGS SECRET

The fathers told me that the inspired Euthymius had received this charism too from God, that from seeing

46. the appearance of the body he beheld the movements of the soul and knew which thoughts each person was wrestling with, and also which he prevailed over and which he was mastered by. Similarly, when he offered the holy gifts, he frequently saw angels concelebrating

46,5 with him. He would recount privately to his companions, 'Frequently, when distributing the holy sacrament to the brethren, I have seen some of those who approach illuminated by communion and others condemned and in a manner made dead by it, since unworthy of the divine light.' Day by day he bore witness to

46,10 this, saying to the brethren, 'Attend to yourselves, brethren and fathers, and let each of you "examine himself and so eat of the bread and drink of the cup," as the Apostle says, for he who does this unworthily

a. Cf. Ex 19:12.

"eats and drinks judgment upon himself."[a] This is why
46,15 the priest offering the bloodless sacrifice to God, before he starts, warns and exhorts everyone by saying,
"Let us lift up our mind and hearts,"[68] and it is on receiving the promise of the people that he has the courage to offer the anaphora to God. And when this is
completed, he raises his hands upwards and holds and
46,20 displays to all the sacrament administered for our salvation, while saying with a loud voice audible to all the
congregation, "Holy things for the holy," just as if one
were to say: Since I am a man who shares your weakness and is ignorant of the deeds and thoughts of individuals, it is for this that I speak this warning in the
46,25 Lord: If anyone stinks of gluttony or consent to impure
thoughts, if anyone has been blinded by hatred or
resentment, if anyone is confused by envy or anger, if
anyone has been overcome by arrogance or boastful-
ness, he should not presume to approach this pure and
holy fire before washing in meet repentance and
cleansing himself "from every defilement of body and
47. spirit, making holiness perfect."[b] For these holy things
are not for the profane but for the holy. So, if you are
confident in your own conscience, "approach him and
be illuminated, and your countenance will not be put to
shame."'[c]

30. HOW THE EMPRESS EUDOCIA
RETURNED TO COMMUNION

47,5 Deceived by Theodosius and separated from the
catholic communion, blessed Eudocia[69] was eagerly
doing all she could to support and strengthen the
Aposchists[70] and combat the orthodox. All the monks

a. 1 Co 11:28-29.
b. 2 Co 7:1.
c. Ps 34:5(33:6).

47,10

47,15

47,20

47,25

48.

48,5

of the holy city and the desert maintained the same apostasy, even though Theodosius had been ousted and Juvenal had recovered his own throne. Because she received letters at various times from her brother Valerius and from her daughter's son-in-law Olybrius urging her to leave the communion of the Eutychianists and return to that of the Catholic Church, and especially because of all her misfortunes at this time, with her son-in-law killed at Rome and her daughter and grandchildren carried off into captivity from Rome to Africa, she began to be distressed and have doubts in her mind: on the one hand she did not want to trample on her own conscience and through sympathy with her kin betray what she thought to be the faith, but on the other she was moved by her love for God and decided it would be better to frequent the inspired men and learn from them which was the more sound faith. So she sent the honorable rural bishop Anastasius with some of her suite to Antioch to see Saint Symeon the Stylite, who was then a great luminary shining out over the world,[71] indicating her thoughts to him by letter and begging to receive from him advice pleasing to God. Saint Symeon sent her a clear answer in the following terms: 'Know that the devil seeing your abundance of virtues has "obtained leave to sift you like wheat"[a] and that the destroyer Theodosius, a receptacle and instrument of the evil one, has plunged your soul, dear to God, into darkness and confusion. But take heart, for your faith has not failed.[b] I am utterly amazed that, having a spring nearby, you ignore it and have labored to draw from the same water at a distance. For you have there the inspired Euthymius. Follow his teaching and guidance, and you will be saved.'

On hearing this advice, blessed Eudocia did not ne-

a. Lk 22:31.
b. Cf. Lk 22:32.

glect it but, learning first of all that the great
Euthymius could not bear to enter the city, she zealous-
ly built a tower at the highest spot in all the eastern
desert,[72] about thirty stades to the south of his laura,
wishing to enjoy his godly teaching more frequently
there. She sent Cosmas guardian of the Cross and the
rural bishop Anastasius to seek him out.[73] These men,
on going to the laura and not finding him there (for on
hearing of their approach he had retired to Roubâ),
Roubâ), went down to him, accompanied by the
blessed Theoctistus. Entreating him with many words,
they persuaded him with difficulty and led him to
Eudocia in the tower she had built, in the place where
the monastery of Scholarius is now situated. She, overjoyed at seeing the saint, did obeisance to him and said,
'Now I know that God through your coming has visited
my unworthiness.' The saint blessed her and said, 'In
future attend to yourself, my child. It is because of
your being led astray by the evilness of Theodosius
that you have suffered evil and hateful things in Italy.
Therefore renounce irrational contentiousness, and in
addition to the other three holy ecumenical councils,
that assembled at Nicaea against Arius, that at Constantinople against Macedonius and the first council
assembled at Ephesus against Nestorius, accept the
definition issued by the ecumenical council that lately
gathered at Chalcedon. Depart from the communion of
Dioscorus and enter into communion with Bishop
Juvenal of Jerusalem.' After saying these words, praying for her, and taking his leave, he departed. She, astounded at the saint's virtue, fulfilled in action what he
had said, as if she had heard it from the mouth of God.
She went to the holy city immediately; and on being
reconciled to the archbishop through the information
provided by the priests Cosmas and Anastasius, she
returned to the communion of the catholic Church. By
her example she drew back to the catholic communion

48,10

48,15

48,20

48,25

49.

49,5   a great number of laymen and monks who had been led
          astray by Theodosius.[74] Of the two archimandrites,
          Elpidius shook off his error and was reconciled to the
          Church, but Gerontius maintained his previous irra-
          tional opposition and drew after him a considerable
49,10   flock, including two monks called Marcianus and
          Romanus who, persevering in error, withdrew from
          Elpidius' community and founded cenobia, one near
          holy Bethlehem, the other at the village of Thekoa.[75]

          Meanwhile blessed Eudocia, summoning the brothers
          of the guardian of the Cross who were at the laura of
49,15   the great Euthymius, had them ordained priests of the
          holy church of the Resurrection; taking Gabrielius un-
          der her wing, she made him superior of the venerable
          convent of the holy protomartyr and first deacon
          Stephen, while Chrysippus achieved eminence at the
          holy Resurrection and left behind many writings wor-
49,20   thy of full approval.[76] Likewise, blessed Bassa called
          Andrew, the brother of Bishop Stephen of Jamnia,
          from the laura of the great Euthymius and appointed
          him superior of the shrine of St Menas[77] which she had
          founded.

                          31. ABBA SABAS

[AD 457]   In the eighty-second year[78] of the life of the great
          Euthymius, blessed Sabas came to him and asked to
50.   live with him. On accepting him, the great Euthymius
          entrusted him for a short time to his own disciple
          Domitian; but then he summoned him and said, 'It is
          not right, my child, for you, being but a youth, to live
          in a laura. It is more beneficial for youths to be in a
50,5   cenobium.' The truth is that the great Euthymius was
          very much on his guard against accepting an adoles-
          cent in his laura because of the activities of the evil
          one.[79] So he sent him with one of the fathers to the
          blessed Theoctistus with the message, 'Receive this

50,10

youth and attend to him, for, as I see, he is going to attain eminence in the monastic life.' This prophecy did not err: the blessed Sabas attained great eminence and his name has circulated from one end of our region to the other. His praises and achievements cannot be recorded in passing, but, if it please God, when I have brought the work in hand to an end, I shall relate some

50,15

few facts about him in a separate work. For it is neither safe for me to conceal the actions and lives, pleasing to God, handed down to me by devout men, nor is it just that, while the lives of the impious have the honor of being recorded by those in the world, those who excelled in piety among us should be relegated to silence and oblivion.

32. MARTYRIUS AND ELIAS

50,20

In this same year, Leo the friend of Christ having succeeded to the throne of Marcian, one Timothy called Aelurus harassed and convulsed the city of Alexandria by murdering Proterius, bishop of the city,[80] in the holy baptistery and usurping the patriarchal throne. Since as a result the whole of the province of Egypt was filled with tumult and confusion, two

51.

archimandrites left Mount Nitria and journeyed to Palestine. They came to the miracle-working Euthymius, drawn by the report that circulated everywhere about him, and settled with him, each in his own cell. One of them was of Cappadocian stock and called

51,5

Martyrius, while the other was called Elias and stemmed from Arabia. The mentally enlightened Euthymius took exceedingly to these two and frequently invited them to come and see him, since he foresaw clearly, by second sight,[81] that they were going to succeed to the see of St James the Apostle, each in his turn. He used to take them with him to the desert

51,10

of Coutila and Roubâ on 14 January; they would stay

with him there till Palm Sunday, in the company of the
famous Gerasimus and the other anchorites, who came
each Sunday and partook of the spotless sacrament
51,15   from the hands of the great Euthymius. Since the cells
of the laura were extremely cramped and uncomfortable, the great Euthymius having ordered them to be
built this way, after a year Elias went down to Jericho
and built himself a cell outside the city, where his holy
and celebrated monasteries are now situated, while
51,20   Martyrius, having found a cave about fifteen stades to
the west of the laura, lived in it as a solitary and there
with God's help founded a most celebrated monastery.[82]

33. HE DECLINES A VISIT FROM THE PATRIARCH

[AD 459]   In the eighty-third year of the life of the great
Euthymius, archbishop Juvenal, having completed
52.   his forty-fourth year as patriarch, came to the end of
his life, and Anastasius, whom I have frequently mentioned, was raised to the see of James by the vote of
the entire people at the beginning of July.[83] On ob-
52,5   taining the see he remembered the prophecy of the
great Euthymius and, having ordained Fidus deacon of
the holy Resurrection, who as lector had previously
visited the laura with him and heard the prophecy, sent
him together with the guardian of the Cross to the great
Euthymius, to inform him of the fulfilment of the
prophecy and to ask leave to come and greet him. The
52,10   great Euthymius replied, 'The constant enjoyment of
your paternal solicitude, most venerable father, is a
source of delight to me. However, although on the previous occasion playing host to you in no way incon-
venienced me, it is now the case that the coming of
your blessedness would overstrain my weakness. I
therefore entreat your holiness not to trouble yourself
52,15   to visit my mediocrity. If you decide to come, I shall

receive you with joy. But if I receive you, I shall have to receive every visitor and shall no longer be able to stay in this place.' On hearing this answer, the archbishop changed his mind, saying, 'If my visit distresses him, I cancel the journey.'[84]

34. ANTIPATRUS BISHOP OF BOSTRA

Terebôn the Saracen and Saracen tribal chief, on going to Bostra on necessary business that had arisen, fell victim to a plot. As the result of the machinations of an assistant tribal chief, he was arrested by the governor there and held under guard for a time. On learning this, the great Euthymius wrote to the thrice-blessed Antipatrus, who at that time directed the church of Bostra and emitted in all directions the beams of his knowledge of God,[85] asking him to exert himself to obtain Terebôn's release from captivity; he sent Gaianus, the brother of Bishop Stephen of Jamnia, with the letter. On receiving the letter of the great Euthymius, the sainted Antipatrus obtained Terebôn's release from every entanglement and, providing him for the journey, sent him to the great Euthymius. Gaianus, however, he detained, in his desire to have with him one of Euthymius' stock, and ordained him bishop of the city of Medaba.

35. THE DEATH OF EUDOCIA

Blessed Eudocia built a huge number of churches to Christ, and more monasteries and homes for the poor and elderly than I am able to count. One of the churches founded by her, named after St Peter,[86] lies opposite the monastery of the great Euthymius, at a distance of about twenty stades. Having ordered a large cistern to be constructed in it, she paid a visit in the holy season of

52,20

52,25

53.

53,5

53,10

Easter to inspect the work on the cistern; and gazing
across, she saw the laura of the great Euthymius spread
out before her, with monastic cells scattered over the
desert. She felt strong compunction and reflected on
53,15   the text of Scripture that says, 'How fair are your
dwellings, O Jacob, and your tents, O Israel.'[a][87] So she
sent Gabrielius, the superior of St Stephen's, to the
great Euthymius, to ask leave to come and benefit from
his prayer and teaching. The great Euthymius replied to
her, 'Do not expect to see me again in the flesh. Why
53,20   are you, my child, distracted about many things?[b] I
believe that before winter you will go to dwell with the
Lord. Resolve therefore this summer to collect your
thoughts and to prepare for departure, and do not continue, while in the flesh, to remember me either by
word or letter, I mean about giving and receiving. But
53,25   when you depart to the Master of all, remember me
there, so that he may receive me too with peace, whenever and howsoever his mercy wishes.' Hearing this,
blessed Eudocia was much distressed, especially at his
saying, 'Do not continue to remember me either by
word or letter,' since she wished to bequeath him a
54.   considerable income in her will. Journeying in haste to
the holy city, she sent for the archbishop, told him
what the great Euthymius had said, and had the church
of the holy protomartyr Stephen consecrated, although
unfinished, on 15 June. She assigned to it a large in-
54,5   come and set Gabrielius in charge of all the administration. Indeed she went round all the churches she had
founded, having them consecrated and assigning a sufficient income to each one. Four months after the consecration, piously disposed in a manner pleasing to
54,10   God, she committed her spirit into the hands of God on
[AD 460]   20 October of the fourteenth indiction.

a. Num 24:5.
b. Cf. Lk 10:40.

36. THE DEATH OF ABBA THEOCTISTUS

In the ninetieth year of the life of the great Euthymius our great father Theoctistus fell gravely ill, as a result [AD 466] of which he fell asleep on 3 September at the beginning of the fifth indiction, 'an old man and full of 54,15 days.'ᵃ The sanctified Euthymius, going down to visit him and seeing him seriously ill, stayed there several days and, when the thrice-blessed one completed his course and departed to God, conducted his funeral. Archbishop Anastasius, learning that blessed Theoctistus had died and that the great Euthymius was staying there for the funeral, snatching the opportunity to 54,20 greet him, hastened down, and after depositing the remains of the venerable father took and kissed the hands of the holy Euthymius and said to him, 'Long have I desired to kiss these holy hands, and behold, God has granted it to me. And I now ask you, venerable father, first to pray to God that your prophecy about me that was fulfilled be safeguarded till the end, and then to write to me frequently and give directions on whatever 55. matters seem good to you.' The great Euthymius, with the grace he possessed from God, replied, 'The request I make of your beatitude is to remember me in your prayers to God.' The archbishop said, 'It is rather I who make this request and shall not cease to make it, 55,5 for I know that the gifts of divine grace are active in you and I have experienced their power.' The elder modestly replied, 'Grant me a request, venerable father, even though an importunate one: look after this monastery.' The archbishop said, 'Even when blessed Theoctistus was alive you were the one who chose this spot and who founded it and offered it to Christ as no 55,10 longer wild but holy,⁸⁸ by the power of the Holy Spirit within you, and so now I entrust to you your own.' Af-

a. Gen 25:8.

ter saying this and taking his leave, the archbishop returned to his own place. The great Euthymius, judging
Maris the uncle of Terebôn, who was virtuous and already advanced in years, to be both worthy of the post
55,15   and capable of leading souls to follow God's will, appointed him superior of the monastery and so returned
to his laura. After continuing as superior for two years,
this Maris died, and the great Euthymius came down
again; he placed Abba Maris in the tomb of the great
Theoctistus and appointed one Longinus, a praisewor-
thy man, superior of the monastery.

37. CHRYSIPPUS, COSMAS AND GABRIELIUS

55,20   After the death of the great Theoctistus, when Bishop
Olympius of Scythopolis died, Cosmas guardian of the
Cross was ordained bishop of the same metropolis,
while Chrysippus was appointed to the ministry of
guardian of the Cross, so that in the case of Cosmas as
well the prophecy of the great Euthymius should be
fulfilled.[89] In consequence, it has occurred to me too, a
55,25   sinner, to utter in my amazement the text of Scripture,
'For the Lord God will not do anything without reveal-
56.   ing his training to his servants the prophets.'[a] The
blessed Cosmas attained great fame in the second province of Palestine by ruling and adorning the church
there for thirty years to the best of his power. His
brother Chrysippus served blamelessly for twelve years
56,5   in the guarding of the holy Cross and became a wonderful writer. Likewise Gabrielius continued for
twenty-four years as priest, as I have said, of the holy
Resurrection and superior of St Stephen's. He built
himself a small hermitage on the eastern slope of the
revered hill of the holy Ascension;[90] he used to with-

a. Am 3:7.

56,10 draw there from the octave of the holy Theophanies[91]
and live in solitude till Palm Sunday, following the
tradition of our holy father Euthymius. At the age of
eighty, having become a worker of miracles, he died in
this very hermitage during the season of Lent and was
56,15 buried there. Being highly intelligent and also studious,
he had learnt to speak and write accurately in Latin,
Greek, and Syriac. So much for the disciples of the
great Euthymius; I now return to our father himself.

38. THE THIRST OF ABBA SABAS

Abba John, bishop and solitary, and Abba Thal-
56,20 lelaeus the priest have told me that once when they
were in the utter desert the blessed Sabas told them the
following story: 'When I was in the monastery, after
the death of the blessed Theoctistus, I went up with
Abba Longinus our superior to the great Euthymius in
the month of January in order to send him on his way
56,25 to the utter desert. Seeing me full of zeal, he took me
with him. After we had spent some days at Roubâ with
Martyrius and Elias (the sainted Gerasimus being there
with us also), the great Euthymius, taking myself and
the blessed Domitian, set off for the innermost desert.
On our journey through it we came to a waterless re-
57. gion where we lived on roots of *melagria*.[92] I, being as
yet without experience of life in the desert, became
extremely thirsty, so that as a result of great thirst I
could no longer walk. Turning round and seeing me
failing, the great Euthymius took pity on me and,
withdrawing from us about a stone's throw, fell on his
57,5 face and besought God with the words, "Lord God of
hosts, grant water to this thirsty land to assuage the
thirst of my brother." After this prayer he took the
trowel we carried to use on the roots of *melagria* and
proceeded to dig a little. When water appeared, he

57,10   called me and showed it to me. As I drank, I came to
myself and glorified God for working such miracles
through his saints.'[93]

39. THE TESTAMENT OF THE GREAT EUTHYMIUS

In addition to the other gifts of divine grace which
the great Euthymius obtained, this too was granted
him, to know in advance the day of his death and what
was going to happen to his monastery. I shall not hes-
57,15   itate to set out clearly the fathers' accounts of his
death. On the octave of the holy Theophanies, when it
was specially his custom to go out to the utter desert,
those expecting to send him on his way and those expecting to go with him, among whom were Martyrius
and Elias, assembled together. On seeing that he had
57,20   not made arrangements or preparations as he was accustomed, they said to him, 'Are you not leaving
tomorrow, venerable father?' The saint replied, 'I shall
stay here this week and depart on Saturday after
nightfall'— foretelling his death. On the Tuesday he
ordered a night service to be held in memory of our
holy father Antony. During this vigil, he took the
57,25   priests to the sacristy and said to them, 'From now on I
shall not perform another vigil with you in this little
flesh, for God has called me. So set off and send Domi-
58.   tian to me, and assemble all the fathers in the morning
to me here.'

When all were assembled round him, he said, 'My
beloved brethren, I myself am setting out on the path
of my fathers;[94] you yourselves, if you love me, must
keep these commandments. In all things aim at pure
58,5   love, the source and goal of every good work and "the
bond of perfection".[a] Just as it is not done to eat bread

a. Col 3:14.

without salt, so it is impossible to achieve virtue without love. For each virtue is made secure through love and humility, with the aid of experience, time, and grace. While humility exalts to a height, love prevents

58,10 falling from this height, since "he who humbles himself will be exalted"[b] and "love never fails".[c] Love is greater than humility, for it was on account of love for us that God the Word humbled himself to become like us. Therefore we ought to confess him from our hearts and address him with hymns and thanksgivings without

58,15 ceasing, specially we ourselves who are separate from the manifold affairs of this life, not only because of our pledges to him but also by reason of the undistracted life we lead, freed as we are from the confusion of the world. Therefore let us make every effort to offer up to him purity of soul, chastity of body, and pure love.'

58,20 After saying this, he asked them, 'Whom do you wish to have for superior?' They unanimously elected Domitian. At this the great Euthymius said, 'That is not possible, for Domitian will only remain in this life for seven days after me.' The fathers, amazed at his foretelling the future with such frankness, asked to have as superior one Elias, steward of the lower mon-

58,25 astery and a native of Jericho. The great Euthymius said to him in the presence of all, 'See, all the fathers have elected you to be their father and shepherd. So attend to yourself and to all your flock, and first of all know this, that it has pleased God to make this laura a cenobium

59. and that this change will soon take place.' He gave them directions as to the place where the cenobium was to be built, about its constitution, reception of guests and zeal in the office of psalmody, and that they should not neglect brethren in distress, specially those oppressed

59,5 by evil thoughts, but encourage and admonish them al-

b. Lk 18:14.
c. 1 Co 13:8.

ways. This he said to the monk appointed superior. To all of them he made this declaration: 'My beloved brethren, do not shut to anyone the door of the cenobium you are about to build, and God will then grant you his blessing. Keep my commandments sacrosanct and, if I

59,10 obtain the right to address God freely, I shall ask from him as my first request for myself to be always with you in spirit and with those after you till eternity.' After saying this, he made them all depart except only Domitian. After three further days in the sacristy he fell asleep on the Saturday night and 'was added

59,15 to his fathers, an old man and full of days.'d

40. HIS DEATH

It is related of him that his expression was angelic, his character unaffected and his behavior most gentle. As for his body, the appearance of his face was round, bright, fair and with fine eyes. He was dwarf-like in

59,20 build, with hair completely grey and a great beard that reached his stomach. All his limbs were unimpaired; neither his eyes nor his teeth had suffered any damage at all, but he died with full physical and mental vigor. His

[AD 473] death occurred on 20 January of the eleventh indiction,

60. in the year 5965 since the creation of the world, from when time began to be measured by the course of the sun, and in the year 465 since the Word of God became

60,5 man from the Virgin and was born in the flesh, according to the chronologies composed by the holy fathers Hippolytus the Ancient, disciple of the Apostles, Epiphanius of Cyprus, and Hero the philosopher and confessor.[95] The chronology of his life in the flesh is as follows. Born following a revelation, he was consecrated to God at the age of three at the beginning of

d. Gen 25:8.

60,10   the reign of Theodosius the Great; on progressing through all the ecclesiastical grades, he came to Jerusalem in the twenty-ninth year of his life; he spent sixty-eight years in the desert and died at the age of ninety-seven in the fifth consulship of the emperor Leo and the sixteenth year of his reign.

60,15   The news, circulating through all the surrounding country, brought together an immense crowd of monks and laypeople. Indeed the most holy archbishop Anastasius also, bringing a great number of clerics and soldiers, arrived at the laura, accompanied by Chrysippus, Gabrielius, and Fidus the deacon. From all parts assem-

60,20   bled the anchorites of the desert, including our great father Gerasimus. Many extraordinary miracles were wrought by God through his holy remains, to the amazement of the archbishop and those present, so that it was not possible to bury them till the ninth hour, when at the order of the archbishop, the soldiers drove off the

60,25   crowd. Then the fathers placed them in a coffin and buried them in a suitable place. Martyrius and Elias wept and lamented the loss of the father. At the recommendation of Chrysippus the guardian of the Cross the archbishop invited them to attend upon him; and leaving Fidus the deacon in the laura with responsibility for

61.   building a burial vault for the translation of the precious remains to a becoming place, he returned to the holy city, whence he sent skilled workmen and every assistance for the building.

41. THE DEATH OF DOMITIAN

     The great Domitian, the authentic disciple of our

61,5   holy father, having won esteem in the cenobium, exhibited manliness in the laura, attained eminence in the deserts, served the holy father for over fifty years, shared his ascetic contests on earth, deserved to reign

with him in the kingdom of heaven, and shown himself
'both pleasing to God and esteemed by men,'[a] did not
61,10   leave the place where lay the precious remains until the
completion of the predicted six days. In the night of the
seventh day the great Euthymius appeared to him in
great glory with shining countenance and said, 'Enter
into the glory prepared for you; for Christ the Lord, in
response to my entreaty, has granted me the favor of
61,15   having you with me.' On hearing this, Domitian went
into the church and, after recounting the vision to the
fathers, fell asleep in joy.

42. THE TRANSLATION OF THE REMAINS

Fidus the deacon speedily erected the burial vault on
the site of the cave where the great Euthymius had
originally been a solitary. Demolishing the cave, he
61,20   built in only three months a great and marvelous
vaulted chamber. In the middle he constructed the
tomb of the saint; on either side he provided tombs for
superiors, priests, and other pious men. The
archbishop, who had sent the tombstone in advance
with a silver crucible[96] and surrounding railings, came
61,25   down to the laura and translated the precious remains
to the place prepared, carrying them with his own
hands. After laying them to rest securely, so that no
one could open the tomb and carry off the remains, he
laid the tombstone in place, fixing the crucible above
the breast. This crucible, from then till this day, pours
61,30   forth every kind of benefit for those who approach
with faith. The translation of the remains took place
on 7 May. Then the archbishop, after celebrating the
62.   *synaxis*, took Martyrius and Elias with him to the holy
city and ordained them priests of the holy Resurrection.

a. Rom 14:18.

43. THE LAURA BECOMES A CENOBIUM

It is now time to relate how the laura of the great
Euthymius adopted the constitution of a cenobium. At
62,5   the end of the first year after the death of the great
[Jan 476]   Euthymius, the most pious emperor Leo died and left
as successor to the throne his grandson Leo, a mere
child. He survived only a few months on the throne
and on his death was succeeded by his father Zeno. At
this juncture one Basiliscus, seizing the throne by
62,10   usurpation and causing Zeno to flee to Isauria, issued
[Jan 475]   an encyclical against the Council of Chalcedon.[97] In
[AD 478]   the sixth year after the death of the great Euthymius,
Archbishop Anastasius died in Christ at the beginning
of July, and the emperor Zeno recovered the throne
62,15   after defeating Basiliscus. At this juncture Martyrius,
whom I have often mentioned above, succeeded to the
patriarchate and wrote an outspoken letter to the emperor Zeno and Archbishop Acacius of Constantinople
concerning the lawlessness of the Aposchists and the
revolution they had effected in the holy city; for at this
time the remaining Aposchists in the holy city, with
63.   Gerontius as archimandrite, were trying to commit outrages similar to those formerly perpetrated by
Theodosius, relying on the encyclical I have mentioned.
Fidus the deacon was sent with the letter to
Constantinople.

This Fidus, on receiving the commission of the patri-
63,5   arch, embarked at Joppa and got on a ship crossing
to Curicus. On reaching the Parthenian sea,[98] he suffered shipwreck at night, with the total loss of the
ship. By the providence of God, who wished him to
be saved, he grasped hold of a plank. Being in such
63,10   dire straits, he remembered God and the great Euthymius
and uttered the following prayer: 'God of hosts, you
who make rough ways smooth, through the prayers of
the holy Euthymius deliver me from these terrible and

fearful straits.' And again he said, 'Holy father
Euthymius, see, here is an opportunity to help. Help me
and rescue me from these straits.' When Fidus had

63,15	said this, the great Euthymius appeared to him walking
on the waters. Fidus being terrified, the great
Euthymius said, 'Have no fear: I am Euthymius the
servant of God. Know that your voyage is not pleasing
before God, for your present journey to Constantinople
brings no benefit to the mother of the churches. Return,

63,20	therefore, and say to him who sent you, "Thus says the
servant of God Euthymius: be entirely without anxiety
over the Aposchists, for God in these days will grant
perfect unity, and in your episcopacy there shall be in
Jerusalem one flock under one shepherd." As for yourself, depart to my laura and build a cenobium in the

63,25	place where you built my burial vault, after razing all
the cells down to their foundations. For it is not the
will of God that there be a laura in that place, but it is
his good pleasure that the laura should rather become a
cenobium.' On hearing this, Fidus promised the saint
so to do. He did not know that what was happening
through the saint was a reality but thought he was see-

64.	ing a vision. But the great Euthymius, veiling him with
his mantle, dismissed him in peace, at which Fidus,
snatched up and becoming airborne, in the manner, I
suppose, of Habakkuk,[a] found himself in the twinkling
of an eye on the shore and then in the holy city, with

64,5	ut any consciousness of things human. Going into his
own house, he took off the mantle given by God with
which he was clad and put on his own clothes, at which
the mantle disappeared. He came to himself and said,
'Now I know in truth that God sent his saint and
rescued me from bitter death.' He then related all this

64,10	to his mother, who was a devout Christian, and was
told by her, 'Whatever you promised the saint, you

---

a. Dan 14 (Bel and the Dragon):36.

must perform without delay.' So going in to the archbishop, he related everything in order. He replied in amazement, 'The great Euthymius is truly a prophet of the Lord, for he foretold this to all of us when about to be perfected in Christ. Set off, therefore, to build the cenobium, and you have me as your fellow-worker in everything.' So taking an engineer, a quantity of skilled workmen, and many assistants, Fidus went down to the laura and built the cenobium, which he surrounded with walls and made secure.[99] The old church he made into a refectory, and built the new church above it; within the cenobium he constructed a tower that was at the same time entirely secure and extremely beautiful, and he also contrived that the burial vault should lie in the middle of the cenobium.

64,15

64,20

The location of the cenobium, beautiful to look at because of its perfect evenness and suitable for the ascetic life of the monks because of its temperate and mild climate, I shall attempt to describe in words. There is a tiny hill surrounded on the east and on the west by two slight hollows that come together at the south side and join each other. On the north side there is an utterly delightful plain that spreads out for about three stades. To the north of the plain there is a gorge that descends virtually from the eastern roots of the revered mount of the holy Ascension of Christ our God; it is in this plain that the tower is situated and the porter's lodge of the cenobium protrudes. The whole place is clement and quite marvellous, and, as I have said, enjoys a mild climate. For it is warmer than cold places and cooler than scorching ones; in addition, it is drier than really humid places and more humid than utterly dry ones.

64,25

65.

65,5

44. THE MONASTERY IS CONSECRATED

65,10   The building and decoration of the cenobium was completed in only three years, thanks to the number and speed of the builders. The fathers wished to consecrate the church and the cenobium on the very day on which the precious remains of our holy father had been translated and placed in the new burial vault. But they were in straits because they had no water; there

65,15   had been little rain in the desert itself and the cistern had not received water. May had already begun, and as those with long experience of it know, this desert is scarcely watered even in winter and there was therefore no reasonable expectation of rain.[100] Being totally at a loss, Elias the superior and Fidus the deacon asked

65,20   Abba Longinus of the lower monastery and Abba Paul, superior of the monastery of Martyrius, to send the animals of both communities, so that, together with the animals of our monastery, they might convey water from Pharan. The animals were got ready to set off in the night after the hour of striking.[101] In this same night the great Euthymius appeared to the blessed Elias

65,25   and said, 'What are the animals doing today?' When he replied, 'They are going to Pharan since we have no water,' he rebuked him with the words, 'Why have you neglected to pray to God, you men of little faith? Is the hand of the Lord too weak to give you water? The God who for a disobedient and mutinous people brought water out of the hard rock[a] and for Samson in his thirst

66.   made water spurt from the jaw-bone of an ox,[b] will he not also give water to you in your need? Yes, I tell you, he will give it to you, if you ask him with faith. So do not send the animals to fetch water, but cast your cares

66,5   on God, and today before the third hour your two large

a. Ex 17:6.
b. Jdg 15:19.

cisterns will be replenished.' On rising, he told the vision to the blessed Fidus and all the others, and sent the animals back to their monasteries. At sunrise, a cloud mounted and there was a massive downpour of rain around the monastery, and there alone; before the third hour the two large cisterns were replenished, at which the rain immediately ceased. Archbishop Martyrius, learning of the miracle that had occurred, arrived in great state for the consecration of the monastery. The vigil was performed with brilliant illumination, and during the celebration of the *synaxis* the relics of the holy and victorious martyrs Tarachus, Probus, and Andronicus were placed under the altar, on 7 May of the tenth year since the death of the great Euthymius. After one year had elapsed, Fidus the deacon was ordained bishop of the city called Dôra.

66,10

66,15
[AD 482]

45. THE REUNION OF THE APOSCHISTS

I think it right to mention in the present account the complete reunion of the Aposchists in Jerusalem, in order to demonstrate clearly that the words uttered at sea by the great Euthymius were at this time fulfilled.

66,20

Archbishop Martyrius, trusting in the vision that had occurred at sea and the promise of the great Euthymius, had shaken off all anxiety. After a few days had elapsed, Abba Marcianus, mentioned above, who had already founded a cenobium in the region round holy Bethlehem, gathered together all the Aposchists there and, stirred by a divine inspiration, said to them, 'How long, fathers, shall we strive to dismember the body of the Church, ignoring the perfect will of God? Let us examine ourselves, lest, supposing we are keeping to the royal road, we are in fact traveling on a road that is no road, for supposition gets in the way of reality. Let us test ourselves whether we are in the

66,25

67.

faith; following the Apostolic precedent[a] let us cast lots representing the bishops and the monks. If the lot falls on the monks, let us remain where we are; but if on the bishops, let us join the Church.' When he had said this, they agreed and cast lots: the lot fell on the bishops. Fully convinced, they all in unanimous agreement went to the holy city, having pledged themselves to reunion with holy Church. They were received by the archbishop, who ordered the holy church of the Resurrection to be illuminated, and celebrated a public festival with the whole mass of monks and citizens; there were great festivities in the squares of Jerusalem in joy at the reunion. The whole mass of Aposchists returned to communion, apart from Gerontius the archimandrite, who had governed the monasteries of blessed Melania for forty-five years, and Romanus, who had founded the monastery at Thekoa. These monks, persisting in their irrational contentiousness, were for this reason expelled from their monasteries; after wandering hither and thither, they died excommunicate. This reunion took place in the reign of Zeno.[102]

67,5

67,10

67,15

67,20

46. HOW THE TENTS WERE DEVASTATED

In the time of the emperor Anastasius[103] the tents of the Saracens set up by our father the sainted Euthymius were devastated by barbarians, and the principal Saracens in them erected other tents near the monastery of Abba Martyrius, where they founded a church. But there also the barbarians attacked them, killing some and taking others prisoner; the remainder were scattered round various villages. There occurred at this time great and terrible disruption in this region, with the barbarians making incursions with impunity.

67,25

68.

a. Ac 1:26.

47. CAESARIUS, LEONTIUS, AND NILUS

The blessed Elias, the good shepherd of Euthymius' flock, died after governing the monastery for thirty-eight years and practising many virtues in it. After one Symeonius of Apamea had ruled this monastery for three years and died in Christ, one Stephen, an Arab by race, succeeded as superior; he had a blood-brother called Procopius, priest of the church of Caesarea, at whose death Stephen made over all the family property to the monastery. In his time an Antiochene called Caesarius, who had gained a high reputation in many city magistracies, came to the holy city and, after spending some time there, fell ill of a terrible bodily affliction. He was brought to the monastery and anointed with oil from the tomb of the miracle-working Euthymius, at which he was totally freed of all bodily disease; on receiving this favor, he presented a substantial alms, and promised to give another each year. On his way back to Antioch he met in Tripoli Bishop Stephen, whom he told about the grace of the great Euthymius and the favor that had come to him. Leontius, a young nephew of the bishop, was thrilled in spirit to hear this, came to the monastery and renounced the world. When he had advanced in the monastic life, he was summoned by Bishop Stephen, who made him superior of the revered shrine of St Leontius the martyr, and left him as his successor as bishop when, not long after, he died. A certain Nilus, priest of the monastery, was sent to Antioch for the alms promised by Caesarius. Passing through Tripoli on the way, he was received by Bishop Leontius and ordained bishop of Orthosias.

68,5

68,10

68,15

68,20

68,25

68,30

48. THE STOLEN MONEY

Our father Stephen, having augmented and enriched the monastery of Euthymius to the best of his powers and leaving it six hundred solidi in minted money from his family property, died on 22 January after having completed twenty-one years as superior. A certain Thomas of Apamea took over the flock of Euthymius in flourishing condition, but diminished it. In his time the illustrious Caesarius paid a further visit to the monastery and, having been invited by him to dine, heard him say at luncheon, 'We have in the sacristy some pieces of the precious wood of the all-holy Cross, which Cosmas and Chrysippus, guardians of the Cross, gave at various times. Our superior Stephen placed some of these pieces in a cross he had made for the monastery all of gold and set with precious stones.' Caesarius said, 'By the Lord, do me the favor of letting me venerate them and of giving me one fragment.' The superior agreed to do this; taking him at this hour of midday to the sacristy, he opened the safe of the treasury, and Caesarius, after venerating, took the fragment. After going into the inner room of the sacristy, he was invited back to the meal. A certain Theodotus, a Galatian, who served in the refectory, was waiting on them; going in and out through the sacristy and finding the safes open, he stole from one of the safes the six hundred solidi mentioned above, which were in three boxes, and continued serving. The superior, however, wishing to send Caesarius on his way, made a bustle in shutting the safes and, not noticing what had happened, sent him on his way with prayer. On rising in the morning, Theodotus pretended to be angry and inveighed against the superior, saying, 'It is impossible to be saved in this place, because there is so much distraction.' And uttering other nonsense, he left the

69.

[AD 534]

69,5

69,10

69,15

69,20

69,25

monastery taking the money. On his way up to the holy city, he stopped opposite the monastery of Abba Martyrius and, taking fifty solidi from one of the boxes, placed the three boxes under a big stone; after marking

69,30 the place, he entered Jerusalem. Hiring beasts of burden to go to Joppa and leaving a deposit, he returned to collect the money. As he approached the stone, a most terrifying snake came out from under the stone and

70. pursued him, which foiled him that day. When he came back again the next day, the same wild beast pursued him for a great distance and would not let him alone. When he came to the spot again on the third day, some bodiless power in the air assailed him, struck him as if

70,5 with a cudgel and knocked him down on the road half-dead. Some people of Lazarium, passing by this spot, found him lying there, carried him into the holy city, and took him into a hospital.

When he had spent some time there with his pains only increasing, he saw in a dream someone of hallowed appearance, who said to him angrily, 'It will be

70,10 impossible for you to rise from this bed unless you return the stolen money to the monastery of Euthymius.' At this he summoned the guest-master of the monastery and confessed about the money. On learning of this, Thomas the superior and Leontius the prior went up to the holy city. When they had heard from the man that no one could approach the spot where the

70,15 money was because of the wild beast inhabiting it, Abba Leontius said, 'Come and point out the stone to us from a distance, for we are not afraid of that snake.' Taking him seated on an animal, they led him to the spot, and found the money safe under the stone without the wild beast's making any appearance. Theodotus

70,20 they let go scot-free, without worrying about the money he had squandered.

After governing the monastery of the great

Euthymius for eight years, Thomas died on 25 March

[AD 542]   of the fifth indiction in the seventieth year since the
death of the great Euthymius. His successor as superior was Leontius, who received me a sinner into the
monastery I so revere.

49. HOW THE WRITER ENTERED THE MONASTERY

71.   Whatever I heard and learnt and my fathers told me
of the inspired Euthymius I have not hidden from their
children in another generation but have reported and
recorded, so as to transmit it to subsequent generations.

71,5   I think it necessary to commit also to writing the miracles that have issued in my time from his tomb and
memorial, while both the recipients and the witnesses
are still alive. The miracles that come forth from his
tomb before the eyes of all are worthy not only to be
admired but also to be recorded, for they will convince

71,10   my readers to harbor no doubts about what I have already said of him.

How and when I was privileged to take up my abode
in the monastery, I shall relate from further back, right
from the beginning. Enrolled among the clergy of the
Church, I renounced the world in the holy monastery
of Your Sanctity in the sixteenth year of the present
divinely protected reign.[104] As you yourself know,

71,15   George, as the best of fathers and most loving of
parents, after receiving the monastic habit from your
hands I departed to Jerusalem with your prayer and
blessing, in the month of November. The pretext for
my departure was the consecration in Jerusalem of the
new church of the all-glorious Mary mother of God,

71,20   but my real reason was the desire to take up my abode
in the desert. Just before leaving the metropolis of
Scythopolis, I received instructions from my devout

mother to take no decisions as regards my spiritual welfare without the advice and permission of the inspired solitary Bishop John, who lived in the laura of

71,25   blessed Sabas and shone in all the godly virtues; 'my fear,' she said, 'is that you be carried away by the error of the Origenists and so lose the basis of your stability.'[a][105] Accordingly, after I had come to the holy city

72.   and venerated the holy and revered places together with the life-giving wood of the all-holy Cross, I also paid a visit to the inspired man I have just mentioned. He told me, 'If you want to be saved, go and live in the monastery of the great Euthymius.' So, after making

72,5   my way through the desert to the Jordan and spending some time with the holy fathers there, I entered the monastery of the great Euthymius in the month of July, being received by Leontius the father of the monastery.

50. PAUL

72,10   In this same period a monk called Paul, who came from the village of Tomessus in the first province of Cilicia, and who was grievously troubled by an impure spirit, was brought along from the monastery of Abba Martyrius and placed in the burial vault by the tomb of the our holy father Euthymius. After a few days Euthymius appeared to him in the middle of the night and expelled the impure spirit. Going to the church at

72,15   the hour of the night office, Paul made confession to God in the presence of all, announcing the miracle that had happened to him. Hearing of his cure, the members of his own cenobium came to fetch him; he, however, did not consent, but with great eagerness joined in the labors of the cenobium. Once, when we were outside in

a. Cf. 2 Pt 3:17.

72,20   the desert to collect faggots,[106] we asked Paul about the
nature and cause of his complaint and how he had been
cured. Deriving confidence from his frank love for us,
he gave us the following account:

'Being entrusted with a task in the cenobium, I took
the keys from the holy sanctuary and, dismissing fear
of God, I purloined some sums, while others I con-
temptuously squandered, ignoring the fact that all the
72,25   goods of monasteries and of other holy houses are
dedicated to God, as coming from offerings. When I
had completed the task and returned the keys to the
holy sanctuary, I was invited by some of the brethren
to a meal and, after drinking wine to excess, I went to
bed. Impure thoughts suddenly assailed me and, find-
72,30   ing me welcoming, disturbed my mind so dreadfully
that I reached a state just as if a woman was with me
and was lying down with me. While I was harboring
73.   these thoughts, suddenly I saw the power of the demon
coming against me like a dark cloud; darkened in my
wits by this, I continued being punished and tormented
by the demon for many days. Seeing that the demon
73,5   was daily growing in insolence towards me, the members of the cenobium brought me here.

'I was placed (he continued) right next to the holy
tomb and, immediately recovering my senses, I begged
the holy father with tears to free me from the demon
afflicting me and cleanse me from his operations. On
the night when you saw me confessing in the church, as
73,10   I was praying with groans and tears at about the fifth
hour of the night, I went into an ecstasy and had a vision as if I was in a glorious and awesome place,
whose glory no one could describe, and I seemed to be
wearing on my head a black woolen cowl, which was
an instrument of thorns (as in Scripture)[a] with a flock
73,15   of wool that pricked me keenly and tortured me hor-

___
a. Mt 27:29.

ribly. I opened my mouth and said, "Have pity on me, holy father Euthymius, and free me from the misfortune that oppresses me." Immediately I saw the saint, radiant with light, with grey hair and dwarf-life

73,20   build, a great beard, a round face and eyes full of joy, wearing a cloak darker and shorter than a habit, and holding a staff in his hand. He said to me, "Why are you bothering me? What do you want me to do for you?" I said in fear, "I beg you to take pity on me." He answered me harshly, "Are you now convinced that nothing can escape God? Have you learnt from your

73,25   sufferings how wicked it is to despise the service of Christ and to behave carelessly in a monastery? Are you now fully aware that everything in monasteries is sacred as coming from offerings? Just as those who make offerings to a monastery are giving to God and receive reward from him, so those who make an improper use of what has been given to God are wronging

74.   him and receive an appropriate punishment from him. If the famous Ananias and his wife, for purloining some of their own property which they had given to the community, received so severe a condemnation that they died as a result of the theft,[b] what pardon will he

74,5   win who purloins the offerings of others? But if you give me your word never again to misappropriate something belonging to a monastery, and also guard yourself from harboring impure thoughts, God will relent and cure you; for he is merciful and desires not the death of a sinner but that he should turn and live.[c] This has happened to you because, when entrusted with

74,10   the care of sacred things, you did not keep trust with God, but gave yourself up to avarice, by purloining what had been entrusted to you, and to vainglory, by shamelessly squandering the things of God, and to lust, by let-

b. Ac 5:1-5.
c. Cf. Ezk 18:23.

74,15

ting yourself be defiled by impure thoughts. This is why, deserted by the grace of God, you have been so buffeted by a towering wave of wickedness as to fall victim to most terrible shipwreck at the hand of a demon."

'On hearing this (he continued), I gave him my word never to wrong a monastery or other house of prayer. Then the saint in a fit of indignation grasped the black cowl and tore it with difficulty from my head. In his hand it took on the appearance of a small Ethiopian

74,20

darting fire from his eyes. Peering down, I saw in the ground in front of him an extremely deep and terrifying pit, into which pit the saint hurled the Ethiopian. Turning towards me, he said to me, "See, you are well! Sin no more, but attend to yourself, lest anything worse

74,25

befall you."[d] Coming to myself, I gave thanks to God, and from that time no evil has approached me.'

Having heard this from Paul, we glorified God and expressed amazement at the grace of the miracle-working father Euthymius.

51. THE SARACEN

75.

Two stades away from the monastery of the great Euthymius are too large cisterns, dug long ago, as the story goes, by the Amorites. They were subsequently restored by the great Euthymius when he was in the flesh; he placed a door in the mouth of one of them to

75,5

serve the fathers of his laura, while he gave leave to the Saracens he had baptized to use the other one during a prescribed season of the year. At this period, because of a lack of water, we had secured the cistern of the monastery. Since two Saracen tribal chiefs in alliance with the Romans Arethas and Asovades had an im-

75,10

placable feud and anarchy resulted, barbarians spread

d. Jn 5:14.

out over this desert and committed many outrages, as is common knowledge.

One day as we were sitting in front of the porter's lodge, two of the barbarians suddenly arrived together with a Christian Saracen called Thalabas, a descendant of the barbarians originally baptized by great Euthymius. They had brought with them a barbarian who was grievously tormented by a demon. Thalabas told us, 'these men came to water their camels and, when they found the cistern of the monastery secured, this one, excited in a somewhat barbarous manner, took a stone and broke the big door. No sooner had he broken it then he fell down smitten by a demon and remained there in convulsions. Learning the cause of this misfortune as I was passing the spot (he continued), I told them, "Carry him to the monastery of the saint and learn by experience that it is impossible for someone to damage property of his monastery without being detected."' Hearing this from Thalabas, we carried the sick man to the burial vault and laid him down by the tomb of the holy father. After he had waited there, the saint cleansed him from the activity of the demon and also illuminated him spiritually; for we learnt that after a few days he received holy baptism.

52. THE NIECE OF THALABAS

The Thalabas just mentioned, an inhabitant of Lazarium, brought to the monastery his brother's daughter, who was troubled by an impure spirit, and for three days he stayed at her side, while she was anointed each day with holy oil from the tomb of our holy father Euthymius. On the third day, after going into convulsions, she was cured. Receiving her back completely cleansed, he went home with joy.

75,15
75,20
75,25
76.
76,5

53. THE SON OF ARGÔB

Another Saracen originating from the same estate, called
Argôb, had a son who was grazing flocks in the desert
when he was seized by a demon and with a loud cry invoked the holy Euthymius. His face all contorted by the
76,10   evil spirit, he was carried to the monastery and placed by
the tomb of the miracle-working father. In a few days he
was cleansed from the demon and the contortion of his
face was corrected.

54. THE WOMAN OF BÊTABOUDISSAE

A woman from the village of Bêtaboudissae, sitting in
her husband's house at midday, was smitten by a most
76,15   cruel demon and remained moonstruck for seven months.
Her husband was grieved and saddened at the unbearable
misfortune of his wife. Remembering the saint, he took
her along to the monastery. Since no woman enters
within, the woman remained for three days and nights in
76,20   front of the monastery, fasting and praying continuously;
each evening she took holy oil from the tomb of the saint
and drank the liquid from his inextinguishable lamp. In
consequence, she was freed from the demon by the saint
appearing to her in the third night and saying, 'See, you
are well! Return to your home.' From then on she re-
76,25   turned in gratitude each year to the monastery, to give
thanks to God and to the saint; she would kiss the jambs
of the main entrance and, as an expression of her thanks,
provide a festal meal[107] for the fathers of the monastery.

55. PROCOPIUS

77.   There is in the monastery a brother of Galatian stock
and with the name Procopius who for many years had

an evil spirit hidden within that constantly terrorized
him and performed other acts against him, as he himself has told us. When he was received in the mon-
77,5   astery and performed an act of veneration at the tomb
of the saint, the spirit was convicted and forced into the
open, as Procopius manifested demonic possession. He
was repeatedly hurled to the ground, and his tongue
was tied, so that he was prevented from speaking to us;
if he was firmly forced to do so, he spoke to us in
Galatian. Why say more? He too was cured by the
77,10   saint, who expelled the demon and loosed the tying of
his tongue. He has remained in the monastery right
until now, outstanding in self-control and patience al-
lied to complete gravity, in a word, bearing the yoke of
Christ to the very best of his ability.

56. THE FOREIGNER

One day as we were sitting in the porter's lodge
77,15   washing *malôas,* we saw a foreigner driven in a great
rush by a most spiteful spirit and coming to the
monastery. He cried out in these express terms: 'What
have you to do with me, Euthymius, servant of God?
Where are you drawing me? I shan't come out!' And
with this the spirit hurled him down in front of the
porter's lodge. We got up and with the help of the
77,20   porter, called Babylas, managed with difficulty and by
force to lead him to the burial vault, while he cried out
as follows: 'Why are you carrying me off to my ad-
versary? Why are you taking me to my enemy? Why
are you dragging me along to the one who burns me?
Oh, violence! I shan't go with you, I'm leaving, I
won't stay!' Accordingly, when we had with great ex-
77,25   ertion brought the foreigner along, the spirit hurled him
down again on the tomb of the saint, so that he lay
speechless till evening. In the morning he got up and

tasted food, in his right mind and speaking intelligibly,
totally freed from every demonic influence. When we
questioned him, asking, 'How did you come here and
why yesterday were you shouting?,' he replied, 'I do
not know what you mean nor how I came here.' When
we heard this, we glorified God who gives glory to
those who love him.

78.

57. ROMANUS

There was a priest in the monastery named Achthabius, originating from the village of Bêtakabea, situated twelve miles from Gaza, who completed forty-five
years in the monastery, showing himself irreproachable
in performing the commandments of the Lord. Abba
Achthabius had a blood-brother in the said village
called Romanus. A man possessed by satanic envy
tried to seize the property of this Romanus. Failing in
his aim and mad with rage against him, he went off to
Eleutheropolis and consorted with a magician in his
desire to kill the man. The magician, on receiving substantial payment, applied diabolical spells. Romanus,
who had gone out into his fields with some workmen,
was seized with paralysis and carried into his house; as
the disease gradually intensified, dropsy set in, his
strength ebbed away, and after a few days he was written off by the doctors. As his family were sitting at his
side weeping, he opened his eyes and told them all to
leave him; then turning himself to the wall, as the great
Hezekiah once did,[a] he prayed as follows: 'God of
hosts, who hast said, "When you turn and groan, then
you will be saved,"[b] look upon me in my unworthiness
and rescue me from the misfortune that presses upon

78,5

78,10

78,15

78,20

a. 2 Kgs 20:2.
b. Is 30:15.

me.' Again he said, 'Holy father Euthymius, have pity
on me and ask God to deliver me from this severe illness.' As he uttered these prayers and others like them,
78,25   he went into an ecstasy and saw a monk with hair completely grey, who said to him, 'What do you wish me
to do for you?' Seized with both fear and joy, he said,
'Who are you, master?' The other replied, 'I am
Euthymius, whom you have just invoked with faith.
79.   Have no fear, but show me your complaint.' When
Romanus pointed to his belly, the figure of the vision,
straightening and joining his fingers, cut open the place
as if with a sword and removed from the stomach a tin
tablet with certain characters on it; this he placed in
front of Romanus on a small table. Rubbing the place
79,5   with his hand, he expunged the cut and cured him,
while he said, 'This has happened to you because for a
long time you have not gone to church or approached
the divine mysteries. This is why you have been oppressed. Someone has gone to Eleutheropolis and hired
79,10   demons against you, who prevailed against you because you were neglecting your own salvation. But see,
God has taken pity on you. No longer neglect your
prayers.' Having said this, he disappeared.

Romanus came to himself and immediately got up.
Excreting everything that had caused the disease, he
recovered his health and, summoning his people,
79,15   related the whole vision. They, on seeing such a sudden change, glorified God for showering such charisms
on his saints. Taking them with him, Romanus came to
the monastery and, after venerating the tomb of the
miracle-working father Euthymius, recounted the
whole story to the blessed Achthabius, to the superior
79,20   and to all of us; after this announcement of the miracle
he returned home. On each anniversary of this miracle
he offers a public feast in his village in memory of the
favor that came to him through the inspired Euthymius.

58. THE VILLAGERS OF PHARAN

Ten stades to the east of the laura of Pharon there is a
79,25   village called Pharan, from which, I imagine, the laura
got its name. A man originating from this village,
called Cyriacus, who had a flock grazing in the desert,
took a further ten animals from a poor man of the same
village in order to graze them together with his own
flock, as the result of some agreement between them.
After some time, the poor man under the pressure of
some need or other wanted to sell his animals, but
80.   Cyriacus gave him eight instead of the ten. When the
other said that the animals he had supplied numbered
ten, Cyriacus denied it. With these two at odds in the
dispute, certain mediators came between them and proposed an oath to them, wishing to resolve the dispute.
80,5   When Cyriacus agreed to swear, the poor man asked
for the oath to be taken at the tomb of Saint Euthymius.
After fixing a day, they set off to the monastery. When
they reached the imperial highway that leads from
80,10   Jerusalem down to Jericho and the monastery came
into view, as the one who received the oath later
recounted to me, he felt a hesitation on seeing his op-
ponent giving himself up to perjury and said to him,
'Come, let us go back, brother. See, I have become
convinced during the time we have spent getting as far
as here.' But the other refused to return. When they
entered the monastery, the wretch swore on the tomb
of the revered father and left the monastery none the
80,15   worse. He thought God had ignored it; but rather he
himself had ignored God and as a true 'fool' said in his
heart, 'There is no God.'[a]

After one day had elapsed, in the second night
around the sixth hour, he was lying alone in his own
house, awake and engrossed in futile thoughts, when he

a. Cf. Ps 14(13):1.

80,20   suddenly saw the door of his house open of itself and an aged monk come in, shining with light and lighting up the house, accompanied by five younger monks and holding a rod in his hand. With stern voice and grim look the apparition said to him, 'Tell me, you reprobate among men, what did you come and do at the mon-

80,25   astery of Euthymius?' When the other was reduced to silence, finding nothing to say in defence, the saint said to the younger men, 'Lift him up.' They immediately seized him and four of them stretched him out. He gave

81.   the rod in his hand to the fifth and said, 'Beat him and say, "No, you perjuror! No, you cheat! Do not despise the forbearance of God."' As he was being tortured by further beating, the saint said to the one administering the beating, 'Well done!' And taking him by the hair, he said to him, 'Have you now learnt, you impious

81,5   wretch, that there is indeed a God who repays each person according to his deserts? Behold, this night we require your soul from you, and the things you have stolen, whose will they be?[b] Since you have despised the patience and long-suffering of God, you have laid up for yourself this store of wrath,[c] so that all may learn from your example to defraud no one and not to

81,10   give themselves over to oaths at all, even if they intend to speak the truth.' So they left him. Panic-stricken, he shouted out, 'Have pity on me in the name of God.' His neighbors flocked to him and, hearing what had happened and seeing his body all bruised from the blows, they were seized with great fear. When he

81,15   begged to be carried to the monastery and acknowledged his many sins against the holy place, they placed him on an ass between two sacks of chaff and brought him to the monastery. Telling us everything that had happened, they showed us the blows on his back, and we

b. Cf. Lk 12:10.
c. Cf. Rom 2:4-5.

saw his back looking as if repeatedly struck by whips of
ox-tendon. Seized with fear at this, the inmates of the
monastery have from that time on allowed no one, as
far as lies with them, to take or exact an oath on the
tomb of the holy father. The villagers stayed one day at
the monastery, but were unable to lay him down in the
burial vault since his stomach was loose, he discharged
blood, and his mouth constantly vomited. So they
departed, taking him half-dead, and on the next day he
died, a lesson to those intending to commit perjury.

59. THE MAN WHO STOLE THE URN

In this same period a foreign traveler came to the
monastery and was hospitably received. Around midnight he went down to the burial vault, unfixed the silver urn of the miracle-working father and made off
with it in the same night, making his exit with the animals of the monastery. Procopius, who had earlier been
healed by the saint and had been entrusted with the
task of porter, on going out early found the thief of the
urn completely immobilized and in a manner nailed
down in front of the monastery. Learning the cause of
his immobility, he led him into the monastery, where
he confessed to us, 'I have walked up and down a distance of almost thirty miles and am totally exhausted. I
was simply unable to cross the boundaries of the
monastery.' Recovering the urn, we were amazed at
the power and the forbearance of the miracle-working
father. As for the man, after supplying him for his journey, since he was in need, we sent him on his way.

60. HOW AND WHEN
THE PRESENT BOOK WAS COMPOSED

Selecting few out of many, I have recorded these events which I saw with my own eyes, and I have joined them to those I have recorded on hearsay concerning the life of our father in the flesh, in order that the readers, including Your Holiness, may know the power of the divine grace that invests the tomb of Euthymius, and reflect how the lustre of his life in the flesh has as evidence the miracles worked after his death. For not only when he was in the flesh did he work miracles among men, but even after his death, when he was united to the angels, he performs great marvels among us; though existing in a superior state, he has not left us, but cherishes and cares for us with assistance even greater than before.

In consequence, I too, his unworthy servant, since I had often been benefited by him in both body and soul and beheld the benefits welling up from his tomb, was astounded in thought and asked myself, How did this holy Euthymius lead his life among men, and with what virtues did he win God's favor, so as to have obtained such divine grace? This question excited in me a fervent desire to study and record his life and conduct in the flesh. I made asiduous inquiry among the most ancient of the inspired fathers in this desert, who had acquired by oral transmission an accurate knowledge of the facts about the great Euthymius and had been contemporaries and fellow-combatants with the all-praiseworthy Sabas; and whatever I managed to learn and gather from each of these, not only of the life and miracles of the great Euthymius but also of the life and conduct of Saint Sabas, I recorded higgledy-piggledy on various sheets in disorganized and jumbled accounts.

A short time afterwards, when the fifth holy ecu-

82,15

82,20

82,25

82,30

83.

83,5

menical council gathered at Constantinople and
anathematised the doctrines of Origen and Nestor-
83,10   ius,[108] the original inmates of the New Laura, espous-
ing the heresy of Origen, left the catholic commun-
AD 554/5   ion and were expelled from the New Laura. On their
departure, orthodox fathers were transferred to the
New Laura from the laura of the blessed Saba and
83,15   other holy and irreproachable monasteries. At this
time, on the advice and by the leave of the wonderful
John, bishop and solitary, I left the cenobium and settled in the New Laura, taking with me the pages I had
written on Euthymius and Sabas. On being instructed
by Your Holiness, who had heard about the said pages,
83,20   to arrange the chapters contained in them harmoniously
in the appropriate style and sequence and to send them
to you, I spent about two years as a hermit in the New
Laura, without ceasing to ponder on the sheets. I was at
a loss how to begin the composition since I was uncul-
tivated and had been through nothing in the way of
83,25   secular education; in addition, I was ignorant of the
divine Scriptures and also slow of speech.[109] But the
God of marvels, who has implanted in all men a
tongue, who gives resource to the resourceless, who
smoothes out difficulties in things and makes the
speech of stammerers distinct, performed through
Euthymius and Sabas his servants a prodigy in the case
of my lowliness, when being at a loss for words and
expressions I had already thought of abandoning my
pages, except that I plied fervent petitionary prayer.
84.   One day I was sitting on my usual seat and holding my
pages in my hands when, around the second hour of the
day, I was overcome with sleep and there appeared to
me the holy fathers Euthymius and Sabas in their cus-
84,5   tomary sacred dress. I heard Saint Sabas say to the
great Euthymius, 'Here is Cyril. He holds your pages
in his hands and displays intense eagerness, and yet,
despite his great and painful labors, he is unable to be-

gin writing.' The great Euthymius replied to him, 'How can he write about us when he has not yet received the grace of opening his mouth in fitting speech?' Saint Sabas said, 'Give him the grace, father.' The great Euthymius consented; taking from his bosom a silver ointment-jar with a probe, he dipped in the probe and three times ministered from the jar to my mouth. Of the substance inserted by the probe the texture was that of oil but the taste was sweeter than honey and truly a proof of the divine saying, 'How sweet to my throat are thy sayings, beyond honey to my mouth.'[a] As a result, when I awoke from that ineffable sweetness, I still had that spiritual fragrance and sweetness on my lips and mouth, and immediately began the preface of the present work. In consequence of so great a grace I proceeded through my account of the great Euthymius, eager in my reliance on so great a grace to fulfil my promise and relate in a second account the facts of the life and conduct of the citizen of heaven Sabas. I ask both of them, in addition to the grace accorded me, to intercede on my behalf and to beg propitiation for my offences, so that both here and in the resurrection to come I, wretched sinner though I am, may be protected from shame and find mercy before the judgment-seat of Christ. To him be the glory with the Father and the Holy Spirit for ever and ever. Amen.

84,10

84,15

84,20

84,25

85.

---

a. Ps 119(118):103.

NOTES

Internal references are by page and line (0,0) in the critical edition (marginally noted in this translation)

1. Abba George received Cyril's monastic profession and remained his friend and guide. The *Lives* of Euthymius and Sabas are dedicated to him. See Introduction, p. xlix. During the excavation of a sixth-century monastery at Scythopolis an inscription was discovered which referred to the 'hegumen and priest George'. If this is the same George, then Beella was a large monastery just outside the city walls with magnificent mosaics. It can be seen today, at the end of a row of factories on the outskirts of the modern Beth-Shan. For a description, see G. Fitzgerald, *A sixth-century Monastery in Beth-Shan (Scythopolis)*.

2. The writers of hagiography often emphasise the need for faith, realising that the events they describe stretch the reader's credibility. Compare Theodoret, *History of the Monks of Syria* Prologue 10, and *Life of Antony* Introduction.

3. John Moschus uses the same comparison. See *The Spiritual Meadow*, Prologue.

4. The Prologue is constructed carefully. In structure it is based on the Prologue to the Life of Pachomius, which also describes the ascetics as descending directly from Christ through the apostles and martyrs. The doctrinal statements are derived from the *Confessio fidei* and *Contra Origenem* of Justinian; and the chapter also contains quotation from Nilus of Ancyra and Basil of Seleucia's *Life of Thecla*. For references, see Flusin, 48, 54, 70-71.

5. The Council of Chalcedon used the words *prosôpon* and *hypostasis* to refer to the unity of the person of Christ. They could be translated as 'face' and 'subsistence'. The thought of the Council's Definition of Faith lies behind this passage, although mediated through the writings of Justinian.

6. Sabas and Theodosius are also called citizens of heaven or *ouranopolitai* (84,24 and 235,27). The title refers both to their status in heaven indicated by the posthumous miracles performed at their tombs and also to the function of the monasteries as cities built in desert places for godly purposes.

7. The story of Euthymius' conception is based on that of Samuel in 1 Samuel 1.

8. Polyeuctus was a Roman soldier martyred for his faith in Melitene.

9. The inception of his third year means that he was two years old.

10. Compare the description of Eudoxius with that of Cyril's father (180,4-6). These events took place seventy years before Cyril was writing. He is filling in the gaps in his knowledge with details of his own family background.

11. Otreius was Metropolitan of Melitene from 374 to 384. He was a friend and correspondent of St Basil. See Basil, *Ep.* 181.

12. The title *scholastikos* could refer to anyone who had achieved a high level of education, but had come to be used mainly for members of the legal profession.

13. Euthymius became lector at the age of two, long before he could read. Again, compare Cyril's childhood spent in the bishop's palace, at 180-181.

14. The only complimentary reference to secular learning in Cyril's writing. In

view of the parallels with Cyril's own childhood, this sentence could imply that Cyril received a classical education.

15. Acacius was Metropolitan by 431, when he attended the Council of Ephesus, and was alive in 437, when he tried to obtain the condemnation of Theodore of Mopsuestia. See Liberatus, *Breviarium* 10. Synodius succeeded Acacius and was present at the Council of Ephesus in 449.

16. One of two occasions when Cyril acknowledges the source of his quotation. It is from Gregory's *Elogium of Basil,* 12.1. A further unacknowledged quotation from the same work occurs in 12,25 - 13,1. See also 229,27.

17. The image of the monk as athlete was common, for example Theodoret, *History of the Monks of Syria* 3.18. It is rare in Cyril, perhaps because he lacked experience of the theatres and hippodromes of the cities. The theatre at Scythopolis had fallen into disuse before his birth. See the report by S. Applebaum in the *Israel Exploration Journal* 10 (1960) 126-2 and 263-4.

18. This was Letoius, who was in correspondence with Gregory of Nyssa in 390.

19. The custom of retiring to greater solitude for an extended Lent was to become common in the Palestinian desert. This passage suggests that Euthymius introduced the custom from Armenia. The lenten journey also served as a means of maintaining contact with monasteries in other parts of the country (108-9). Monastic writers often referred to Elijah and John the Baptist as initiators of the ascetic life, but this is the only reference to them in Cyril.

20. The call to the monastic life is a call to pilgrimage. Pilgrimage came more naturally to the people of Asia Minor, where the terrain encouraged a nomadic mobile way of life, than to those of Egypt, where the agriculture of the Nile valley led to greater stability.

21. The Church of the Resurrection, the focus of the pilgrim's devotion, was built by the Emperor Constantine and completed some time before 348. Euthymius would have entered through the atrium and passed through a covered apsidal basilica to the courtyard with the stone of Golgotha at its southeast corner and the tomb to the west.

22. The Laura of Pharan lies about seven miles northeast of Jerusalem beyond Anathoth and was, according to tradition, founded by Chariton in about 275. The form of monastic life of Pharan was to inspire Euthymius' later foundations (16,26 and 26,16). See Vailhé, 94.

23. The words used to describe the bonds of affection linking Euthymius and Theoctistus are borrowed from Theodoret, *History of the Monks of Syria* 26.4.

24. Coutila is the area of desert which leads to the north-west shore of the Dead Sea. It is flatter and more barren than the mountainous grazing area in which most of the monasteries were to be situated.

25. 'Familiar access' translates *parresia*. This is an important concept in Cyril's understanding of the monks' ascetic life. In its classical origins, the word referred to the freedom of speech enjoyed by the citizen and denied to the slave. Here it is used to describe the intimacy of the saint's relationship with God and the efficacy of his prayers. In the *Lives* of Euthymius and Sabas a dramatic rain miracle provides assurance that the saint has achieved *parresia* (38,1-39,16 and 167,25-169,24). Cyril's use of the concept is derived from Theodoret's *His-*

tory of the Monks of Syria, from which this sentence is quoted (1.3).

26. This monastery in the Wadi Mukellik has been excavated by D. Chitty. It is described in Chitty, 'Two monasteries in the wilderness of Judaea'. The cave in which the ascetics settled is clearly distinguishable.

27. Lazarium was the village now known as Bethany, about seven miles distant. The plants which Euthymius and Theoctistus fed on also provided food for sheep and goats.

28. Compare the *Life of Antony* 48, where Antony reassures a nervous visitor, 'I too am a man like you'.

29. The renunciation of the world is an important step, in Cyril's view. It describes the first stage of the monastic life in which the virtues of obedience, humility, and abstinence are practised. In the second stage, attention shifts to the goal of *parresia*, where solitude and prayer are the relevant disciplines. See note 24.

30. These monasteries are about two miles northeast of Bethlehem. Metopa is now Umm-Tuba; the remains of Marinus' monastery are probably those at Abu Ghunneim, and those of Luke's monastery are at Khirbet Luqa. See P. Virgilio Corbo, *Gli Scavi Di Kh. Siyar El-Ghanam*, 144,148: and Ovadiah 98.

31. One of Cyril's few passages of ascetic teaching. It contains little that is original and draws on ideas and phrases from the *Life of Pachomius,* the *Life of Antony* and Theodoret's *History of the Monks of Syria*.

32. Aspébetus is in origin a title: *Spahbedh* or commander of an army. It has evolved into a proper name.

33. Isigerdes I reigned from 399 to 420, and, although he was generally sympathetic to the Christian faith, persecuted the church for a brief period towards the end of his reign. Isigerdes II, who came to the Persian throne in 438, was consistently hostile to the church and was involved in a border dispute with Anatolius the commander-in-chief. In spite of Cyril's reference to Anatolius (19,7), the chronology requires that this event took place under the first Isigerdes.

34. *Magi* are Persian priests. In Egypt the word was used to refer to 'sorcerers' or 'magicians', and this derogatory use has influenced Cyril.

35. Roubâ is to the south of Coutila.

36. This mountain must be Masada, the rock on which the Zealots made their last stand against the Romans before committing mass suicide in AD 73. There are the remains of a fifth-century church on the summit. From it, the journey westwards across the desert leads to the wilderness of Ziph and the village of Caparbaricha. This journey took Euthymius further to the south than any other of the monks described by Cyril.

37. *Malôa* is a desert plant which was often eaten by monks (e.g. 77.14-15). It is mentioned in Job 30.14 and is to be identified with the shrubby Orache which grows on river-banks and by the roadside. Its leaves are still eaten when other food is in short supply.

38. The comparison between 'mania' (madness) and the dualist heresy of Manes was popular in the literature of the time (for example, Epiphanius, *Panarion* 66,1). Presumably a popular blend of superstition and ancient religious practices is referred to here rather than a formalised system of beliefs.

39. The remains of the settlement can still be discerned in the area between Khan el-Ahmar and the Wadi Mukellik. They are described by R.P. Federlin in R. Genier, *La vie de St Euthyme le Grand*, 94-104.

40. Gifts from visiting pilgrims and others were an important source of income for the monasteries. Theodore of Petra, (*Life of Theodosius* 27,10-15), records wealthy residents making regular tours of the desert distributing money to all the monastic houses.

41. The first eleven recruits, only one of them from Palestine, show the cosmopolitan nature of the Palestinian monks.

42. A rural bishop or 'chorepiscop' was appointed to assist the bishop of a large or prominent diocese in his duties. Since fifteen rural bishops signed the canons of Nicaea in 325 and only six signed those of Chalcedon in 451, it seems that the office was dying out. Perhaps the growing importance of the position of archimandrite compensated for this decline. For further description of rural bishops, see A.H.M. Jones, *Later Roman Empire*, 879. Passariôn was an important figure in the early history of Palestinian monasticism. He founded an almshouse outside the east gate of the city and cenobium on Mount Sion (*Life of Peter the Iberian* 35). Hesychius wrote extensive commentaries on the Bible. Little is known of his life. 'The sainted' translates *ho en hagiois*, an honorific title used repeatedly by Cyril.

43. The indiction was a form of taxation. The method for calculating it evolved into the standard chronological framework by which events were dated. The indiction years ran from 1 September to 31 August and were counted in cycles of fifteen. So the fifteenth indiction year was followed by another first indiction. Most of Cyril's dates are given in this form.

44. Now follow three dramatic stories in which miraculous signs demonstrate the principles which govern the life of the laura—hospitality, obedience and stability.

45. If these four hundred Armenians had a similar background to the followers of Barsaumas, then Euthymius' desire to provide them with food is understandable. See Introduction, p. xxiii.

46. The 'steward' or *oikonomos* held an important position, since the laura was expected to provide a livelihood for the monks. The mule carried the work of the monks to Jerusalem to be sold and brought back necessary provisions. The responsibility of the muleteer for bartering and trade explains Auxentius' reluctance to accept.

47. Cyriacus lived to be 108. He was the only one of Cyril's informants who had known Euthymius personally.

48. The story of Marôn and Clematius is derived from Cyril's literary sources. The Egyptian anecdote is also to be found in the *Apophthegmata Patrum* (F. Nau, in *Revue de l'Orient Chrétien* 13 (1908) 278). Other parts of the section are influenced by Palladius' *Lausiac History*, Paul of Elousa's *Life of Theognius*, and Theodoret's *History of the Monks of Syria* (references in Flusin).

49. 'Insolence' translates *parresia*. This is the only example in Cyril of the negative use of *parresia* which is frequent in Egyptian ascetic writings. Freedom can be abused and then speech becomes impudently over-familiar.

50. The Council of Ephesus condemned the teaching of Nestorius and gave

formal approval to the title *Theotokos* or 'God-bearer' for the Virgin Mary. Nestorius was deposed from the Patriarchate of Constantinople by Cyril of Alexandria's party before the Syrian bishops led by John of Antioch arrived.

51. Acacius was a strong Monophysite. After the Formulary of Union which reconciled Cyril and John of Antioch, Acacius complained to Cyril that it accepted the 'doctrine of two sons' (see Cyril's *Ep.* 40 *ad Acacium*; PG 77:184 B).

52. The Formulary of Union (433) reconciled John of Antioch and Cyril of Alexandria.

53. Domnus became Patriarch of Antioch ten years later in 441. He opposed the extreme Monophysitism of Eutyches, but was forced to withdraw his opposition by Dioscorus at the 'Latrocinium' of Ephesus. He was deposed at the same council along with other bishops but, unlike them, was not reinstated by the Council of Chalcedon. He returned to the laura of Euthymius where he was among those who sheltered Juvenal after the Council of Chalcedon.

54. Arsenius had educated Arcadius and Honorius, the sons of Theodosius I, and after the death of Theodosius in 395 settled in Egypt. The virtues which Cyril attributes to Arsenius are echoed in the sayings attributed to him in the *Apophthegmata Patrum*.

55. No other evidence exists for the Patriarch of Jerusalem's everyday dress being white. See P. Devos, 'Cyrille de Scythopolis'.

56. This edifying story is found in the anonymous section of the *Apophthegmata Patrum*, N491. See Flusin, 58.

57. The same cry is emitted by a devil in the *Life of Antony* 6.

58. This episode took place in January. The winter rains should have been at their height. To have reached mid-January without rain would have been alarming, but sudden violent storms are not uncommon at this time of year.

59. The dogmatic views expressed in this chapter are the expression of the orthodoxy of the Desert in Cyril's lifetime. Several of the statements are quotations from Justinian's *Confessio fidei*. See Flusin, 70-1.

60. Euthymius was unlikely to have met a Sabellian or an Arian in the desert. Sabellius, who probably taught at Rome in the early third century, emphasised the unity of God so strongly that the three persons seemed aspects or modes of being of the one God. Arius safeguarded the divine unity by the alternative method of reducing the Son and the Spirit to the status of separate and subordinate beings. The threat from these heresies had receded in the fifth century. Nestorius and Eutyches represent contrary heretical Christologies: the first emphasises the duality in Christ and the second the unity. The purpose of the passage is to state that Euthymius' orthodoxy is irreproachable.

61. Dioscorus succeeded Cyril of Alexandria as Patriarch in 444. His ascendancy, established at the 'Latrocinium' of Ephesus in 449, was short lived as the accession of the Emperor Marcian in 450 led to the summoning of another council at Chalcedon in 451, at which Dioscorus was deposed.

62. The Council of Ephesus held in 449 was called the *latrocinium* by Pope Leo, who described it as '*non iudicium sed latrocinium*,' not a just trial but a highway robbery', in Ep. 95 to Pulcheria (edited by E. Schwartz in *ACO 2.4*). At the Council, Patriarch Flavian of Constantinople was manhandled so brutally that he died a few days later. The Council was a brief moment of triumph

for Dioscorus and the Monophysites.

63. Theodosius had a reputation as a trouble-maker. Evagrius reports that he was expelled from his monastery in Egypt for stirring up trouble (*Ecclesiastical History* 2.5). But the monks of Palestine, who thought that Chalcedon had made heretical innovations, were a sympathetic following. An alternative view of these events is presented by John Rufus in his *Plerophoria*.

64. Gerasimus was a famous anchorite and a close associate of Euthymius (see 56,27: 60,20: 224,25). He established a monastery near the Jordan south east of Jericho, which combined the cenobite and laurite ways of life. After a time in the cenobium the monks would graduate to one of the seventy or so anchorites' cells in the neighbourhood. A life of Gerasimus was compiled, probably in the late sixth-century, and contains passages from Cyril of Scythopolis and John Moschus, as well as original writing. The view that this life should be assigned to Cyril has been abandoned. See Flusin, 35-40 and H. Grégoire, 'La Vie Anonyme de S. Gérasime'.

65. The liturgical fan or *flabellum* was held by the deacon and was used to keep flies away from the eucharistic elements. It was in use from the fourth century.

66. The sanctuary was separated from the narthex by a rail from which curtains might be hung; see 186,5. This suggests that the iconostasis was a later development.

67. Terebôn, as a layman, was standing in the narthex. Gabrielius, as a eunuch, had, until then, remained in the porch with women and children, because of his un-bearded face.

68. A formula used in the Syrian liturgy of St. James. The liturgy of St John Chrysostom has only 'let us lift up our hearts'.

69. Eudocia dominated the church in Jerusalem. The wife of the Emperor Theodosius II (408-450), she left Constantinople and settled in Jerusalem after estrangement from her husband (444). She used her vast wealth to restore the walls of the city and build many churches, monasteries and charitable institutions. See 53,5; John Moschus, *Spiritual Meadow* 185; and Evagrius, *Ecclesiastical History* 1.21-22.

70. *Aposchists*, meaning 'those cut off from' the Church, is Cyril's favoured word to describe Monophysites. Used in Egypt to refer to extreme Monophysites who seceded from the Church, it here points to Cyril's concern that Monophysites should be in communion with the Patriarch of Jerusalem.

71. By now Symeon was approaching the end of his life. He died in 459. His column at Telanissus was almost fifty miles from Antioch.

72. At Jebel Muntar, which was later the site of one of Sabas' monasteries. See 127,15-129,2.

73. Cosmas was one of the three Capadocian brothers who were Euthymius' first monks. Anastasius was later Patriarch (35,1).

74. Eudocia's renewed relationship with Juvenal did not lead her to desert the Monophysites. According to a Monophysite source she persuaded Romanus to build a monastery on land at Eleutheropolis which belonged to her. See John Rufus, *Narratio de obitu Theodosii* 26.10-23.

75. Cyril has made a mistake here. Romanus' monastery at Thekoa was not founded at this time. See Chitty, *The Desert a City*, 99 n. 77.

76. Chrysippus' surviving writings include sermons on the Mother of God, St

Theodore, Michael the Archangel, and John the Baptist. He died in 479.

77. St Menas was an Egyptian martyr who died about 300. His shrine near Alexandria was a centre of pilgrimage and healing. Churches dedicated to him are found throughout the Byzantine empire.

78. This is a mistake. It should read the '81st year' (457). See 50,20 and 51,22.

79. The practice of not allowing beardless men to live in the laura originated in Egypt. See 114,12. Earlier Euthymius had reluctantly accepted the young Cappadocian brothers (25,22-25) but he has now developed the practice of sending young men to a nearby cenobium, a practice which Sabas continued. Compare *Apophthegmata Patrum,* Eudemon 1.

80. Proterius had been the archpriest of Dioscorus and was consecrated Patriarch after his deposition at Chalcedon, but popular support for Dioscorus and opposition to Constantinople rendered his position untenable. Imperial troops protected him for a while, but after the death of the Emperor Marcian he was lynched by the crowd and Timothy Aelurus or 'The Weasel' took his place. See Evagrius, *Ecclesiastical History* 2.5: 2.8, and *Life of Peter the Iberian* 64-8.

81. Compare 35,1-25. The gift of clairvoyance seems to have applied especially to episcopal appointments and the time of death. See 53,21 and 57,12-13.

82. A cell could house several monks; Sabas built a cell for Jeremiah and two other monks, 105,8. Presumably it was not lack of comfort that drove these two hardened ascetics away but lack of accomodation for their followers. No trace remains of Elias' monastery. Martyrius' monastery is often located at Khirbet Murasas, because of the similarity of the name to that of Martyrius. But this hill does not command a view of the Jericho road and the alternative location at Deir-es-sidd is to be preferred. See 69, 26-27, and Vailhé, 'Les premières monastères de la Palestine' 197-8.

83. The dates in this sentence are unsure. Euthymius' eighty-third year is 459, while Anastasius' accession to the patriarchate is generally dated to 458; compare 49,23 with n.72. And Juvenal could not have been patriarch as long as forty-four years, since his predecessor, Praylius, was still in office in 417. See Schwartz 51 note.

84. A similar story is told of Arsenius, on whom Euthymius modelled his behaviour: *Apophthegmata Patrum*, Arsenius 8.

85. Bostra is in Arabia. Antipatrus was Bishop after 451 and wrote a refutation of Origen. See 189,20.

86. The ruins of Khirbet Musrasas probably mark the site of this monastery. See n. 76, Ovadiah 111 and Vailhé 77.

87. The same verse of Scripture is quoted in a similar context in the *Life of Antony* 44.

88. A play on words: *hagion ex agriou.*

89. For the prophecy about Cosmas see 26,4-5.

90.The ruins of Wadi-er-Rawabe could well be Gabrielius' hermitage. See V. Corbo, 'Il romitorio egumeno Gabriel', and Ovadiah 176.

91. The Theophanies is the feast known in the West as Epiphany.

92. The *melagria* root (also mentioned at 96,15; 209,10; 210,10; 227,9; 228,19) was a staple food during these excursions into the desert. It is the same as the

food of John the Baptist, *meli agrion*, misleadingly translated as 'wild honey' (Mt 3:4).

93. The same story is told in the *Life of Sabas* 94,13 - 95,5.

94. These are also St Antony's dying words, *Life of Antony* 91.

95. This extensive chronographical information is provided only for the dates of death of Euthymius and Sabas. This emphasises that Cyril sees them not as influential historical persons but as the chosen instruments of God. The moment of death is the fulfillment, not the end, of their work, and their intercessory power becomes even more efficacious because of their greater closeness to God. Of the chronographers mentioned by name, only the chronography of Hippolytus survives; see Schwartz 346-7.

96. The crucible contained oil which was used to anoint the sick. See 68,15 and 76,1.

97. Basiliscus was Leo's brother-in-law who profited from the unpopularity of the Isaurian Zeno to seize the throne in January 475. The Encyclical, issued in April 475, affirmed Nicaea, Constantinople, and both councils of Ephesus, and anathematized Chalcedon. See Evagrius, *Ecclesiastical History* 3.3-4.

98. Curicus is on the coast of Cilicia. The Parthenian Sea is the Eastern Mediterranean between Egypt and Cyprus.

99. The site of Euthymius' monastery of Khan-el-Amar has been excavated by D. Chitty, who praises Cyril's topographical accuracy: 'It was from what he tells us that we were led to find the cemetery of St. Euthymius and the line of the walls of the church of his Laura in the vault under the church of the Coenobium' (Chitty, *The Desert a City*, 131). For a full account of the excavations, see D. Chitty, 'Two monasteries in the wilderness of Judaea' and 'The Monastery of Euthymius'.

100. What rain there is in the desert falls between November and March.

101. The monks were, and in many monasteries still are, summoned to worship by striking a wooden block, called the *simandron*, with a mallet.

102. A different account is given by the Monophysite historian Zacharias Rhetor. He says that the union was the result of an agreement to base the faith on Nicaea and anathematize Chalcedon. This was the solution to the dispute put forward by Basiliscus' Encyclical and, later, by Zeno's Henoticon (482). So Cyril's account needs to be treated with caution. The relevant passages of Zacharias' *Ecclesiastical History* are conveniently collected at Schwartz, 367-8.

103. Anastasius was Emperor from 491-518.

104. The years of the Emperor's reign are counted from the 1st January after the accession, so the 'sixteenth year' is 543. Cyril made his monastic renunciation before his old friend George, to whom he dedicated his two main *Lives*, and then went to Jerusalem in November. He entered Euthymius' monastery in July 544. This chronology was established by E. Stein who corrected errors in Schwartz's dating. See E. Stein, 'Cyrille de Scythopolis'.

105. Justinian's Edict against Origen had been published in Jerusalem the previous year, and the Origenist retaliation was reaching its height. See the *Life of Sabas* 192,12 - 194,12 for Cyril's memories of this turbulent period.

106. 'Faggots' translates *mannouthia* (as at 92,8 and 130,30). The meaning of

this word is uncertain. Du Buit (in Festugière, *Les moines d'Orient* III/1, 48) suggests the alternative 'thistles'.

107. 'Festal meal' translates *agape*. It was the custom to show gratitude for a blessing received by providing a generous meal. This would have been enjoyed by visitors as well as by monks. The same word is used at 69,16; 130,26; 165,9.

108. The Second Council of Constantinople met in 553. The circumstances leading up to it are described more fully by Cyril at 198,7-200,16 and by Evagrius, *Ecclesiastical History* 4.38. Its purpose was to condemn certain writings of Theodore of Mopsuestia, Theodoret, and Ibas of Edessa and so to eliminate the possibility of a Nestorian interpretation of the Council of Chalcedon. It also provided an opportunity for the condemnation of Origenism.

109. We should not take Cyril's protestations here too literally. The claim to be ignorant and uneducated, and to write as a result of a divine commission, are commonplace features of writing of the period, both Christian and pagan. For a full list of parallels see A.-J. Festugière, 'Lieux communs' 126-31.

THE SECOND MONASTIC HISTORY
OF THE DESERT OF JERUSALEM
COMPOSED BY CYRIL PRIEST AND MONK
AND SENT TO ABBA GEORGE
SOLITARY AND MONASTIC FOUNDER
IN THE PLACE NEAR SCYTHOPOLIS CALLED BEËLA

THE LIFE OF OUR PIOUS FATHER SABAS

PREFACE

B LESSED BE THE GOD AND FATHER of our Lord
Jesus Christ, who has prompted your virtuous
Perfection to instruct my nothingness to record
and send to you the lives pleasing to God of our holy
85,15   fathers and precursors Euthymius and Sabas, and who
through their intercession has in his ineffable mercy
instilled into me in my misery a drop of eloquence to
open my mouth to fulfil such profitable instructions.

Concerning the revered father Euthymius I have already said some slight things unworthy of his greatness
of spirit; for I could not discover more since eighty
86.   years have already passed since his departure to God,
and these few facts I assembled with difficulty, hasten-
ing hither and thither and gathering and collecting
them, as if rescuing them out of some abyss of distant
time and oblivion, lest the edifying stories about him
86,5   become extinct with time. But now the fitting moment
calls me to bring to fulfilment the remainder of your
instructions and to record a few facts about our celebrated father Sabas, which with thought and labor I
gathered from truthful and pious men who were his
disciples and fellow-combatants and who to this day
86,10   imitate his life and illuminate our path to God. Already
in my previous work I undertook to do this; admittedly,
I am not ignorant of my own unworthiness and defi-

93

cient education, but I embark on matters that surpass
them not in presumption of will but through fearing the
danger of disobedience and thinking of that terrifying
86,15   threat that runs, 'You wicked and slothful servant, you
should have taken my money to the bankers.'[a]

I therefore beg future readers of this laborious work
and Your Holiness, George, best of fathers and most
loving towards your offspring, first to beg Christ the
Master to grant me in my misery forgiveness for my
86,20   contemptible life and many sins and then to disbelieve
nothing of what I have already said or am about to say.
It is on this account that I have noted precise details of
time and place, of persons and names, so as to make
close investigation of the truth in these matters.[1] With
86,25   consequent trust in the help and assistance of God, I
shall begin my account of Sabas.

1. BIRTH AND CHILDHOOD[2]

Sabas, who has become a citizen of the heavenly
mother-city, had as his fatherland the country of Cappadocia and the village of Mutalasca, subject to the
87.   metropolis of Caesarea. This village was formerly un-
heard of because of its small size and lowly rank but
has become well-known to everyone because of this
godly youth who stemmed from it; likewise
Ramathaim was formerly insignificant and contemp-
87,5   tible but became famous throughout creation from the
time it gave birth to Samuel, dedicated to God from
infancy.[3] Sabas had well-born Christian parents called
John and Sophia, of whom he was born, as we know
plainly from the accurate chronology of his life, in the
[AD 439]   seventeenth counsulship of Theodosius. Not long

a. Mt 25:26-27.

87,10   afterwards, when his father was sent to serve in Alexandria in the regiment called the Isaurians[4] and emigrated from Cappadocia with his wife, this holy child, being about five years old, was by divine providence left behind with his parents' property in the village of Mutalasca just mentioned to live with his

87,15   maternal uncle called Hermias, who had a wife of evil character. In consequence the boy became unhappy and fled to one Gregory, his uncle on his father's side, who lived about three miles away in a village called Scandus.

2. ENTRY INTO THE MONASTERY OF FLAVIANAE

Soon afterwards,[5] with his uncles Hermias and

87,20   Gregory quarreling with each other over both him and his parents' property, Sabas, being predestined by God from the womb and foreknown before his creation like the great prophet Jeremiah,[a] despising all the things of this life without exception, offered himself to the monastery of Flavianae, twenty stades distant from the

87,25   village of Mutalasca. On being admitted by the archimandrite and enrolled in the community there, he received a strict education in the monastic life and had

88.   in a short time learnt both the psalter and the rest of the observance of the cenobitic rule. His uncles just mentioned, who had come to an agreement, tried repeatedly to make him leave the monastery in order, they said, to take charge of his parents' estates, and urged him to

88,5   enter into marriage; but, guarded by God, he chose rather to be an outcast in the house of God than to give himself to the turbulence of the world. Consequently, he utterly refused to leave this holy way of life. He thought of the Gospel saying of the Lord that runs, 'No

a. Jer 1:5.

88,10   one who puts his hand to the plough and turns back is
fit for the kingdom of heaven.'[b] And he pondered in
himself such thoughts as the following: 'I must flee
from those who advise me to leave the way of the Lord
as from snakes, for "bad company corrupts good
morals."[c] And I am afraid of being weakened by per-

88,15   sistent entreaty and of earning the curse of the
prophet that runs, "Accursed are they who turn from
thy commandments."'[d] Such was Sabas from childhood in his love of piety.

3. HE RENOUNCES APPLES

Once when he was working in the monastery garden,
he was seized with desire to eat an apple that looked,

88,20   before the appointed season, ripe and utterly delicious.
Inflamed with desire, he plucked the apple from the
tree; but with reflection he valiantly mastered himself
and administered a pious rebuke to himself in these
words: 'Beautiful to look at and ripe to eat was the
fruit that caused my death through Adam, when he preferred to the intelligible beauty that which looked

88,25   delectable to the eyes of the flesh and supposed the
satiety of the belly preferable to spiritual enjoyment, as
a result of which death entered the world. But I must
not be weighed down by spiritual torpor and turn away
from the beauty of self-control. For just as blossom
precedes every fruit-bearing, so self-control precedes

89.   every good work.' Having thus conquered his desire
through the power of reflection, he cast the apple to the
ground and trampled on it with his own feet, trampling

b. Lk 9:62.
c. 1 Co 15:33.
d. Ps 119(118):21.

on his desire at the same time as on the apple. From
this moment he imposed a rule on himself not to eat
apples till the day of his death.

4. HIS ASCETIC LABORS

89,5   Henceforth, receiving power from on high, he devoted himself to self-control, as suppressing impure
thoughts and repelling the heaviness of sleep. In addition to self-control he also practised physical labor,
remembering the Davidic chant to God that runs,
'Behold my self-abasement and my toil, and remit all
89,10   my sins.'[a] In consequence he displayed complete zeal
and eagerness in abasing the soul through fasting and
taming the body by strenuous toil. Although he had
sixty or seventy fellow-combatants in the said
monastery of Flavianae, he surpassed them all in
humility, obedience and labors in pursuit of piety.

5. PROOF OF HIS FAITH

89,15   The stories of the ascetic combats of his boyhood
include the following. Once in wintertime the baker of
the monastery spread out his wet clothes in the warmth
inside the oven in order to dry them while there was no
sunshine. He then forgot about them, and a day later,
when the bread ran out, some of the fathers were set to
89,20   work at baking, with whom was the amazing Sabas. As
they were heating the oven, the baker remembered his
clothes and was distressed about them, since the fire
was now intense and no one dared to enter the oven,
which was large and, as I have said, fully heated. The

a. Ps 25(24):18.

89,25

young old man, fortified with unwavering faith and arming himself with the sign of the cross, leapt into the oven and, bringing the clothes, came out unharmed. On seeing this extraordinary miracle, the fathers gave glory to God, saying, 'What will this youth be like, if

90.

he has received such grace in early youth?' I heard this story from his cousin Gregory the priest,[6] and I have recounted it in order to show my readers how rich he was from boyhood in faith, understanding and the highest virtues.

6. HE DEPARTS TO JERUSALEM

90,5

Eager to advance from glory to glory and planning ascents in his heart, after completing ten years in this monastery, he conceived a desire, pleasing to God, to repair to the holy city and live in solitude in the neighboring desert, for it was necessary that this desert be colonized through him and that the prophecies made

90,10

out it by the eloquent Isaiah be fulfilled.[a] Going to the archimandrite he begged to be sent on his way with a blessing. The archimandrite refused, but then received the revelation of a divine vision that said to him, 'Give Sabas leave to go, so that he may serve me in the desert.' At this he summoned him in secret and said to him, 'I, my child, have been won over by a divine vi-

90,15

sion and give you leave to go. As for you, depart in peace, with no one in the community knowing, and may the Lord be with you.'

[AD 456]

Accordingly, guided by God, he came to Jerusalem in the eighteenth year of his life towards the end of the pious reign of Marcian and of the episcopate in Jerusalem of Juvenal. He was received by a Cap-

a. Is 41:18-20, 51:3.

90,20 padocian elder at the monastery of the sainted Passariôn, which at that time was governed by the archimandrite Elpidius;[7] here the servant of God Sabas spent the winter. He was urged by the elder to be enrolled there, but refused; likewise, when enticed by other orders[8] offering daily sustenance in various places, he totally resisted the allurements of each one, being a lover of

90,25 solitude from boyhood and dedicated to God.

7. HE GOES TO EUTHYMIUS

Hearing from almost everyone about the ascetic contests at this time, in the desert to the east of the holy city, of the godly Euthymius, who was shining like a

91. star and sending out everywhere his miraculous rays, he was thrilled in spirit and conceived a desire to behold the saint. Going to the blessed Elpidius and imparting his wish to him, he was sent on his way with a blessing and accompanied by a guide. Coming to the

91,5 place indicated and staying with the fathers there, on the Saturday he saw the great Euthymius as he was coming to the church, and begged with tears to be numbered among his monks. The great Euthymius gave him the following advice: 'My child, I do not think it right for you as a youth to stay in a laura, for

91,10 neither does it benefit a laura to have a youth nor is it suitable for a youth to live among anchorites. So go, my child, to the monastery below, to Abba Theoctistus, where you will be able to obtain great benefit.' Blessed Sabas replied, 'I know, revered father, that God, who controls all things and wishes my salvation, has led me to place myself in your holy hands. Whatever you or-

91,15 der me, I will do.' At this the great Euthymius sent him to the blessed Theoctistus, with instructions that Theoctistus should take care of him as of one who was

going, by the grace of Christ, to attain eminence in the monastic life. It was not aimlessly, as it seems to me, that the great Euthymius acted in this way; rather, foreseeing by second sight that Sabas was going to be
91,20 archimandrite of all the anchorites in Palestine, nay more, that he was going to found the greatest and most famous laura, surpassing all those in Palestine, and would himself be the leader and lawgiver of all those who withdraw by themselves, he gave him a rule by
91,25 the example of his own case not to receive an adolescent in a laura, but to transmit this rule to the superiors of other lauras as long-standing and in force with the ancient fathers; for it is obvious that everything which belongs to antiquity is worthy of respect.

8. HIS VIRTUES IN THE CENOBIUM

On coming under the blessed Theoctistus, our father Sabas gave himself over entirely to God. The property
92. he had from his family he placed in the hands of the superior and stripped himself for combat, spending the day in physical labor and passing the night without sleep in giving praise to God, making humility and obedience the root and foundation of his life, and
92,5 showing aptitude and great zeal in the office of the holy liturgy by being the first to go into church and the last to leave it. In addition to these spiritual virtues he was also tall and noble in body; when all the others chopped in the desert and carried to the cenobium one
92,10 load of faggots, he would chop and carry three loads a day. In addition, he would give eager assistance to the servants of the monastery, drawing water, bringing wood, and performing all the other services. He was also for a considerable time muleteer, and performed blamelessly and unimpeachably a whole variety of

92,15   tasks entrusted to him, with the result that the fathers
            of the cenobium were amazed to find such virtue and
            aptitude in one so young in age.

                        9. VISIT TO ALEXANDRIA

                There was in the cenobium a brother of Alexandrian
            birth called John, who for a long time pressed the
            sainted Theoctistus to give him leave to go to
            Alexandria to make a proper disposition of his family
92,20   property, since he had learnt that his parents had died.
            On being given leave he asked to be accompanied by
            Abba Sabas, as a trustworthy friend able to endure
            hardship; the blessed Theoctistus, yielding to John's
            request, sent Abba Sabas with him to Alexandria.
            When they arrived in Alexandria and were pondering
92,25   how to investigate John's family affairs, the blessed
            Sabas was recognized by his mother Sophia and his
            father John, who had changed his name to Conon and
            was in command of the Isaurian regiment. They urged
            him to stay there; enlist in the army and become
93.   *senator*[9] of the regiment, but he repulsed them with the
            words, 'Having once enlisted in the service of God the
            king of all, I cannot cancel this service, and those who
            try to draw me from it I cannot bear to call my parents.
            For I shall abide by my commitment to God till my last
93,5   breath, hoping to die in the holy life of asceticism.'
            Since their many machinations were not able to
            weaken his resolve and keep him with them, they
            wanted to give him twenty solidi for his expenses; he,
            however, did not accept this gift, but seeing them very
            upset he took just three *solidi* in order to oblige them.
            He then left Alexandria immediately with his compan-
93,10   ion John, and on returning to the cenobium placed the
            three *solidi* in the hands of the great Theoctistus.

10. HE BECOMES A SOLITARY

When he was already completing his tenth year in the cenobium, it came to pass that the thrice-blessed [AD 466] Theoctistus died on 3 September of the fourth indiction.[10] The great Euthymius came down to the 93,15 place and, after burying the victorious body, appointed one Maris, worthy of admiration, to succeed as superior. When Maris had ruled the monastery for two years and died in a manner pleasing to God, the great Euthymius came down again and, having laid him in the tomb of the blessed Theoctistus, entrusted the charge of the cenobium to one Longinus, a man of virtue.

93,20   It was at this juncture that our father Sabas, having [AD 469] completed the thirtieth year of his age and surpassed all the senior monks of the cenobium in fasting and vigils, humility and obedience, asked Abba Longinus to allow him to live as a solitary in a cave outside the cenobium in the cliff to the south. Abba Longinus 94. noting his exceptional virtue, stability of character, purity of conduct, and zeal and concentration at prayer, reported the matter to the great Euthymius, who replied, 'Do not hinder him from combating as he wishes.' So he gave him leave to live as a solitary in 94,5 the said cave for five days of the week. On receiving the permission he so longed for, our father Sabas maintained for five years the following pattern of life: in the evening of the Sunday he would leave the cenobium taking palm-leaves, the labor of the week, last the five 94,10 days without taking any food at all, and then on the morning of the Saturday return to the cenobium bringing with him as the handiwork of the five days fifty completed baskets.

11. WITH EUTHYMIUS IN THE DESERT[11]

94,15 Knowing he was living this life, the great Euthymius used to take him with him on 14 January to the utter desert of Roubâ together with blessed Domitian, having complete confidence in him and naming him the 'boy elder',[12] while as an excellent trainer he exercised and advanced him in the higher virtues. There they would remain till Palm Sunday, severed from all human society.

94,20 On one occasion the great Euthymius, wishing to traverse the desert that stretches from Roubâ beyond the Dead Sea to the south, set off with Domitian and Sabas as companions. When they reached a waterless region and had spent some time there, blessed Sabas, becoming extremely thirsty because of the intensity of the burning heat, fainted and could no longer walk, the

94,25 humidity in the pit of his stomach being, I imagine, consumed by the intensity of the burning heat. Taking pity on him, the elder withdrew about a stone's throw and fell on his face, beseeching God in these words; 'Lord God, grant water to this thirsty land to assuage the thirst of my disciple.' After this prayer he called him and, on digging with a trowel for the third time, showed him flowing water. On drinking it Sabas came

95. to himself, and from this water received power from God to bear the trials of life in the desert.[13]

After a short time had elapsed, our great father Euthymius both fell asleep and rested in peace, the Lord making him dwell apart in hope,[a] in the fifteenth

95,5 year of Anastasius' episcopacy at Jerusalem.

a. Cf. Ps 4:8(9).

12. DIABOLIC TEMPTATIONS IN THE DESERT

At this time blessed Sabas, having completed the
thirty-fifth year of his life and seeing the life of the
cenobium altered, since the fathers of the monastery
had died, withdrew to the eastern desert of the sainted
Gerasimus, who was at that time shining like a star and
sowing the seeds of piety in the desert of the Jordan.
Our father Sabas now lived in the desert of Coutila and
Roubâ, and chanted in his actions the Davidic saying,
'Behold, I have wandered afar and lodged in the
desert.'ª He devoted himself to solitude, fasts and
ceaseless prayer, making his mind a spotless mirror of
God and the things of God, in accordance with the
saying, 'Be still and know that I am God.'ᵇ The devil
became envious and contrived many temptations
against him, wishing to draw him away from this pattern of life. On one occasion, when in the middle of the
night he was lying on the sand, the devil tried to terrify
him by taking the form of snakes and scorpions. But
after a moment of timidity he detected the devil's
malice and, making the sign of the cross, shook off his
timidity and confidently leapt up, exclaiming, 'Even
when you are able to frighten me, you will then be
defeated, since with me is the Lord God, who gives us
power over you with the words, "Behold, I have given
you authority to tread underfoot snakes and scorpions
and every power of the enemy."'ᶜ As he said these
words, the poisonous beasts vanished instantly.

On another occasion, Satan appeared to him again in
the likeness of a most terrifying lion, advancing against
him and bristling threateningly. Seeing the terrifying
onset of the beast, he said, 'If you have received

Marginalia: [AD 474] · 95,10 · 95,15 · 95,20 · 95,25 · 96.

a. Ps 55:7(54:8).
b. Ps 46:10(45:11).
c. Lk 10:19.

authority against me, do not delay. But if not, why do
96,   you labor in vain?[14] You will not be able to separate
me from God, for he himself has bidden me have confidence with the words, "You will tread on the asp and
the basilisk and trample on the lion and the dragon."[d]
At these words this beast immediately vanished. And
96,10   from then on God made every poisonous and carnivorous beast subject to him, and he received no hurt
from living with them in the desert.

13. THE GRATEFUL SARACENS

At this same time he met four Saracens who were
faint with hunger. Having compassion on them, he told
them to sit down and emptied his sheepskin bag in
96,15   front of them, which contained nothing but roots of
melagria and hearts of reeds. After they had eaten and
had their fill, the barbarians asked what cave of Roubâ
he lived in; and some days later, when they were well-
supplied again, they brought him loaves, cheeses and
dates. In admiration at the gratitude of the barbarians,
yet filled with compunction, our father Sabas said with
96,20   tears, 'Alas, my soul! What trouble these barbarians
have taken to express their gratitude for a service that
was nothing! What should we ungrateful wretches do,
who enjoy day by day such divine graces and favors
from God and yet waste our lives in negligence and in-
dolence, not troubling to give thanks to God the giver by
performing his divine commandments and offering
uninterruptedly "the fruit of lips confessing his name"?'[e]
97.   He remained some time in this state of compunction,
spending whole days and nights in prayer to him.

d. Ps 91(90):13.
e. Heb 13:15.

14. A SARACEN INCURSION

In this desert of Roubâ there came to him, and stayed
with him, a monk worthy of mention called Anthus, who
97,5   had lived for some time with the thrice-blessed Abba
Theodosius in the church of the Cathisma.[15] While
they were living in this desert, they were set upon by
Saracens, six in number, barbarous in character and
mischievous in intent. Incited by malice, they sent
97,10 one of their number to try out the blessed ones, presumably planning to attack and take both prisoner if
they put up resistance to this single man. The blessed
fathers, on seeing their plight, in no way yielded to
panic, but ascending to God with the eye of the soul
prayed earnestly to be delivered from the plot of these
97,15 wicked barbarians. Instantly the earth opened and
swallowed the barbarian intending to test them, at
which the rest, on seeing the terrifying miracle, fled
97,20 panic-stricken. From then on our father Sabas received
the divine grace of never being in fear of barbarian
plots; and this was the first time that our father Sabas,
through living with blessed Anthus, became known to
the blessed Abba Theodosius, before the foundation of
his holy and celebrated monastery.

15. HE SETTLES IN A CAVE NEAR SILOAM

When our holy father Sabas had completed four
years in this desert and was visiting other still more
desert places, he came to the high hill where blessed
97,25 Eudocia had once enjoyed the teaching of the great
Euthymius. While he was praying to God through the
night, there appeared to him an angelic form in daz-
98.   zling apparel who showed him a gorge descending
from Siloam to the south of this hill and said, 'If you

really want to colonize this desert, stay here and ascend the east side of that gorge, where you see facing you an intact cave. Make it your home, and he who "gives

98,5 their food to the animals and to the young ravens that invoke him"[a] will himself take care of you.' So ran the vision; he, on coming to himself and observing the gorge to the south that had been indicated, descended the hill full of joy and by God's guidance found the

98,10 cave just as he had been told in the vision. When he had ascended, he made it his home, at the beginning of

[AD 478] the fortieth year of his life. It was the year in which Archbishop Anastasius of Jerusalem, having completed the nineteenth year of his patriarchate, died at the beginning of July, leaving Martyrius as his suc-

98,15 cessor, and in which Emperor Zeno of the Romans slew the usurper Basiliscus, whose usurpation had lasted twenty months, and recovered his throne.

When our father Sabas had made the said cave his home at this time, he hung a rope at the mouth of the cave to use when ascending or descending because of the difficulty of the ascent. Water he obtained about

98,20 fifteen stades away at the cistern called Heptastomus.[16] Some time later, four Saracens came to the place and found themselves unable to ascend to the cave; the sanctified Sabas, on seeing them from above, let down the rope and told them to ascend. On ascending and

99. finding he had nothing, these barbarians were struck with admiration for his virtue and voluntary poverty; after their departure they returned every few days bringing him dry rolls, cheeses and dates and anything else they came across.

a. Ps 147(146):9.

16. HIS FIRST DISCIPLES[17]

99,5
[AD 483]
In this gorge he spent five years alone by himself in solitude, conversing with God and purifying the eye of his thought so as 'with unveiled face to behold as in a mirror the glory of the Lord,'[a] since the evil spirits had already been conquered by his ceaseless prayers and nearness to God. In consequence, he was

99,10
[AD 483]
now, in the forty-fifth year of his life, entrusted by God with the charge of souls; he was persuaded by the word of God not to devote time pointlessly to enemies who had been defeated but to transfer his spiritual energies from a warlike disposition to husbanding those who had grown rank with evil thoughts, for the

99,15
benefit of the many, in accordance with the words of the prophet, 'Beat your swords into plowshares and your spears into pruning hooks.'[b] So he began to receive all those who came to him. Many of the scattered anchorites and 'grazers'[18] came to join him, among

99,20
whom were the sainted John, later superior of the New Laura, the blessed James who afterwards founded the Laura of the Towers by the Jordan, Serverianus, respected for monastic attainments, who some time later built the monastery near Caparbaricha, the great Firminus who founded the laura in the region of Mach-

99,25
mas, in addition Julian surnamed Curtus who created the laura called after Neelkeraba by the Jordan, and also others with them whose names are in the book of life.[19] Each of these as they came to him he provided

100.
with a suitable spot consisting of a small cell and cave. By divine grace his community grew to seventy persons, all inspired by God, all bearers of Christ; if one were to call them a choir of angels or a band of athletes

a. 2 Co 3:18.
b. Is 2:4.

100,5   or a city of the pious or a new choir of seventy apostles,[c] one would not err in appropriateness. And he was their superior, guide, and shepherd.

First of all he built a tower on the hill on the northern edge of the gorge after the bend, in order to take possession of the place while it was unoccupied. Next he
100,10   made a beginning in founding the laura, with the grace and assistance of the Holy Spirit guiding him. In the middle of the gorge he built a little oratory, in which he set a consecrated altar, and when he received a visit from a stranger with priestly ordination, he would get him to perform the anaphora in the oratory. He himself
100,15   would not accept ordination, for he was of great meekness and true humility, imitating in this respect Christ, true God, who offered himself for imitation to the willing with the words, 'Learn from me for I am meek and humble of heart.'[d] Looking at this model, he humbled
100,20   himself, making himself both the least and the servant of those under him.

As having experienced everything, he taught and admonished each one of them to put up valiant resistance to the wiles of the devil and not to yield at all nor succumb to any discouragement as a result of the manifold wickedness of the demons. It is necessary, he would say, that one who is purified and has consecrated him-
101.   self to God should be fortified by hope in the good things to come, for it is characteristic of a soul without manliness to succumb to discouragement. With these and similar words and actions he nurtured their souls and did not cease to water them; giving them wings, he
101,5   taught them to fly and made them scale heaven.

c. Cf. Lk 10:1.
d. Mt 11:29.

17. DISCOVERY OF A SPRING

Since they were in straits because of the lack of water, he prayed one night in these words: 'Lord God of hosts, if it is your will that this place be colonized for the glory of your holy name, deign to provide us with the relief of a little water.' While he was making
101,10   this prayer in the little oratory, he heard the hoof-beat of a wild ass in the gorge below. Peering down (it was full moon), he saw a wild ass digging deep into the earth with its hooves; when it had dug a large hole, he saw it lowering its mouth to the hole and drinking. Re-
101,15   flecting that rather God was making a visitation and bringing forth water for his servants, he immediately climbed down and, digging the place, found flowing water. And lo, in the middle of the laura this water exists to this day, providing much relief to the fathers; neither in winter is it over-abundant, nor in summer, despite almost everyone's drawing from it, does it run short.

18. THE CHURCH BUILT BY GOD

101,20   On another night blessed Sabas had left his cave and was walking in the gorge alone, reciting Davidic psalms, when suddenly on the western slope of the gorge, where his precious remains now lie between the two churches that now exist, he saw resting on the
101,25   earth a pillar of fire whose head reached into heaven. Seeing this fearful sight and feeling afraid and joyful at the same time, he pondered on the scriptural account of the ladder that appeared to the patriarch Jacob, as he recited, 'How fearful is this place! This is none other than the house of God.'[a] Persevering in prayer at this

a. Gen 28:17.

spot till daybreak, he rose in fear and great joy to see
102.
the spot where the pillar of fire had appeared, and
found a large and marvelous cave that had the shape of
a church of God. On the eastern side there is an apse
made by God, while he found on the north side a large
chamber with the lay-out of a sacristy and to the south
102,5
a wide entrance that admitted sufficient illumination
from the rays of the sun. After setting this cave in order
with divine assistance, he gave instructions for the office to take place here on Saturdays and Sundays.

102,10
And so little by little the community multiplied with
the help of God and reached the number of one hundred and fifty fathers. With the community multiplying
and various cells being built here and there in the
gorge, he now obtained beasts of burden to support the
laura and serve those living in it. He provided for them
with a view to their having within the monastery all the
102,15
necessities of life, in order that those who wanted to
withdraw from the tumult of life outside should not be
compelled by these needs to go out into the world.
They in turn were most willing to be shepherded and
guided by him, as they bore fruit worthy of their calling, making their bodies spiritual even before the
awaited incorruption. He postponed, however, con-
secrating the said cave, that is, the church built by God,
because he did not wish to be ordained priest or in any
102,20
way to be appointed a cleric; for he said that the desire
to be made a cleric is the origin and root of thoughts of
love of power.[20]

Above the church built by God there is an extremely
high and abrupt crag; on this our father Sabas built
himself a tower,[21] finding a secret passage like a spiral
staircase within the holy cave, leading up from the
102,25
sacristy to the tower. Here he would stay for the office
and the rest of the administration. Since his fame
spread everywhere, many came to him bringing plenti-

103.   ful offerings, particularly when they saw his angelic
              mode of life and his existence detached from matter.
              The blessed man preferred to spend most of the offer-
              ings on buildings and the maintenance of the place;
              whatever he thought pleasing to God, this he did, and
103,5   none of his subjects presumed to oppose him in any-
              thing. Martyrius at this time had been entrusted with
              the episcopate; he had known Sabas from the time of
              the great Euthymius and had a great love for him.

                        19. HE IS ORDAINED PRIEST

              The sainted Martyrius was near the end of the eight
              year of his episcopate when he departed to God on 13
103,10   April of the ninth indiction, and Sallustius succeeded to
[AD 486]   the episcopate, in the forty-eighth year of the life of our
              father Sabas. There sprang up in his laura some who
              were fleshly in thought and, in the words of Scripture,
              'lacking the Spirit.'[a] For a considerable time they con-
              cocted intrigues and caused him trouble of every kind;
103,15   after all, it was possible for Judas to be tolerated among
              the Apostles, and Gehazi for a time with Elisha,[b] for Esau
              to be born of Isaac, and Cain to be the brother of Abel.
              These men of whom I am speaking, in consort together,
              went up to the holy city and approached Archbishop
              Sallustius, asking him to give them a superior.[22] The
              archbishop said to them, 'What place are you from?'
              They replied, 'We live in a gorge of the desert.' The
103,20   archbishop asked, 'In what gorge?' Being pressed, they
              replied, 'In the one called by some that of Abba
              Sabas.' The archbishop said, 'Where then is Abba
103,25   Sabas?' They answered, 'He is incapable of directing
              the place because of his extreme rusticity.[23] To add a

              a. Jude 19.
              b. 2 Kgs 5:20-27.

further point, neither is he himself ordained nor has he let someone else become a cleric. How then can he govern a community of a hundred and fifty persons?'

104.   A certain Cyricus, worthy of mention, priest and superior of the holy church of the Resurrection and guardian of the Cross, who was present on this occasion and had heard what was said, asked them, 'Did you accept him into this place, or was it not rather he who

104,5   accepted you?' They replied, 'He indeed accepted us, but because of his boorishness he is unable to govern us, now that we have multiplied.' The thrice-blessed Cyricus asked again, 'If he, as you say, brought you together in this place and colonized this place which was a desert, how could he govern still more both the place he has colonized and you whom he brought to-

104,10   gether in union? God, who assisted him in bringing you together and founding the place, will assist him still more in governing it.' At this point the archbishop dismissed them with the words, 'Go away for the time being, reflect, and come back tomorrow.'

          Then, sending for blessed Sabas as if for some other

104,15   reason, and summoning his accusers as well, he ordained him priest in front of their eyes, and said to them, 'See, here you have your father and the superior of your laura, elected by God from above and not be man, for by laying on hands I have simply confirmed the divine election.' After saying this, he took the blessed Sabas and these men and came to the laura,

104,20   accompanied by the above-mentioned guardian of the Cross Cyricus. He dedicated the church built by God and fixed a consecrated altar in the apse built by God, placing many relics of holy and victorious martyrs under the altar, on 12 December of the fourteenth indic-

[AD 491] tion in the fifty-third year of the life of blessed Sabas,
105.   in the year that the emperor Zeno died and Anastasius succeeded to the throne.[24]

20. ARMENIANS AT THE LAURA

105,5

In this same year was accepted into the laura an inspired man adorned with divine charisms, Armenian by birth and called Jeremias, bringing with him two disciples who shared the same combats and way of life, called Peter and Paul. Because of their piety our father Sabas was utterly delighted at their coming, and gave them a cave and small cell to the north of the cave where he had lived at first, when he was alone in the gorge. He told them to perform the office of psalmody in Armenian in the little oratory on Saturdays and Sundays. In consequence, the Armenians gradually multiplied in the laura.[25] One of the above-mentioned disciples of blessed Jeremias, the inspired Paul, who to this day is eminent in the godly virtues in the Great Laura, tells many wonderful stories about Sabas and transmitted to me many of the stories contained in this account.

105,10

105,15

21. JOHN BISHOP AND SOLITARY

In this same year that the church built by God was consecrated, the Holy Spirit led to the laura our inspired father John bishop and solitary, who has transmitted to me most of the profitable stories about Euthymius and Sabas and urges me to record them. He was enrolled in the laura by our sainted father Sabas. He was at the age of thirty-eight and had become a sanctified temple of the All-holy Spirit, abounding in divine charisms and a bearer of light. He is still now in the flesh,[26] living angelically and illuminating our path to God. His virtues and attainments cannot now be described in passing, but, if it please God, when I have completed the work in hand, I shall relate in a separate work a few facts about him, both those familiar to almost

105,20

105,25

106.

all and those I have heard his own holy tongue relate;
they are many and potent. For it is not right to relegate
106,5   them to silence and oblivion, since he is famous and celebrated for his life and virtue in almost all our land.

22. HOW HIS BEARD WAS SINGED

This solitary and bishop John, great in virtue, told me
that our sainted father Sabas was eager to follow in
every way the manner of life of the great Euthymius.
106,10   So, since the latter had been accustomed at an appointed time in January to retire to the utter desert and
spend Lent there, he would depart, slightly altering the
custom, after the commemoration of Saint Antony; he
would celebrate the commemoration of the great
Euthymius, which is celebrated on 20 January, and
106,15   then immediately retire to the utter desert, withdrawing
from all human society until Palm Sunday. This he did
almost every year.

It is recounted that, having set off in this way and
crossing the desert of Zóara by the Dead Sea, he saw in
the sea a tiny dry island, and conceived a desire to go
106,20   to it and live in solitude on it during the days of fasting. On his way to it, he happened, through the envious
plot of demons, to stumble on a porous part of the sea,
where a hot vapor was given off. This burnt his face,
together with his beard and other parts of his body, so
that for many days he lay speechless, until some divine
107.   power visited him and cured him, fortifying him
against the impure spirits. The only after-effect was
that from then on, because of his beard, as I have said,
being burnt and ceasing to grow, he remained scantily
bearded, so that, when he returned to the laura after
completing Lent, the fathers did not recognize him ex-
107,5   cept by his voice and manner. He used to give thanks

to God for the removal of his beard, reckoning it to be
a divine providence, so that he should be humbled and
not take pride in the hair of his beard.

23. THE DISCIPLE AND THE LION

In the following year he set off to the utter desert, as
was his wont, accompanied by a disciple called
107,10   Agapêtus. After a few days had passed, Agapêtus lay
down prone one night as a result of the exertion and
lack of food. When he had fallen asleep and blessed
Sabas was engaged in mental prayer, an enormous lion
came up and sniffed at Agapêtus from head to foot.
Our father Sabas entreated God on his behalf, at which
107,15   the lion, driven off by the prayer of the elder as by a
whip, went away, after gently striking Agapêtus' face
with his tail and waking him up. Agapêtus, on opening
his eyes and seeing the fearsome lion, leapt up panic-
stricken and fled to his teacher, but the great old man
received him with the following words of admonition:
107,20   'Drive heavy sleep from your eyes and carelessness
from your heart, "to save yourself as a gazelle from the
snares and as a bird from the trap."'[a]

24. SABAS AND THE ANCHORITE[27]

The inspired solitary also told me the following
story. On some other occasion, just before setting off
for the utter desert, he gave Agapêtus his sheepskin
107,25   bag with ten morsels of dry bread weighing around ten
ounces. They set off off and made for the Jordan and,
journeying along the west bank of the Jordan on their
108.   way to northern parts, came to a precipitous place, at

a. Pr 6:5 (LXX).

the top of which was a cave. Filled with compunction, presumably through a revelation from God, blessed Sabas took Agapêtus and with difficulty climbed up. Going into the cave, they found within an anchorite 108,5 with second sight. After both had prayed, the anchorite, somewhat startled, said, 'Servant of God Sabas, who showed you this place? See, with the help of God I have spent thirty-eight years in this cave without ever meeting a human being. How now did you come here?' 108,10 The blessed Sabas answered him, 'The God who revealed to you my name also showed me the place.'

After the two had embraced each other, Sabas and his companion went on their way, journeying a good distance across country between the Sea of Tiberias and the Jordan and praying at Chrosia, Heptapêgus and the 108,15 other revered places there as far as Panias, where they turned back.[28] When they came near the anchorite's cave, the blessed Sabas said, 'Let us ascend, brother, and greet the servant of God.' On ascending, they found him on his knees facing east. Thinking that he was praying, the elder waited a long time. When the day passed without his stirring, the blessed one said, 108,20 'Commend us to Christ, father.' When he did not reply, he drew near and touched him, only to find that he had died. And he said, 'Come, my child, let us bury him. It is for this that God has sent us.' After paying their respects to the body and performing for it the customary 108,25 office, they laid it to rest in the cave itself and walled this up with big stones, at which they completed their journey.

And so they came to the laura on the eve of Palm Sunday. Sabas had lasted all the days of fasting with- 109. out food, satisfied with communion on Saturdays and Sundays; the ten morsels he took along supplied the needs of Agapêtus.

25. HIS FAMILY INHERITANCE

In the above-mentioned year of the consecration of the church built by God, John surnamed Conon, the father of our Abba Sabas, died in Alexandria, after attaining authority and distinction in the Isaurian regiment. On learning that her son Sabas had become famous for monastic attainments, blessed Sophia, who was already well advanced in age, sold all her possessions and came to Jerusalem with a considerable sum of money. She was received by the blessed Sabas, who persuaded her to renounce all the things of this world. When a short time later she died, he conducted her burial and laid her to rest in a holy tomb. Her wealthy he secured for his own laura. It was with this wealth that he acquired the guest-house[29] at Jericho with the gardens there, also buying a water-supply for them, and built the guest-house in the laura to serve the fathers, and achieved much else besides.

109,5

109,10

109,15

26. THE MIRACLE OF THE CLOUD

When the guest-house of the laura was being erected, our father Sabas sent a brother to Jericho with the laura's pack-animals to bring wood for the works. After he had gone there and loaded the animals, this brother was on his way to the laura across the desert. The burning heat being then intense, he became extremely thirsty and fell down in a faint in the middle of the road. Remembering the holy elder, he made this prayer: 'O Lord, the God of my Abba Sabas, do not forsake me.' Immediately, the God who once guided Israel in a pillar of cloud[a] spread a cloud to shield him,

109,20

109,25

a. Ex 13:21.

that provided him with refreshing dew and gave him strength. And so, accompanied by the cloud, he reached the laura.

27. THE FOUNDATION AT CASTELLION

110.

[AD 492]

110,5

110,10

110,15

110,20

110,25

In the fifty-fourth year of the life of the great Sabas, in the second year since the consecration of the church built by God and Bishop John's arrival at the laura, on 21 January of the fifteenth indiction, our sainted father Sabas went to the hill of Castellium, which is about twenty stades north-east from the laura.[30] This hill was terrifying and unfrequented because of the large number of demons who lurked there, so that none of the shepherds in the desert dared to go near the place. The revered old man, however, making the Most High his refuge and sprinkling the place with oil from the all-holy Cross, stayed during the season of Lent; and by his ceaseless prayers and divine praises the place was tamed. He underwent on this hill many trials inflicted by the demons. Doubtless he himself, as a man subject to fear, would have wished to withdraw, but He who had formerly appeared to the great Abba Antony[31] appeared also to him, bidding him have confidence in the power of the Cross; so, taking courage, he overcame by faith and endurance the insolence of the demons.

While he was persevering in uninterrupted prayer and fasting, towards the end of Lent, when he was keeping vigil one night and begging God to cleanse the place from the impure spirits that lurked there, suddenly the demons began to make a beating sound and to display apparitions in the likeness sometimes of snakes and wild animals and sometimes of crows, wishing through such apparitions to terrify him. Since they were thwarted by his perseverant prayer, they departed from the place, shouting in human speech the words, 'What violence from you, Sabas! The gorge you colonized does not satisfy you, but you force your way

111. into our place as well. See, we withdraw from our own territory. We cannot resist you, since you have God as your defender.' With these and similar words, they withdrew from this mountain with one accord at the

111,5 very hour of midnight, with a certain beating sound and confused tumult, like a flock of crows. There were shepherds in the desert round that mountain, who were out in the fields, keeping watch over their flock;[a] marking the tumult of the crows and hearing their cries, they were extremely frightened and said to each other, 'It must be some holy men staying at Castellium

111,10 who have put the demons living there to flight. Let us make our way to the hill and see what has happened and, if there are holy men there, let us pay our respects to them.' At dawn they ascended the hill of Castellium and, finding the holy old man utterly on his own, told him what they had seen and heard in the night. The

111,15 holy man said to them, 'Go, my children, in peace and do not be in fear of them.' This gave them courage, and he sent them on their way in peace.

After completing the days of fasting, he returned to the laura. After celebrating the Easter festival, he went back to Castellium, taking some of the fathers, and be-

111,20 gan to clear the place and to build cells from the material he found there. In clearing the place, they found underneath the debris a large, vaulted, inhabitable room made of wonderful stones; after digging it out and setting it in order, he made it into a church, and from then on he aimed at making the place a cenobium, which indeed has taken place.[32]

a. Cf. Lk 2:8-15.

111,25   While he was toiling at Castellium with the brethren
and had no food supplies, in the month of August, the
sainted Marcianus, who ruled a cenobium near holy
Bethlehem,[33] received a revelation about the godly old
112.   man's situation. One night he saw a dazzling angelic
form that said to him, "See, you, Marcianus, sit at ease,
with everything to feed the body, while the servant of
God Sabas toils away at Castellium with some of his
112,5   brethren for the love of God, hungry and furnished
with no food supplies. But resolve without delay to
send them food, so that they do not lose heart.' The
great Marcianus arose at once and ordered the animals
of the cenobium to be saddled; loading them with various comestibles, he sent them to Castellium with some
112,10   of the brethren. On receiving these brethren together
with their load, the godly old man appropriately recited
the expressions of thanksgiving of David and Daniel
for God's providential care and became still more
zealous in building the cenobium. Meanwhile the
sainted Marcianus lived on after the revelation just
mentioned for only four months and then passed to the
112,15   life without old age or pain on 23 November of the first
[AD 492]   indiction; this is the precise year of the foundation of
Castellium and of the death of the godly Marcianus.

Our great father Sabas, convinced that God was
pleased with his toil, completed the building of the
112,20   cenobium with great zeal and eagerness. Gaining a
large community there, he appointed one Paul, an ancient anchorite, together with his disciple Theodore,
administrator of the place. On Paul's death Theodore
took over the administration, and took as assistants his
brother Sergius and Paul his uncle, who were of
112,25   Melitene by birth. They, after being excellent superiors
of Castellium in turn, obtained the episcopal sees of
Amathus and Aila.[34] So much for Castellium.

28. THE FORMATION OF NOVICES

113.   After founding the cenobium of Castellium, our father Sabas took great pains to transfer to it men who
had advanced to eminence in the monastic life. Whenever he received men from the world wishing to make
their renunciation, he would not let them dwell either
113,5   at Castellium or in a cell at the laura; he had founded a
small cenobium to the north of the laura and placed in
it men who were austere and sober-minded, and told
those making their renunciation to stay there, until they
had learnt the psalter and the office of psalmody and
113,10   received a strict monastic formation.[35] He always used
to say, 'A monk enclosed in a cell must be gifted with
discernment and zealous, a combater, sober, self-
controlled and disciplined, a teacher not needing teaching, capable of curbing all the members of his body
and of keeping a secure watch on his mind. I know that
such a man is called single-minded by the scriptural
113,15   saying, "The Lord gives the single-minded a home to
dwell in."'[a] When he judged that those who had made
their renunciation had learnt the office of psalmody
accurately and become capable of keeping a watch on
their minds, purifying their thoughts from recollection
of the things of the world, and putting up resistance to
alien desires, it was then that he provided them with
113,20   cells in the laura. If they were rich, he told them to
build one themselves, affirming, 'Whoever in this
place builds or rebuilds a cell, counts as building a
church of God.'

a. Ps 68:6(67:7).

29. SABAS AND THEODOSIUS

While teaching and enforcing these rules, our father Sabas would never allow an adolescent to live in his community who had not yet covered his chin with a beard, because of the snares of the evil one. Whenever

114. he received an adolescent of immature age who wished to make his renunciation, he would welcome him and then send him to the thrice-blessed Abba Theodosius, who had earlier retired from the church of the Cathisma and advanced to monastic perfection under two men who had received their formation from the holy Euthymius, Marinus, founder of the monastery

114,5 called after Photinus, and Luke of Metopa;[36] he had then settled about thirty-five stades to the west of the laura and founded there with the help of Christ a very famous cenobium. Our father Sabas, when sending a

114,10 brother to the great Abba Theodosius, as has been said, would first give him the following admonition: 'My child, it is unsuitable, indeed harmful, for a laura like this to contain an adolescent. This is the rule made by the ancient fathers of Scetis and transmitted to me by our great father Euthymius. For seeing me wanting to

114,15 settle in his laura when an adolescent, he sent me to the blessed Theoctistus, saying that it is out of place and harmful for an adolescent to live in a laura. As for you, go off to Abba Theodosius, and you will obtain benefit there.' The great Abba Theodosius, on receiving a brother sent by him, would exert himself in every way to look after him, for the sake of the one who sent him.

114,20 For they were one in soul and one in mind, breathing each other more than the air, so that the people of Jerusalem called their godly concord and unity a new apostolic pairing of Peter and John.

30. SABAS AND THEODOSIUS
BECOME ARCHIMANDRITES

114,25

In consequence, the sainted Archbishop Sallustius, when about to die in Christ, made them both archimandrites[37] and exarchs of monks, at the request of the whole monastic order. I shall relate in a few words the cause of their promotion. After the deaths of Elpidius and Elias, the successors of the sainted Pas-

115.

sarion, who had been archimandrites in succession, one Lazarus succeeded to their office; likewise, after the death of Gerontius who had succeeded to blessed Melania and separated from the catholic communion, one Anastasius[38] succeeded to his office. There re-

115,5

sulted a degree of anarchy, and among the monks at that time there prevailed multiplicity of rulers, which naturally gives birth to disorder and faction. In consequence, with the monastic order in a state of confusion, with Lazarus and Anastasius, archimandrites by succession, having already slackened in monastic strictness and devoted themselves to earthly cares and

115,10

worldly profits, especially when Anastasius succeeded to the throne of Zeno and gave full freedom to the Aposchists, at this juncture the sainted Sallustius was stirred into action and made the above-mentioned Abba Marcianus archimandrite. When a short time later Mar-

115,15

cianus died in Christ, all the monks of the desert assembled in the episcopal palace around the sick patriarch, and by common vote Theodosius and Sabas were appointed archimandrites and exarchs of all the monasteries under the holy city, as being true hermits, without possessions, adorned in life and speech, and abounding in divine charisms. From then on Abba

115,20

Theodosius was leader and archimandrite of the whole cenobitic order, having to second him in directing cenobitic concerns the sainted Abba Paul, superior of

115,25

the monastery of blessed Martyrius, while our father Sabas was made ruler and lawgiver of the whole anchoritic mode of life and of all those who chose to live in cells.

31. SABAS FOUNDS HOSPICES IN JERUSALEM

116.

[AD 494]

116,5

After occupying the throne of Jerusalem for eight years and three months, Archbishop Sallustius died in Christ on 23 July of the second indiction, and Elias, often mentioned in my account of the holy Euthymius, succeeded to the patriarchate, in the fifty-sixth year of the life of blessed Sabas. Patriarch Elias built a monastery near the episcopal palace and brought together in it those ascetics of the holy church of the Resurrection who had been scattered in the district around the Tower of David,[39] assigning to each of them a cell with every bodily comfort. When they had been gathered together, as has been said, our father

116,10

Sabas purchased various cells from them and made them into a hospice for the laura.

To the north of the cells he purchased were other cells, which he wished to purchase on behalf of foreign monks. He tried to find a sufficient quantity of money, but had only one half solidus. Relying on faith in God, he gave the half solidus as a deposit, with the words,

116,15

'If I do not pay you in full tomorrow, I forfeit the deposit.' On the same day, before sunrise, as he was thinking about this and praying mentally, a completely unknown stranger came up to him, gave him one hundred and seventy solidi, and immediately withdrew, not

116,20

even giving his name. Astonished at the prompt assistance of God, the blessed one gave the price of the cells and founded a second hospice for the relief of monks coming from abroad. He also acquired two

hospices for Castellium, one in the holy city not far
from the Tower of David and the other in Jericho in
one of the gardens he had bought.

32. CONSECRATION OF THE NEW CHURCH

117.   At the same time God sent our father two blood-
brothers of Isaurian origin, named Theodulus and
Gelasius, whom in my opinion one would not err in
calling after Bezabel and Oholiab, the architects of the
117,5   Tabernacle.[a] With their assistance our new Moses built
what was lacking to his famous laura and to the holy
monasteries near it. First he built a bakery and an in-
firmary in the laura, and erected above them the great
church of the mother of God and ever-virgin Mary,
117,10   hymned by all, since the church built by God was
cramping the expanding community and the Armenians
too were expanding and feeling cramped in the little
oratory; between the two churches he constructed a
forecourt, where earlier he had seen the vision of the
pillar of fire, and he constructed large cisterns in the
117,5   gorge. When the great church had been built and fully
appointed, the sainted Archbishop Elias came down to
the laura and dedicated the church, fixing in it a consecrated altar, on 1 July of the ninth indiction in the
[AD 501] sixty-third year of the life of the great Sabas. He then
117,20   transferred the Armenians from the little oratory to
performing the office of psalmody in the Armenian
language in the church built by God, telling them to
recite the Gospel and the rest of the sequence in the
office on their own in Armenian and then join the
Greek-speakers at the time of the holy sacrifice in order to partake of the divine mysteries. But when some

a. CF. Ex 31:1-7.

118.   of them tried to recite the Trisagion hymn with the addition 'who was crucified for us' concocted by Peter
nicknamed the Fuller,[40] the godly man was rightly indignant and ordered them to chant this hymn in Greek
118,5   according to the ancient tradition of the catholic
Church and not according to the innovation of the said
Peter, who had shared the opinions of Eutyches. Peter,
having twice seized the see of Antioch in violent manner, only to be expelled by the laws of the Church,
again a third time, after the usurpation of Illus in
118,10 Isauria in the reign of Zeno, by imperial authority
seized the same throne contrary to law, since the
anathemas against him had not been cancelled, and
threw all the east into confusion, at which he was ana-
[AD 485] thematized by Felix, pope of Rome, both for his
heterodoxy and for his said addition to the Trisagion.
118,15 So it was justly and piously that our father Sabas rejected the addition concocted by him and followed the
tradition of the Church. He also decreed that on Saturdays the office should take place in the church built by
God and on Sundays be performed in the church of the
Mother of God, and that there should be a vigil from
eve till dawn without interval in the two churches both
118,20 on Sundays and on feasts of our Lord.

33. WITHDRAWAL TO THE LION'S CAVE

When by the grace of God he had in a short time enlarged the laura, increased the community, founded the
cenobium of Castellium, and become exarch of all the
118,25 other lauras and anchorites, his disciples and accusers
mentioned above, all the more envious at the founding
of Castellium, suborned others in the community and,
now forty in number, were driven by some evil demon
to foment sedition against him. Our father Sabas, gen-

tle towards men although a fighter against demons, yielded to them and withdrew to the region of Scythopolis; he settled in a desert spot by the river called Gadarôn, and stayed there for a short time in a cave where an enormous lion was wont to withdraw.

119. Around midnight this lion returned and found the blessed one sleeping. Taking hold of his patchwork habit with its mouth, it began to pull at him, striving to remove him from the cave. When he got up and began the night psalmody, the lion went out and waited out-

119,5 side the cave; when the old man had completed the office and lay down in the place where the lion was wont to lie down, it came in again and, taking hold of his patchwork habit, began to pull at him, trying to re- move him from the cave. So, with the lion pressing him to leave the cave, the old man said to it in confi-

119,10 dence of spirit, 'The cave is spacious enough to pro- vide plentiful lodging for both of us, for we both have the one Creator. As for you, if you want, stay here; if not, withdraw. I myself was fashioned by the hand of God and privileged to receive his image.' On hearing this, the lion felt some kind of shame and withdrew.

34. THE DISCIPLES OF HIS EXILE

119,15 In a few days he became famous there, and received visits from some of the people of Scythopolis and Gadara,[41] including a young man of Scythopolis, Basil by name, a relative of the local celebrities Severus and Sophronius; stirred by divine compunction, he came to Sabas, made his renunciation and received instruction from him in strict asceticism.

119,20 Some robbers, learning about Basil, made a sudden descent on the two of them in the middle of the night, suspecting that Basil had money; finding they had none of the goods of this world, they went away edified on discovering their life and poverty. They promptly encountered two enormous lions, and in their terror they adjured the beasts with these words: 'By the prayers of Abba Sabas, whose virtue we have just been admiring, leave the road, to let us cross.' On hearing the name of Abba Sabas, the beasts took to flight, as if driven by a whip, while the robbers, amazed at the miracle, reflected, 'The elder is truly a servant of God, if he works miracles even at a distance.' With one accord they returned to him, fell at his feet, and recounted the miraculous occurrence. Promising God no longer to harm anyone, they renounced all lawlessness and from then on devoted their time to their farming.

As this story spread abroad, many hastened to him, while in a few days he built a cell and attracted two other brethren. When he saw himself beset by people of this world, he secretly retired, commending the brethren to God. When in time they died, one Eumathius, an Isaurian, inheriting their cell, made it into a cenobium and built up a community in it. Of this community is the venerable Abba Tarasius, the heir of Eumathius in both virtue and the office of superior; he too is an Isaurian by birth and has lived in monastic perfection.

35. HIS SECOND EXILE

On returning to his own laura, the sanctified Sabas found that the forty mentioned above, those prone to share in evil, had suborned others and become sixty. He was distressed and wept copiously at the damage inflicted on his community, and was amazed how envious and prompt is wickedness in effortlessly drawing the lax to itself. At first he opposed patience to their irascibility and love to their hate, controlling his

120,20   speech with spiritual understanding and integrity. Subsequently, however, when he saw them grow bold in
wickedness and resort to shamelessness, not bearing to
walk in the humble path of Christ but alleging excuses
for their sins and inventing reasons to justify their pas-
120,25   sions, he left scope for divine anger and withdrew to
the region of Nicopolis, where he lived as a solitary for
many days under a single carob-tree, living on carobs.
On learning this, the bailiff of the place came out to see
121.   him and built him a cell in this very place; this cell, by
the help and favor of Christ, became in a short time a
cenobium.

   While he was living in this region, those valiant
monks, taking advantage of his long absence, reported
round the laura, 'Our abbot, in wandering round the
121,5   desert, has fallen prey to wild animals.' Beguiling the
rest, they went to the holy city to the sainted
Archbishop Elias and said, 'Our abbot, withdrawing to
the desert by the Dead Sea, has been eaten by lions.
Give instructions that we be given a superior.' But
Elias, as a true high-priest of God, knowing from the
121,10   time of Saint Euthymius the ways of the godly Sabas
since youth, answered them, 'I do not believe you, for I
know that God is not so unjust as to let his servant fall
prey to wild animals. But go, search instead for your
abbot, or else keep quiet until God reveals him.'

   When the Feast of Dedication[42] came round, Abba
121,15   Sabas, as was customary for superiors, went up to the
holy city with some brethren of the monastery near
Nicopolis, for, as has been said, he had founded a
monastery there and attracted brethren to it, since God
assisted him at every juncture, in every place and in
every matter. With some of the superiors he went in to
121,20   see the archbishop. Seeing the old man, the patriarch
was overjoyed and, taking him aside, bade him return
to his own laura. When Sabas asked to be excused and
utterly declined, the archbishop became annoyed and

121,25 said, 'Believe this: if you do not heed my bidding and advice, you will never again see my face. I cannot bear to see the fruit of your labors directed by others.' When the archbishop had said this, our father Sabas consented to yield to his command; but he was compelled to mention the revolt of the sixty conspirators and their wish to cause trouble. At this the patriarch, stirred into action, wrote to those in the laura the following letter:

122. I wish you to know, beloved brethren, that your father is alive and has not been eaten by lions. He came to me for the feast, and I have kept him and forbidden him to abandon his own laura, which he 122,5 himself labored to found with the help of God. You are therefore to receive him back with due honor and to be subject to him in every way. For you did not choose him, but he accepted you; this is why you must be subject to him. If any of you are stubborn, arrogant and disobedient, and cannot bear to 122,10 be humbled, then do not stay there. It would be intolerable for him not to recover his own monastery.

So our father Sabas, not knowing how to disobey, made one of the disciples with him, of Nicopolis by birth and named Severus, superior of the monastery near Nicopolis; he, after ruling this monastery for 122,15 many years, was succeeded by Domnus when he died. Domnus died after a long time, leaving Sabarôn as his successor. This Sabarôn we know as having grown old there and ruled the place to this day.

36. FOUNDATION OF THE NEW LAURA

Taking the letter of the patriarch, the sanctified Sabas 122,20 returned to his laura. When the letter had been read out in church, those valiant sixty, fiercely indignant and blinded by their own wickedness, made a league by common accord and arrayed themselves against the holy father as if for war. While some of them got ready the clothing and baggage for the whole party, the rest took axes, shovels, spades and levers and, ascending to his tower, demolished it to the foundations in fierce rage, and threw its boards and stones down into the

123.   gorge. Then with their baggage they withdrew and, going to the laura of Souka,[43] asked to settle there. On learning about them, the sainted Aquilinus, who had then been appointed superior of Souka, rejected them and would not receive them. When they failed to be re-

123,5   ceived, they withdrew to the gorge to the south of Thekoa, where they found water and traces of cells once built by the Aposchists.[44] Here they stayed, built themselves cells, and named the site the New Laura. After their departure in this manner from the laura of the old man, the remainder could offer as fruit to God their

123,10   purity of heart without hindrance, like grain that grows once the weeds have been rooted out.

A short time later, Saint Sabas, learning where his disciples who had deserted were staying, took the animals of the laura and of Castellium loaded with provisions and set off thither to visit hem. Some of them,

123,15   seeing him arrive, said to each other, 'See, here comes the squinter.' The holy old man, perceiving that they were in great straits from having neither a church nor a head but communicated on Sundays at the prophet's shrine of holy Amos at Thekoa, and that they were subject to the disorder of anarchy and, furthermore, in dis-

123,20   pute and at variance with each other, took pity on them and referred their case to the patriarch, asking him to give them assistance. The patriarch handed him one pound weight of gold coin and also gave him authority over that place and those living in it as being   123,25 of his own community. So the godly old man returned

to them with skilled workmen and all the requisites and, spending five months with them, built them a bakery and church, which he furnished and then con-
[AD 507]   secrated in the sixty-ninth year of his life.

Sending for the above-mentioned anchorite John
124.   from his own laura, Greek by birth and gifted with the charism of prophecy, he made him superior of the New Laura. This John was inspired by God to prophesy what has happened to the New Laura in our own time;
124,5   for when he was about to die in the Lord, and the leaders of the community were sitting by him, he burst into tears and said, 'Behold, the days will come when the inmates of this house will become extremely proud and depart from the orthodox faith, but their pride will be humbled and they will be persecuted for their inso-
124,10   lence.' After saying this, he attained the haven of rest, after governing this laura in a manner pleasing to God for seven years and displaying miraculous powers. The fathers there on the advice of our father Sabas appointed a Roman named Paul, a simple-minded and
124,15   detached man, resplendent with godly virtues. But Abba Paul, after ruling the New Laura against his will for six months, fled to Arabia and subsequently, going to Caparbaricha to the above-mentioned Severianus who was building a cenobium there, died in that place. The fathers of the New Laura informed the godly old
124,20   man of the flight of Paul and, by repeated entreaty, obtained as superior his above-mentioned disciple Agapêtus.

Agapêtus on becoming superior of the New Laura found four monks in the community, admitted there by the simple-minded Paul out of ignorance about them, who whispered in secret the doctrines of Origen; their
124,25   leader was a Palestinian called Nonnus, who, pretending to be a Christian and simulating piety, held the doctrines of the godless Greeks, Jews, and Manichees,

125.

that is, the myths concerning preexistence related by Origen, Evagrius, and Didymus. Fearing lest the corruption of heresy should spread to others, the blessed Agapêtus, with the agreement of the sainted Archbishop Elias and at his bidding, expelled them from the New Laura; on being expelled, they went off to the plain, to sow their pernicious weeds there.[45] Af-

125,5

ter some time had passed and the archbishop had fallen victim to a conspiracy, as will shortly be related, Nonnus and his companions went to the holy city and asked his successor as patriarch to be allowed to return to the New Laura. Adorned with godly discretion, he summoned both Saint Sabas and the blessed Agapêtus, and asked if it was possible for them to be admitted.

125,10

Agapêtus replied, 'They corrupt the community by fomenting the doctrines of Origen, and I would prefer rather to leave the place than to mix these men with the community entrusted to me.' The archbishop said, 'You have made a good judgment and one agreeable to God.' So, learning that the archbishop would not give

125,15

them permission, these men returned to the plain. When blessed Agapêtus had governed the New Laura well for five years and then died, the monks of the New Laura appointed one Mamas superior. At this juncture Nonnus and his companions, hearing of Agapêtus' death and Mamas' appointment, came and

125,20

were privately admitted by Mamas into the New Laura, maintaining in their souls their wicked fictions but keeping them totally secret from the hearing of the monks out of fear of our sainted father Sabas; for, as long as he was still alive, there was only one confession of faith among all the monks in the desert. Enough has been said for the present about the monks of the

125,25

New Laura; I return to the account in sequence of the achievements of the godly old man.

37. FOUNDATION OF THE CENOBIUM OF THE CAVE

Resplendent were the divine charisms of our inspired father Sabas. His manner of life was glorious, his conduct virtuous, and his faith orthodox. This has already been shown in part by what has been said, but it will be shown more perfectly by what is still to be told, if the Word of God guides my words.

This sanctified Sabas, already revealed at Castellium as victor against the spirits of evil, raised a further abode of piety, with the help of the Holy Spirit within him, in his eagerness to make the desert into a city.[46] After the withdrawal of those valiant ones and the foundation of the New Laura, when the devil wished to ensnare the disciples of Sabas and was himself ensnared by Sabas, Sabas raised a further trophy against him. After returning from the New Laura and enjoying a short period of solitude, he took as companion in the season of Lent one Paul, an elder conspicuous for many attainments, and went to a gorge fifteen stades distant from the Great Laura, near Castellium to the west. Finding in its northern face a large and intact cave, he settled in it with Paul until Palm Sunday. After Easter, taking Theodulus, Gelasius, Paul himself and others with them, he came to the place and, in a word, with the help of God made the cave into a church, and gradually established a distinguished cenobium there, which he named 'of the Cave.'[47] He appointed the blessed Paul administrator of the place, assigning to him from the laura three brethren, George, Cyriacus, and Eustathius. Through the good pleasure of God the place grew and greatly expanded. Why should I say more? Before our eyes lies the cenobium of the Cave, which was founded with great labor by our father Saint Sabas. When the blessed Paul died in Christ,

126.

126,5

126,10

126,15

126,20

126,25

127.   Cyriacus and Eustathius succeeded in turn as superior
          and after their departure from life Sergius succeeded as
          superior; for George had been sent to Alexandria and,
          meeting Archbishop Zoilus,[48] had been ordained
          bishop of Pelusium. So much for the monastery that
          received the name 'of the Cave'.

127,5   One Marcianus, priest at the holy Resurrection and
          superior of holy Sion, made frequent visits to our
          sainted father Sabas, bringing him many offerings.
          Carried away by faith, he would toil with his own
          hands, together with his children Antony and John, in
          helping those laboring at the building of the sacred
127,10   place I have just mentioned; so great was the man's
          faith. Archbishop Elias came to love him and ordained
          him bishop of Sebaste, and Antony bishop of the
          church of Ascalon, while he made John deacon at the
          holy Resurrection.[49] But I must return to my account of
          the achievements of the godly old man.

38. FOUNDATION OF THE CENOBIUM
OF THE TOWER

127,15   The tower built by blessed Eudocia on the highest
          hill in the whole eastern desert, as I have already men-
          tioned in my account of Euthymius, passed to certain
          monks who supported the madness of Dioscorus
          and Eutyches. At the second union[50] they shared
          the expulsion of Gerontius and Romanus, and were
127,20   succeeded in inhabiting this tower by two other monks,
          champions of the heresy of the impious Nestorius, who
          did not profess that the holy Virgin Mary is strictly and
          in truth the Mother of God, and did not even hold
          Christ as true God to be one of the holy and con-
          substantial Trinity.[51] Our great father Sabas was dis-
          tressed at having these men on the peak surmounting

his three monasteries and was considerably annoyed at
128.   them. It so happened that he saw at this time the following vision. He had a vision of himself in the holy
church of the Resurrection during the celebration of the
eucharist, and of these monks being thrown out with
great threats by some vergers, while he was pressing
128,5   the vergers to allow them to receive communion. In a
stern voice they replied to him as follows: 'They cannot receive communion, for they are Jews in not confessing Christ to be true God or holy Mary to be the
Mother of God'. From this moment the old man took
pity on them and addressed earnest prayer to God on
128,10 their behalf, that they might come to recognize the
truth and recover from the heresy of Nestorius. He continued for some time to visit them frequently, urging
and admonishing them, and expounding the doctrines
of true piety. So it was that our father Sabas, after
laboring at many prayers and many admonitions, induced them with the help of God to anathematize the
128,15 doctrines of Nestorius and enter the communion of the
catholic Church.

   After gaining them in this way, he commended them
to the blessed Theodosius; and one of his disciples, an
admirable man, Byzantine by birth and called John,
who had left the first *schola* of the *scholarii*[52] for the
solitary life and followed successfully the monastic life
128,20 in the Great Laura, he appointed administrator and superior of this tower, since adorned with godly prudence
and capable of taking charge of the place. Providing
him with brethren from the laura and all the requisites,
he went up to the place, and expended labor and care
until with the help of God he had made the tower into a
128,25 cenobium. Into this cenobium the *scholarius* attracted a
large community, and it is to this community that belongs the venerable Abraamius, bishop of Cratea. The
scholarius completed thirty-five years in this

129.

monastery, and was outstanding for monastic attainments and orthodox doctrines. Our sainted father Sabas devoted much labor to building and founding this cenobium, and did not cease till death to visit the place and shower it with benefits.

39. JAMES' SELF-WILL AND CURE

129,5

129,10

129,15

129,20

A monk of the Great Laura, of Jerusalem by birth and called James, had the self-will, when the great man went out to the utter desert, to take some monks of the laura and begin to build a small oratory and cells by the above-mentioned cistern of Heptastomus,[53] planning to found a laura there. when the fathers of the laura waxed indignant and tried to stop the work, he asserted quite falsely that the order was the holy father's; the fathers on hearing this were distressed, but did not stop the work. When the great father returned for the feast and saw the work, he summoned James and said, 'God is not pleased with your work, my child, founding another laura in the same district as the laura, specially when the fathers of the laura do not approve but are indeed extremely concerned at its being on the road and by our cistern. Even if someone were to say that the building is going to be subject to the laura, I do not want the laura to extend so far. But listen to what the prophet advises those who through inexperience or folly attempt what exceeds their power and worth: "Beat your ploughshares into swords and your pruning-hooks into spears."[a] For what is the advantage in agriculture when the land is in the grip of war? How can you, who have not yet overcome the passions of flesh and soul, undertake the formation of others, when

a. Joel 3:10.

you are still under the sway of pleasure and vainglory?' When James opposed this and would not yield, the

129,25   elder said to him, 'My child, I am giving you, the advice I judge will benefit you. But since you persevere in disobedience, you will learn by experience that Scripture says truly, "Every wicked man stirs up opposition, and the Lord sends a pitiless angel against

130.   him."'[b] When the saint had said this and retired to a small tower, James was seized with a terrible shivering and fever and was tormented by the disease for seven

130,5   months. In November he was despaired of, and asked the fathers to be carried and taken into the church of the laura and to be placed at the feet of the saint in order to receive forgiveness before dying. When this was done, the saint said to him, 'Do you recognize the penalty for self-will and opposition? Have you learnt from your own arrogance?' When with difficulty he man-

130,10   aged to open his mouth and say, 'Forgive me, father,' the saint said, 'God will forgive you'. Giving him his hand, he raised him up and told him to partake of the spotless mysteries. When he had done so, he immediately took food and recovered his strength, so that all were astonished at the sudden change in James. From then on he no more returned to that building.

130,15   Archbishop Elias, on learning of this, sent some men to demolish James' building. Our sainted father Sabas, took some capable monks of the laura and built about five stades to the north of the demolished building an oratory and cells round it; he appointed as administrators there two monks of the Great Laura called

130,20   Paul and Andrew, who were blood-brothers of Greek birth, planted other brethren there, and founded the place as a laura, calling it Heptastomus. He had been given the site by someone called Zanagôn, who origi-

b. Pr 17:11.

130,25   nated from the village of Betabudissae. He took all
          necessary care of the place and, when there was a festal
          meal at the monastery, he would send some of the food to
          the monks there, out of the great care he took of the place.

40. JAMES AND THE DISH OF BEANS

              When some time had passed, the above-mentioned
          James was charged with looking after the guest-house
130,30   of the Great Laura and had to cook for those who went
          out to the desert to collect faggots. Once when he had
          cooked a quantity of beans, which we call *pisarion*,
          and had prepared too much on two successive days, he
131.   later threw the left-overs through a window down into
          the gorge. The elder, on seeing this from his tower,
          went down secretly, neatly collected the discarded
          pisarion, and spread it out to dry. Later in the year he
131,5   invited James, on finishing his period of service, to a
          meal on his own; he cooked the dry *pisarion*, dressed it
          well and served it. While they were eating, the elder
          said, 'Forgive me, brother, I do not know how to dress
          food well, and perhaps you did not enjoy the dish.' The
          other replied, 'I enjoyed it immensely, venerable
          father. I have not tasted so delicious a dish for a long
131,10   time.' The old man[54] answered, 'Believe me, my child,
          this is the *pisarion* you threw from the guest-house into
          the gorge. Know this, that he who is unable to dispense
          a pot of vegetables so as to satisfy the needs of those in
          his charge without ever wasting any of the vegetables
131,15   is not able to govern a community. As the Apostle
          says, "If a man does not know how to run his own
          household, how can he take care of God's Church?"'[a]
          At these words James went off to his cell much
          benefited.

          a. 1 Tim 3:5.

41. THE DEATH OF JAMES

131,20   This same James in the solitude of his cell was fiercely tempted by the demon of fornication. After struggling for a considerable time and losing heart for the struggle, as the demon's kindling intensified, in either ignorance or forgetfulness of the rules of the divine and ecclesiastical canons, he took a knife and

131,25   recklessly castrated himself. Unable to bear the flow of blood and the pain, he began calling for his neighbors. They assembled and, on seeing the wound, called a doctor of the laura and tended him. On hearing of it, the sanctified Sabas expelled James from the laura,

132.   once he was cured, as guilty of virtual suicide. The great Theodosius received him into his monastery; after inquiring into the affair, he took him to the laura and asked the elder to receive him back with a suitable penance. The sanctified Sabas gave him orders to keep

132,5   to the solitude of his own cell, never going out of it and never admitting anyone for a meeting with the sole exception of the brother serving him. James accepted the elder's order, and for a long time besought God with tears. It was then revealed to the elder that God accepted James' repentance. He saw a man radiating

132,10   light, who showed him a corpse outstretched in front of James, who was standing at prayer. The latter was told, 'Your prayer has been heard, James. Stretch out your hand and raise up the man outstretched.' When he had raised the corpse, the radiant figure said to the elder, 'See, the corpse has been raised. You also must loose

132,15   the chain that weighs on the man who raised it.' On coming to himself and interpreting the vision, the elder gave permission for James to enter the church. On entering, he embraced Sabas and the fathers; then, after returning to the blessed Theodosius and embracing him, on the seventh day after the vision he died in joy.

42. FOUNDATION OF THE CENOBIUM OF ZANNUS

132,20   There were at the Great Laura two blood-brothers
united as true brothers in their attitude towards God
and abounding in godly virtues, who originated from
the region of Hebron and were called Zannus and Ben-
jamin. With one voice they asked the sanctified Sabas
to give them an anchoritic cell which he had built for
132,25   himself at about fifteen stades' distance from the laura
to the south-west. The great old man, knowing them to
be laborers of God, yielded to their request and gave
them the cell. They continued to occupy both the
anchoritic cell and their own one in the laura. Toiling
and moiling in this anchoritic cell, they made it into a
133.   cenobium, while our sainted father Sabas gave them
assistance and provided them with food and other services. When brethren had gathered there, he took
charge of building the church, which he consecrated,
and gave the rules of his other cenobia to this one also.
133,5   This cenobium, named after the blessed Zannus,
flourishes by the grace of God to this day.[55]

43. THE DEATH OF ANTHIMUS

There was an elder in the laura who had passed his
life with many monastic attainments; he originated
from Bithynia and was called Anthimus. He began by
building himself a small cell on the other side of the
133,10   gorge to the east opposite the tower of our sainted father Sabas, and lived there for thirty years. On reaching
old age he grew weak and became bed-bound. When
the blessed Sabas saw him reduced to extreme bodily
weakness, he urged him to take a cell near the church
133,15   so that someone could minister to him easily. The elder
refused in these words: 'I have trust in God that my

soul shall be taken by God its creator in the very cell where I have been privileged to live from the beginning.' After some time had passed, the saint arose one night before the hour of striking and heard a sound of
133,20   psalmody as if made by a large assembly; thinking that by some accident the office was taking place in the church, he was astonished at something contrary to custom taking place without his approval. Going down in haste, he found the church shut. Then, returning again to his tower, he heard a multitude chanting in
133,25   mellifluous song this sole verse, 'I shall pass through the place of the wondrous tabernacle to the house of God with the voice of rejoicing and thanksgiving, of the sound of those keeping festival.'[a] Realizing where the sound of psalmody came from, he roused the pre-
134.   centor and made him sound the summons. Going with incense and candles to the cell of the elder, he found no one there except only the elder himself, dead. This amazed all those who had accompanied the elder; they tended the corpse and carried the precious remains to
134,5   the church. After performing the customary office over him, they laid him in a holy grave, as they glorified God for glorifying his saints.

44. BROTHER APHRODISIUS

A brother of the monastery of blessed Theodosius, Asian by birth and called Aphrodisius, who had been
134,10   given the office of muleteer, was able unassisted to lift from the ground the load for a mule, that is, twelve measures of corn, and place it on his own shoulders; for in bodily size he surpassed all in the cenobium. It happened that once on the road he lost his temper,

a. Ps 42:4(41:5).

134,15

struck with his hand the face of the mule and broke it; when the animal instantly fell down dead, Aphrodisius lifted its load and the saddle onto his shoulders and returned to the monastery. Expelled by the great Theodosius for killing the animal, he went down to the Jordan and laid his offence before the sainted John the Egyptian, who was then refulgent with virtues at

134,20

Choziba.[56] On being told by him, 'If you want to be saved, go to our Abba Sabas and do what he tells you,' he went to Sabas in haste, confessed his offence and begged to hear a word of salvation from him. Our father Sabas gave him a cell with the words, 'Be content

134,25

with your cell, do not visit any other cell or go outside the laura, exercise control over your tongue and belly, and you will be saved.' Accepting this command and not infringing it in any respect, Aphrodisius for thirty

135.

years neither went outside the laura nor visited a cell, never possessed an earthern or copper pot, an oven or mattress, drank no wine or mixed drink, and did not possess two tunics. Instead, he slept in straw on a rush-mat and patchwork cloak and, getting palms from the steward, supplied the guest-master with ninety

135,5

completed baskets each month. Taking the left-overs of the cooked food, whether greens or pulses or roughage, he would put them in a single bowl and take a little from the bowl each day, and was satisfied with this. If the food in the bowl began to smell or produced

135,10

worms, he did not throw it away but simply added more cooked left-overs. His wailing throughout the night left his neighbors no peace.

Having completed thirty years, as has been said, in this mode of life, without ever falling ill or getting discouraged or harming his stomach, he received the charism of second sight and had foreknowledge of the

135,15

day of his death a week in advance. Going into the church, he asked our father Sabas for a one day's leave of absence to visit the monastery of blessed Theodosius. The elder, knowing that his day was near, sent as his companion Theodulus, priest and brother of Gelasius, with the following message to the blessed Theodosius: 'Behold, I earlier received Aphrodisius as 135,20 a man and now by the grace of Christ I have sent him to you as an angel.' The blessed Theodosius received him with joy and embraced him and, after inviting him kindly to a common meal, sent him on his way in peace. Returning to the laura, Aphrodisius after a short illness died in joy. The fathers tended his corpse and 135,25 buried him with the priests. The blessed Sabas gave orders for his precious remains to be laid crosswise so that they would be recognized for a long time and venerated by the fathers who went down to the graveyard.

45. THE CURE OF GERONTIUS

136.   Medaba is a city on the east side of the Jordan, subject to Arabia; its inhabitants used to visit our sainted father Sabas, in order to draw many spiritual benefits and give his cenobia and lauras offerings of grain and 136,5 pulses. Among them was a man called Gerontius, who, beset with bodily illness and for this reason tarrying in the holy city, conceived a desire to pray at the holy church of the Ascension. Seated on some animal, he set off, accompanied by servants. While ascending the mountain, the animal shied through some accident and 136,10 Gerontius had a fall; he was so injured that a masseur who came along despaired of his cure. His younger brother Porphyry, saying nothing to anyone, came down to the laura to beg Saint Sabas to go up and visit Gerontius. Hearing of the accident that had befallen Gerontius and much distressed by it, the old man im- 136,15 mediately went up to the holy city and visited Geron-

tius. By making earnest prayer on his behalf and
anointing him with oil from the holy Cross he restored
him to health, so that all were astonished at such a sudden change and extraordinary miracle.

46. THE MIRACLE OF THE WINE

136,20   After a long time had elapsed, the son of this Gerontius, named Thomas, on a visit to the Great Laura's
guest-house at Jericho, it being late evening and in a
time of famine, found Saint Sabas there and also
Theodore and Paul, the administrators of the
monasteries of Castellion and of the Cave. The blessed
136,25   Sabas was overjoyed at seeing him and said to the
guest-master, 'Make us dinner.' As they were dining,
the guest-master, asked if he had wine, replied that he
had none at all, but said that he had a gourd of vinegar
137.   for dressing pulses. The saint said, 'Bring the gourd to
me here. Blessed be the Lord that we are able because
of him to make merry, for Christ our God, who himself
turned water into wine, is able to turn vinegar also into
wine.' At these words of the saint the gourd was
137,5   brought in and the vinegar was found to have changed
into excellent wine. Thomas was overwhelmed at this
extraordinary miracle, and blessed Sabas said to the
guest-master, 'Bring hot coals immediately and throw
on incense, for God has visited us in this hour.' The
137,10   wine of the gourd was so blessed that for three days all
drank freely from it. Thomas was amazed at the mir-
acle and begged the elder for permission to take the
gourd to his own house; the saint gave the gourd and
Thomas took it with him when he departed. He continued drinking the abundant wine, both himself and his
companions, all the way to Medaba.
137,15   This was related to me by Abba Gerontius, the pre-

sent administrator of the monastery of Saint
Euthymius, the son of Thomas and grandson of Gerontius, who adds to the story the following: 'We had this
gourd in our house for many years and, when anyone
was unwell, the people of the house filled it with water
137,20 and sprinkled the patient.[57] This mere sprinkling relieved the sick person of all bodily illness.'

47. A LESSON IN GUARDING ONE'S EYES

Once when journeying with a disciple from Jericho
to the Jordan, this champion of piety Sabas fell in with
some people of the world among whom was a girl of
winning appearance. When they had passed by, the
137,25 elder, wishing to test the disciple, asked, 'What about
the girl who has gone by and is one-eyed?' The brother
replied, 'No, father, she has two eyes.' The elder said,
'You are wrong, my child. She is one-eyed.' The other
insisted that he knew with precision that she was not
138. one-eyed but had indeed extremely fine eyes. The elder
asked, 'How do you know that so clearly?' He replied,
'I, father, had a careful look, and I noted that she has
both her eyes.' At this the elder said, 'And where have
you stored the precept that says, "Do not fix your eye
on her and do not be captured by her eyebrows"?[a]
138,5 Fiery is the passion that arises from inquisitive looks.
Know this: from now on you are not to stay with me in
a cell because you do not guard your eyes as you
should.' He sent him to Castellium and, when he had
spent sufficient time there and learnt to keep a careful
watch on his eyes and thoughts, he received him as an
138,10 anchorite into the laura.

a. Pr 9:18a (LXX), 6:25.

48. THE MIRACLE OF THE GOURDS

The cook of the laura once boiled gourds on behalf of some workmen and at dinner-time tasted them and found them bitter, which placed him in difficulty, since he had nothing else to offer them. Running to the elder, he threw himself at his feet and announced what had

138,15 happened. The saint, having come and sealed the pot with the sign of the cross, said to the cook, 'Proceed! Blessed is the Lord. Serve this at table.' Instantly the gourds became sweet and all ate and were satisfied, giving glory to God.

49. THE LION, FLAVIAN, AND THE ASS

This holy old man was once traveling from Roubâ to

138,20 the monastery of Calamôn of the Jordan[58] when he encountered an enormous lion which was limping and fell at his feet, showing him its paw and by a gesture asking for help. On perceiving the pain the beast was in, our father Sabas sat down and, taking hold of its paw, drew out of it a thorn that was sticking in. Re-

138,25 lieved of the pain, the lion got up and went away. From then on it followed the elder during the season of Lent, performing kindly services.[59] At this time the sancti-

139. fied old man had a Syrian disciple called Flavius who had below in Roubâ an ass to serve him. When Sabas sent him on a commission, he would get the lion to keep watch over his ass. So in the morning the lion

139,5 would go off with the halter of the ass in its mouth, let it graze the whole day, and in the evening take it to water and then bring it back. Some time later, while the lion was performing this office, Flavius, who had been sent on a commission, apparently neglected his salvation and was carried away by presumption; in his con-

sequent state of abandonment, he fell into fornication.
139,10　On the very same day the lion struck down the ass and
made it his food. On discovering this, Flavius realized
that his own sin was the cause of the ass's being eaten
and, no longer daring to appear before the elder, gave
himself up for lost, acting wrongly. Going away, he
settled on his own property, lamenting his sin. The
139,15　godly old man, however, in imitation of the Master's
mercy did not despise him but carried out a lengthy
search for him. When by the grace of Christ he found
him, he admonished and exhorted him, raised him from
his fall and restored him. Flavius went into reclusion,
repented from the bottom of his soul, and became extremely well-pleasing to God.

50. MISSION TO CONSTANTINOPLE

139,20　　　In the sixty-third year of the life of the great Sabas,
[AD 511]　Archbishop Elias, wishing to send some of the
monastic superiors to Constantinople, summoned our
father Sabas and besought him to go with them and
strive with all his might to protect the mother of the
churches from disturbance, since the emperor
139,25　Anastasius, in utter exasperation, was attempting to
reverse and overturn the whole state of the churches of
Palestine. The cause of the emperor's rage and exasperation at the archbishop I shall relate in a few
words, going right back to its origins.

　　　When blessed Elias obtained the see of Jerusalem,
140.　in the third year of the reign of Anastasius, the Church
[AD 494]　of God was in confusion through a threefold
division.[60] The bishops of Rome were at variance
with those of Byzantium because of the inclusion in
the sacred diptychs of the name of Acacius, who had
140,5　been bishop of Constantinople, on the ground of his

not following their own strictness, while those of
Byzantium were at variance with those of Alexandria
on the ground of their anathematizing the Council of
Chalcedon and accepting the communion of Dioscorus
who had been deposed by it; Elias was in communion
140,10 only with Euthemius of Byzantium, while the western-
ers, as has been said, had seceded, and Palladius of
Antioch, to please the emperor, had anathematized the
dogmatic decree of Chalcedon and accepted the communion of the Alexandrians. At this juncture, Bishop
Euphemius of Constantinople, who had given synodical approval to the dogmatic decree of Chalcedon, was
140,15 removed from his see on the basis of a false accusation. While the bishops of Alexandria and Antioch approved the expulsion of Euphemius, Elias, who had not
yet completed his second year as bishop, felt unable to
give his approval; but on finding the ordained
Macedonius orthodox from his synodical letters, he
accepted him into his communion, a fact which at the
140,20 beginning considerably disturbed the emperor.[61] So
there was accord between Macedonius and Elias. But
when after the death of Palladius Flavian obtained the
see of Antioch and was reconciled to them, the
emperor, bold against piety alone, could not bear their
concord, but was madly eager to banish them. First,
charging Macedonius with various false accusations,
141.   he expelled him from his see and promoted Timothy to
it; he demanded the assent of Flavian and Elias, who
approved the synodical letters of Timothy but not those
deposing Macedonius. At this juncture, with the emperor vehemently excited against both of them, a fierce
141,5   storm hung over both churches.

It was because of this that blessed Elias, as has been
said, sent our father Sabas and other superiors with him
to Constantinople, with the following letter to the
emperor: 'The elite of the servants of God, good and

141,10 faithful and leaders in the whole desert, including our Lord Sabas, the colonizer and guardian of our desert and luminary over all Palestine, I have sent to entreat your Majesty.' Such was the letter of Archbishop Elias. Our father Sabas obeyed the hierarch out of eagerness to help, if he could, the catholic, orthodox faith which

141,15 at this time was tempest-tossed and endangered. When he had been sent on his way and was completing the journey, the emperor Anastasius, possessed with uncontrollable fury against the patriarchs Flavian and Elias, gave orders that there was to be a council at Sidon of the Oriental and Palestinian bishops, and that the presidents of the council were to be Soterichus of

141,20 Caesarea of Cappadocia and Philoxenus of Hierapolis, who had been signal in anathematizing the dogmatic decree of Chalcedon and embracing Eutyches and Dioscorus and their heresy.

51. SABAS' FIRST INTERVIEW WITH ANASTASIUS

When our sainted father Sabas, with the fathers sent with him reached the imperial city and sent word to the

142. emperor, they were all ordered into his presence. God, who glorifies those who glorify him, wishing to manifest the grace that accompanied his servant Sabas, disposed that the following should happen. As they all entered the palace and reached the so-called

142,5 *silentiarion*,[62] the *silentiarii* at the doors, while admitting all the rest, repelled this great luminary who through humility of spirit judged himself the last, they did not admit him since he looked like a beggar and viler than all, when they saw him wearing dirty and much-patched rags. The emperor Anastasius gave the

142,10 fathers a friendly welcome and asked for the holy Sabas praised in the letter. The fathers looked round in

all directions, not knowing how he had been separated
from them. When the emperor ordered careful search
to be made for him and a commotion arose among the
cubicularii, the *silentiarii* went out and found him
142,15   standing apart in a corner of the hall called the Consis-
tory, reciting Davidic psalms by himself. Seizing him,
they led him in. When he entered through the curtain,
the emperor saw an angelic form leading the way for
him. Standing up and receiving him with due honor, he
142,20   bade all sit down; for he was a lover of monks, even
though induced by some blackguards to make war on
the correct faith.[63]

Then as various topics were raised, each of the other
superiors showed concern for his own monastery, as
one of them asked for lands surrounding his monastery
and another strove to obtain some other imperial order.
142,25   The emperor, after obliging each of them, said to Saint
Sabas, 'As for you, venerable father, if you have no
petition, why did you undertake such a troublesome
journey?' The elder replied, 'I have come here prin-
143.   cipally to venerate the feet of Your Piety, while I am
still in the body, and next to entreat you, on behalf of
the holy city of God Jerusalem and its most pious
archbishop, to bestow peace on our holy churches, with
the clergy in them remaining free of annoyance. If be-
143,5   cause of the peace of the churches we can live in the
tranquillity in which the virtues are naturally attained,
we shall pray night and day for Your Serenity, as relying on your pious laws.' The emperor ordered a thousand *solidi* to be brought and said, 'Take these, father,
and pray for me, for I have heard that you take care of
143,10   many monasteries in the desert.' The great Sabas
answered, 'I wish to spend the winter here and be allowed to venerate Your Piety.' At this the emperor let
the other superiors return to Palestine, but bade him
143,15   spend the winter there and enter the palace freely without being announced.

52. SECOND INTERVIEW WITH ANASTASIUS

A few days later, the emperor summoned him and said, 'Your archbishop has made himself a champion of the Council of Chalcedon, that approved the doctrines of Nestorius. He has in addition unsettled Flavian of Antioch and dragged him down with himself. In consequence, when the dogmatic decree of Chalcedon was about to be canonically anathematized by the council lately assembled at Sidon, he alone frustrated it, in league with Flavian of Antioch. Moreover, as regards his own views, he tricked Our Majesty in his letter to us, where he used these very words: "We reject every heresy that introduces some novelty contrary to the orthodox faith; we do not even accept what was done at Chalcedon, because of the scandals that resulted from it." With these words he deceived us as regards his own views, when we decreed that the council should be dissolved without result. We are well aware, however, no less now than formerly, when he refused to approve the decrees deposing the Nestorians Euphemius and Macedonius, that he is a champion of the Council of Chalcedon and the whole Nestorian heresy. Consequently, we decree his deposition from the episcopacy as a corrupter and the appointment of a man who is orthodox and worthy of that holy and apostolic see, in order that the revered region that played host to God may not be sullied by the doctrines of Nestorius.'

So spoke the emperor. Our sainted father Sabas replied, 'May Your Serenity rest fully assured that the archbishop of our holy city of God, educated in the doctrines of piety by the ancient luminaries and miracle-working fathers of our desert, rejects equally both Nestorius' division and Eutyches' confusion and, following the middle road of the orthodox Church, allows deviation, in the scriptural phrase, neither to the right nor to the left.[a] We know that he emits the godly doctrines of Saint Cyril, archbishop of Alexandria, and anathematizes those who opposed or oppose his doc-

144,20 trines. We therefore beseech Your Serenity to protect from annoyance the holy city of Jerusalem, in which the great mystery of piety was revealed, with our hierarchy remaining undisturbed.' Perceiving the holiness, integrity and spiritual understanding of the old man, the emperor

144,25 said, 'Truly, venerable father, it is well written in divine Scripture that "he who walks in integrity walks confidently."[b] But pray for us and be without anxiety. For your Holiness' sake we decree nothing against your archbishop, and I shall endeavor to do you every service when sending you off on your way.'

53. HE SEES THE LADIES OF THE COURT

145. Leaving the emperor's presence, the old man went to see the Augusta Ariadne[64] and, after blessing her, exhorted her to hold firmly onto the faith of her father the great emperor the sainted Leo. She replied to him, 'You speak well, venerable father, as there is One who

145,5 hears us.' On leaving her presence he left the city, fleeing from city tumult, and settled in the suburb of Rufinus, tenanted by Demostratus.[65] The patrician Juliana, the grand-daughter of the emperor Valentinian,[66] and Anastasia, the wife of the patrician Pompeius, who at present is conspicuous on the Mount

145,10 of Olives for monastic attainments,[67] visited him frequently where he was staying, to pay their respects to him and enjoy his godly teaching; for these ladies were

a. Cf. Dt 5:32.
b. Pr 10:9.

of great faith and outstanding both for orthodoxy and
the other virtues.

54. THIRD INTERVIEW WITH ANASTASIUS

145,15

Summoned again a short time afterwards, he went
into the emperor's presence and, when the subject of
the holy city was raised, made the following request:
'The whole Roman empire thanks Your Serenity for
having been already freed these thirteen years from the
iniquitous *collatio lustralis*.[68] We now beseech you to
reduce the *superflua discriptio*[69] relating to indigent
and insolvent persons, imposed on the holy church of
145,20 the Resurrection and the landowners of the holy city. I
shall describe the cause of this *superflua discriptio*.
The then *tractores* and *vindices* of the taxes of Palestine, exacting a hundred pounds of gold from poor and
insolvent persons that could not be obtained, were
compelled to transfer this exaction onto the taxpayers'
145,25 syndicate in Jerusalem in proportion to the means of
each member. When the hundred pounds of gold were
apportioned in the manner related, the holy church of
the Resurrection, the remaining revered places and the
landowners were registered for *superflua discriptio*. It
is this *superflua discriptio* that we ask to be reduced.'
Yielding to this request out of respect for the old man's
146. holiness, the emperor summoned the praetorian prefect
Zôticus and gave instructions for the reduction of the
said *superflua discriptio* on the Palestinian tax-register
and the bestowal on the holy city of this concession.

When this had been approved, one Marînus,[70] a most
146,5 unjust man, who by God's leave was controlling the
affairs of state and was guiding and influencing the
easily swayed mind of the emperor in accordance with
his own wishes, learned of the emperor's decision on

the concession. He immediately came in and prevented the arrangement of this concession from proceeding,

146,10 calling the people of the holy city Nestorians and Jews and unworthy of the emperor's favors. At this Saint Sabas, truly filled with the Holy Spirit, said to Marînus, 'Stop undoing the good will of the emperor, stop your war against the holy churches of God. Stop your great avarice and wickedness, and be on your

146,15 guard. For if you disregard me, in a short time you will cause yourself terrible misfortune and bring no small danger on His Majesty and the whole city. You will be stripped of everything in a moment of time, and your house will be burnt with fire.' Having said this to

146,20 Marînus in the presence of the emperor with sagacity and candor, the holy elder asked leave to return to Palestine. Receiving a further one thousand solidi from the hand of the emperor[71] and taking his leave, he

[AD 512] sailed to Palestine in May of the fifth indiction.

This was how in the time of Anastasius the remission of the *superflua discriptio* relating to the indigent

146,25 was prevented. A part of it, however, was remitted in the pious reign of Justin, following a petition by our father Sabas and the other superiors of the desert, and a

147. complete remission of the rest of it occurred in the present God-protected reign of Justinian through the mediation of father Eusebius; this we will treat later. The prophecy addressed by the godly old man to Marînus did not err: a few months later, as the result of

147,5 a popular riot,[72] the house of Marînus was burnt with fire and every detail of the saint's prophecy was fulfilled. This was told to me by mother Anastasia, who brings honor on the monastic habit on the Mount of Olives and is resplendent with divine charisms, having heard it from her husband Pompeius, nephew of the emperor.

55. HE RETURNS FROM CONSTANTINOPLE

147,10   Our father Sabas sent a great quantity of money from Byzantium to his home village of Mutalasca, to have his parents' house made into a church of Saints Cosmas and Damian, which was done.

One Mamas, archimandrite of the Aposchist monks near Eleutheropolis, together with one Severus, leader of
147,15   the Acephaloi,[73] had gone to Constantinople to combat the orthodox faith; there he spoke very boldly in the emperor's presence and had a bitter disagreement with Severus himself. Our father Sabas brought him with him to Jerusalem and urged him to renounce the heresy of the Acephaloi and enter the communion of the
147,20   catholic Church. Having repeatedly exhorted him to this effect, he took him to the patriarch Elias and got him to accept the Council of Chalcedon and enter the communion of the catholic Church, anathematizing Eutyches and Dioscorus, and by his own example leading many to do the same. This contributed significantly
147,25   to the emperor Anastasius' annoyance with the patriarch Elias.

The godly old man distributed the money he had brought from Byzantium to the monasteries under him. When the disciples who had been with him at Byzantium were much aggrieved at the distribution of the
148.   money, he said to them, 'Ours was the bodily labor, but they strove for us spiritually and God rescued us through their prayers.' This he did, in my opinion, following the example of David, who distributed equal shares to those who had labored in war and those who
148,5   had guarded the camp.[a]

a. Cf. 1 Sam 30:24.

56. REVOLT AT JERUSALEM
AGAINST THE ACEPHALOI

But now the time calls me to add to the private attainments and struggles of the godly old man the public
combats for the faith both of himself and of the holy
fathers who attained distinction with him in this desert.

148,10   The patriarchs Flavian and Elias had been at Sidon,
as has been said, and by flattering and diplomatic letters to the emperor[74] had secured the dissolution of the
council assemble at Sidon against the orthodox faith, at
which they returned to their own sees. Soterichus and
Philoxenus and their party in exasperation stirred the
emperor to uncontrollable anger as having been

148,15   deceived by the cunning simulation of the patriarchs.
Armed with the authority they desired and distributing
large sums to the people of Antioch, they caused
Flavian trouble of every kind, and by virtually throt-
tling him forced him to anathematize the Council of
Chalcedon; they then expelled him from his see and

148,20   condemned him to exile. The emperor, overjoyed at
hearing this, sent Severus, leader of the Acephaloi, to
be bishop of Antioch. On seizing the patriarchate,
Severus exhibited great cruelty towards those not in
communion with him. He sent his synodical letters to

148,25   Archbishop Elias and, on not being recognized, stirred
[AD 513]   the emperor to anger; in May of the sixth indiction he
again sent the same synodical letters to Jerusalem together with certain clerics and an imperial force. On
learning this, our sainted father Sabas went up to the

149.   holy city with the other superiors of the desert. They
drove those who came with Severus' synodical letters
from the holy city and, collecting the mass of monks
from all directions in front of the holy church of
Calvary, shouted out together with the people of
Jerusalem, 'Anathema to Severus and those in com-

munion with him,' while the *agentes in rebus*,[74a]
149,5   magistrates and soldiers sent by the emperor stood by
and listened.

This Severus, possessed by fearful arrogance and
relying on imperial power, subjected the Council of
Chalcedon to countless anathemas and, striving to
strengthen the heresy of Eutyches, proclaimed one cor-
149,10   ruptible nature of the Master Christ the Son of God
after he became flesh and man from the Virgin. Being
enamored of upheaval, he concocted many novelties
contrary to the correct dogmas and decrees of the
Church. He accepted the impious robbery of the Sec-
149,15   ond Council of Ephesus and said it was on a par with
the council previously assembled at Ephesus, while he
declared equal as teachers the great and inspired Cyril,
archbishop of Alexandria, and Dioscorus, who received
into communion the heretic Eutyches for being of the
same mind and deposed and killed the most holy and
orthodox Flavian, archbishop of the imperial city.
149,20   Thereby advancing in impiety, the same Severus shar-
pened his tongue to blaspheme against God, and in his
words divided the Godhead one and indivisible in
trinity: alleging and affirming that person is nature and
nature person, recognizing no difference between these
149,25   terms, he had the effrontery to say that the holy and
adorable consubstantial trinity of the divine person is a
trinity of natures and Godheads and Gods.

This destructive corrupter of souls the emperor Anastasius was pressing Archbishop Elias to receive into his
communion. When he refused to do this in any way at
150.   all, the emperor bubbled over with rage and sent along
one Olympus of Caesarea, *dux* of Palestine,[75] with the
diplomatic letter written from Sidon which professed
disapproval of the Council of Chalcedon, in order by
150,5   any and every means to oust Elias from his see. Olympus arrived with an imperial force and, by employing

many methods and strategems and displaying the said
letter, ousted Elias from his see and banished him to
Aila,[76] while John the son of Marcianus, who had
promised to accept Severus into communion an
150,10   anathematize the Council of Chalcedon, he made
bishop of Jerusalem, on 1 September at the beginning
[AD 516] of the tenth indiction. The sanctified Sabas and the
other fathers of the desert, on learning that John had
made this promise, gathered together and adjured him
not to receive Severus into communion but to bear the
brunt of the battle on behalf of the Council of Chal-
150,15   cedon, with all of them for his allies. And so John
broke the promise he had made to the *dux*, out of respect for the fathers. The emperor Anastasius, furious
at learning that John had canceled his compact, sent
Anastasius son of Pamphilus and *dux* of Palestine
150,20   (Olympus was now out of the way) to make John receive Severus into communion and anathematize the
Council of Chalcedon, or oust him from his see. On
arriving at Jerusalem, Anastasius descended suddenly
on the archbishop and threw him into the public prison;
this delighted all the inhabitants of the holy city, since
150,25   he had plotted against Archbishop Elias and betrayed
him. One Zacharias, governor of Caesarea, entered the
prison secretly and advised John as follows: 'If you
151.   want to act well and not be deprived of your see, be
induced by no one to receive Severus into communion,
but pretend to make a compact with the *dux*, in these
words: "I shall not now postpone fulfilling my offer
but, lest some will say that I acted by forcible con-
151,5   straint, please release me from here, and in two days'
time, on the Sunday, I shall willingly carry out your
orders."' Convinced by these words, the *dux* restored
him to his church.

On being released, however, the archbishop summoned all the monks to the holy city overnight, gather-

151,10   ing them from all sides: those who counted the multitude announced that the total came to ten thousand
monks. Since no church could hold so great a congregation, it was decided that all should assemble at
the church of the holy protomartyr Stephen, which was
capacious enough to receive the multitude;[77] in addition they wanted to meet the emperor's nephew
Hypatius, who had at this time been released from
being held prisoner by Vitalian and come to Jerusalem
151,15   because of a vow.[78] When all the monks and city-
people had assembled in the revered convent just mentioned, the *dux* Anastasius and the consular Zacharias
joined them. When Hypatius arrived and went with the
multitude into the convent of the protomartyr Stephen,
151,20   and the *dux* was expecting the will of the emperor to be
done, the archbishop ascended the pulpit, accompanied
by Theodosius and Sabas, the chiefs and leaders of the
monks, and the whole congregation shouted out many
times, 'Anathematize the heretics and confirm the
council.' Without delay the three with one voice
anathematized Nestorius, Eutyches, Severus, Soteri-
152.   chus of Caesarea in Cappadocia, and everyone who did
not accept the Council of Chalcedon. When the three
had proclaimed this, they descended, but Abba
Theodosius ascended again and uttered the following
declaration to the congregation: 'If anyone does not
152,5   accept the four councils like the four Gospels, let him
be anathema.' After this outcome, the *dux* in fear of the
multitude of monks fled to Caesarea. Hypatius assured
the fathers with oaths, 'I came here not in communion
with Severus but out of desire for the honor of your
communion.' And he made an offering of a hundred
pounds of gold coin to each of the holy churches of the
152,10   Resurrection, Calvary and the venerable Cross, and
gave Theodosius and Sabas a hundred pounds of gold
coin to distribute to the monks of the region. When the

emperor Anastasius learned what had happened at
Jerusalem, he prepared by force to condemn to exile
both Archbishop John and Theodosius and Sabas, who
152,15   had ascended the pulpit with the archbishop.

57. PETITION TO THE EMPEROR

When this plan became known in Jerusalem, those
captains of the monks, combatants for piety, and gener-
als and champions of orthodoxy Theodosius and Sabas
assembled together all the monks of the desert and,
152,20   being of one mind, wrote and sent to the emperor the
following petition or plea:

*TO THE MOST DEAR TO GOD and most pious emperor,
by God's will Augustus and Imperator, Flavius
Anastasius the lover of Christ, a petition and supplication from the archimandrites Theodosius and
Sabas, other superiors, and all the monks inhabiting*
152,25   *the holy city of God, the whole desert round it and the
Jordan.*
*The universal king of all, God and Master Jesus
Christ, the only-begotten Son of God, has entrusted the
scepter of empire over all, after himself, to your rule*
153.   *dear to God, out of a desire to bestow the great gift of
peace through Your Piety on all his most holy churches
and in particular on the mother of the churches, Sion,
in which the great mystery of piety for the salvation of
the world was manifested and accomplished and then,*
153,5   *beginning from Jerusalem, through the divine and
evangelical preaching raised up the light of the truth to
all the ends of the earth.*[a] *Of this venerable and extraordinary mystery of Christ, through the victorious*

a. Cf. Ac 1:8.

*and venerable Cross and the life-giving Resurrection
and indeed all the holy and revered places, we the inhabitants of this holy land have all received, from the
original beginning through the blessed and holy*
153,10 *Apostles, the true and not illusory confession and faith.
This in Christ we have kept, and by the grace of God
always shall keep, unharmed and inviolable, "not
frightened in anything by the opponents," according to
the apostolic exhortation,*[b] *nor "tossed to and fro by*
153,15 *every wind of doctrine through the cunning of men,
through the malice"*[c] *of those who by soul-destroying
and deceitful sophistries "deceive the hearts of the
simple-minded"*[d] *and disturb the pure and unadul-
terated flow of the true faith with their evil opinions.*
153,20 *Since Your Christ-loving Imperial Highness was born
and reared by the grace of God in this holy and unim-
peachable faith and received from God, as we believe,
authority over virtually all lands under the sun, we are
amazed at how in the time of your rule, dear to God,
such disturbance and turmoil has poured over the holy
city of God Jerusalem, increased to such excess*
153,25 *that the mother of all the churches, Sion, and the holy
shrine of the Resurrection of our God and Saviour, the
refuge and retreat of all those from the whole world*
154. *who have been wronged or need salvation, have become a public market and profane place, in that the
high-priest who presides in the image and place of
God, the ministers who serve round him, and even
those who have entered on the solitary life, are before
the eyes of pagans, Jews and Samaritans openly and by*
154,5 *force expelled from holy Sion itself and the venerable
shrine of the Resurrection, swept through the midst of*

b. Phil 1:28.
c. Eph 4:14.
d. Rom 16:18.

*the city to profane and impure places, and compelled
to do things harmful to the faith, with the consequence
thereafter that those who are present or have been present for the sake of prayer return to their own lands*

154,10   *filled with scandal instead of with benefit and
edification.*

*If it is on behalf of the faith that all this trouble has
been stirred up against the holy city of God Jerusalem,
the eye and luminary of the whole world, the recipient
of the word of the gospel, if indeed , according to the
prophetic saying, "out of Sion shall go forth the law*

154,15   *and the word of the Lord from Jerusalem,"[e] and if her
inhabitants touch as it were with their own hands the
truth each day through the venerable places in which
was wrought the mystery of the incarnation of our
great God and Saviour, how then, more than five hundred years since the coming of Christ, are we of*

154,20   *Jerusalem to learn the faith? In consequence, it is easy
to perceive that the correction proposed now, forsooth,
to the earlier faith in Christ is the teaching not of the
authentic Christ but of Antichrist, who seeks to confound the unity and peace of the churches of God and
fills all with turmoil and anarchy. The originator and
perpetrator of all this is Severus, Acephalos and Apos-*

155.   *chist from the original beginning, who for the destruction of his own soul and of the commonwealth has by
God's leave for our sins been appointed bishop of Antioch and has anathematized our holy fathers who in
every way confirmed the apostolic faith defined and
transmitted to us by the holy fathers assembled at*

155,5   *Nicaea and baptize all in it. Shunning and utterly
rejecting communion and union with this Acephalos,
we entreat Your Piety to have pity on Sion, the mother
of all the churches and protector of your rule dear to*

e. Is 2:3.

155,10
God, who is being so ignominiously maltreated and ravaged. Deign to decree that the storm hanging over the holy city of God be entirely prevented.

If life and death depend on our account of the faith, it is death that we prefer. We shall never in any way or for whatever reason enter into communion with the enemies of the Church of God and their futile anathe-

155,15
mas; instead, we shall maintain with God's help the apostolic faith, "in which we stand and exult in the hope of the glory of God."[f] We the inhabitants of this holy land all share with God's help one mind and one

155,20
faith; in one spirit and mind we gladly accept four holy councils equal in glory and bearing the venerable impress of the Gospels, assembled by divine inspiration at various times and places against the multifarious errors of the heresies in question, yet differing only in expression and not in meaning, like the image and meaning of the Gospels engraven by God. Of these holy councils surpassing is the radiance of the above-

156.
mentioned choir of the three hundred and eighteen holy fathers that assembled at Nicaea against the most godless Arius; this council was followed in all respects by the three other holy councils, i.e. that of the one hundred and fifty which assembled against the enemy of

156,5
the Spirit Macedonius, the later one that convened at Ephesus against the accursed man-worshiper Nestorius, and equally the subsequent one that gathered in the city of Chalcedon to confirm the anathema against the impious Nestorius and to expel and anathematize the godless Eutyches. Since through these four holy councils we the inhabitants of this holy land have all

156,10
received, as we have repeatedly said, the unique, apostolic faith and with God's help are firmly rooted in it, no one will be able in whatever way to unite us to any-

f. Rom 5:2.

one who is of a different mind and does not obey these
councils, even if countless deaths are impending.

156,15   For the assurance of Your Majesty, let us add to the
above the following. Anathema, as with every heresy
against Christ our God, be Nestorius and anyone who
holds his views or considers the one Lord Jesus Christ,
the Son of God, the only-begotten, crucified for us, to
be two sons or who splits up the divine and incom-
prehensible union into two separate natures or who in
156,20   any way or for whatever reason assents to such madness. Anathema, together with him, also to Eutyches,
who treats the divine incarnation as mere illusion or
involving change, who anathematized and totally denied the difference between the divinity and the humanity of the one sole Jesus Christ, true God, in the hypostatic union free of both division and confusion, and
157.   who was anathematized together with the godless Nestorius himself by the above-mentioned holy fathers.

Your Serenity, on receiving favorably the written assurance of this petition from the humility of us all, will
deign to decree that from now on must cease the reck-
157,5   less misdeeds and continual disruptions perpetrated
each day against this holy city of God and our most
pious archbishop John by the enemies of the truth in
the name, allegedly, of Your Piety, once Your Majesty
has been convinced before God and the elect angels
157,10   that in no way nor for any reason do we accept union
with the said Aposchists, without a lawful and canoni-
cal decision, and that neither do we agree to any innovation respecting the faith for whatever reason nor
will we accept the forcible ordination at whatever time
of one of the Acephaloi. If some such misfortune should
occur on account of our sins, we assure Your Piety
157,15   before the holy and consubstantial Trinity that the
blood of all of us will willingly be shed and all the holy
places be consumed with fire before such a thing come

to pass in this holy city of God. For what benefit is there in the bare title of the holy places if they are so ravaged and dishonored? "The peace of God which

157,20 *passes all understanding will guard"*[g] *his holy Church and put an end to the scandals pressing upon it, at the command of Your Majesty, to his glory and for the vaunting of your reign, dear to God.*

158. Our fathers sent a copy of this petition to John, at this time on the death of Timothy ordained bishop of Constantinople. On receiving the supplication, the emperor Anastasius, being under pressure from the attacks of

158,5 Vitalian's barbarians, was advised to leave them at rest for the time being,[79] and so John was not ousted from the see of Jerusalem. But I must now bring to an end the collective combats of our holy fathers and, returning to the sequence of the account devoted solely to

158,10 our holy father Sabas, relate by the grace of God his noteworthy personal achievements.

58. CONFIDENCE IN TIME OF FAMINE

This angel on earth and heavenly man Sabas, the wise and knowledgeable teacher, the advocate of orthodoxy and accuser of heresy, who proved to be a

158,15 faithful and prudent steward,[a] who multiplied the talents of God,[b] who was clothed with power from on high,[c] by the favor of God the Father, the assistance of Christ, and the inspiration of the Holy Spirit colonized the desert with a huge number of monks, and founded

g. Phil 4:7.
a. Cf. Lk 12:42.
b. Cf. Mt 25:14-17.
c. Cf. Lk 24:49.

in it, in the manner above described, seven famous monasteries, which are as follows: among the lauras, his Great Laura, which has first place above all the 158,20 lauras of Palestine, the New Laura, second after it in rank, and the one called Heptastomus; among the cenobia, those of Castellium and of the Cave and those named after Scholarius and Zannus. He gave no 159. less assistance to the two ancient cenobia of our holy fathers Euthymius and Theoctistus.

Though exercising the care and oversight of these seven monasteries, he totally declined to secure them an income. Nevertheless, relying on faith and confi- 159,5 dence in God, he never fell into despondency through anxiety, and this specially in the time of the famine. At the same time as the exile of Archbishop Elias the sky was closed from raining on the earth for five years, and in addition to the drought there was a fierce infestation of many locusts and countless caterpillars, so that the 159,10 whole face of the earth failed. In the year after the locusts, came a further infestation of locusts, who covered the sky and ate all the trees of the field. There resulted severe famine and loss of life, so that the people of Jerusalem said that these ills had descended on account of the sin committed over Archbishop Elias. At 159,15 this time our sainted father Sabas exhorted the leaders of his monasteries never to be anxious about things of the flesh; and he reminded them of the saying of the Lord that runs: 'Do not be anxious, saying, What shall we eat? or, What shall we drink? or, What shall we wear? For your heavenly Father knows that you need all these things. But seek first the kingdom of heaven, 159,20 and all these things shall be added to you.'[d] These were the thoughts and teaching of this godly old man. God provided his every need without stint, so that it was

d. Mt 6:31-33.

those who relied on property and income who fell short rather than the monasteries in his care.

159,25   In this same time of famine the steward of the Great Laura came to him and said, 'Father, we cannot, strike the summoning-block this Saturday or Sunday, since we have nothing, not even water for the assembled fathers to rinse their mouths.' The elder answered him, 'I shall not prevent the liturgy of God. If you lack any of the requisites, the precentor will send to the city a precious vessel or vestment by the monk responsible for offerings. He will sell it to buy what you lack, so that

160   we can perform the liturgy of God.' But faithful is he who said, 'Do not be anxious about tomorrow.'[e] On the Friday there arrived some victualers of the holy city, those called 'the sons of Sheshan,'[f] with a convoy of

160,5   thirty animals, bringing wine, loaves, grain, oil, honey and cheese. They filled the storeroom with good things of every sort and prepared a great banquet for the fathers. The elder chided the steward in these words: 'What have you to say, lord steward? Are we to stop the striking because the fathers do not have water to rinse their mouths?' The steward came to his senses

160,10   and threw himself at his feet, begging to receive forgiveness. The elder blessed him and admonished him with the words, 'Never doubt but, fortified by faith, cast all your anxiety on God, for he cares about you.'

59. THE SHEPHERDS NEAR THE CAVE

    On one occasion the fathers living in the monastery

160,15   of the Cave came to the holy elder to say that they suffered much annoyance from some shepherds who re-

e. Mt 6:34.
f. 1 Chr 2:31.

peatedly pastured their flocks on the monastery estate
and impudently demanded victuals, 'with the result
that they leave us no peace.' On learning this, the elder
wrote to rebuke them and tell them no longer to go

160,20   near the monastery. When they disobeyed, suddenly
the udders of their animals stopped bearing milk, as a
result of which the newly born kids and lambs were
perishing of hunger. At this the goatherds, coming to
their senses and reasoning that disobedience was the
cause of the deaths among their animals, came at a run
to the elder and, falling at his feet, promised him no

160,25   longer to go near any of his monasteries. Accepting
this undertaking, the elder uttered prayer on their behalf and sent them away with a blessing. When they
returned, they found the milk coming forth without
hindrance and, on inquiry, learnt that the milk had be-

161.   gun to flow and come forth at the very hour that the
elder uttered prayer and blessed them. Filled with
wonder, they gave glory to God.

60. DEATHS OF ELIAS AND ANASTASIUS

Our sainted father Sabas, in the eightieth year of his

[AD 518] life, around the summer solstice of the eleventh indic-
161,5   tion, went to Aila to see Archbishop Elias, by divine
providence, and took with him Stephen superior of the
monastery of the great Euthymius, and Euthalius superior of the monasteries of blessed Elias himself at
Jericho. They were received joyfully by Elias, who
kept them with him for some days. During this time he

161,10   would not appear to them from the end of vespers till
the ninth hour of the following day; at the ninth hour
he would emerge, communicate with them and eat, and
retire again after vespers. With this as his pattern, it
happened that on 9 July he did not emerge as usual;

when the three fathers waited, without communicating
161,15   or eating anything, he emerged at the sixth hour of the
night and said, 'As for yourselves, do eat. I myself do
not have the leisure.' When Saint Sabas detained him
and forced him somehow to say what the matter was,
he burst into tears and said, 'At this very hour the emperor Anastasius has died, and I must depart without
161,20   fail after ten days and be judged together with him.' He
made dispositions concerning his own monasteries,
that after the death of Euthalius Nestabus and
Zacharias should succeed in turn as superior, so that no
one should presume to separate these monasteries from
each other. After making these dispositions and passing eight days after the vision content with communion
only and mixed drink,[80] he fell mildly ill. After Sabas
and his companions had kept at his side for three days,
162.   then, on 20 July, after communicating, praying and
saying the Amen, he both fell asleep and rested in
peace,[a] after a total lifespan of eighty-eight years.

Noting the day, the blessed Sabas, on returning to
162,5   Jerusalem, learnt that in the night of 10 July when
blessed Elias had the vision, thunder and lightning en-
veloped the imperial palace, and consumed the emperor Anastasius and him alone. He fled in panic from
room to room, till the wrath of God overtook him in
one of the bedrooms, hurled him down and killed him,
162,10   a victim of sudden death. When Anastasius had died in
this way, Justin, on succeeding to the throne, immediately issued decrees ordering all those exiled by Anastasius to be recalled and for the Council of Chalcedon
to be inserted in the sacred diptychs.[81] When the
decrees of the emperor Justin reached Jerusalem, there
162,15   gathered an infinite multitude of monks and laypeople,
there assembled in haste Saint Sabas and the synod of

a. Cf. Ps 4:8(9).

bishops, and, at a festival on 6 August, the imperial decrees were published and the four councils inserted in the sacred diptychs.

61. SABAS AT CAESAREA AND SCYTHOPOLIS

162,20

At this juncture Archbishop John of Jerusalem persuaded our sainted father Sabas to proceed to Caesarea and Scythopolis with some other superiors of the desert in order to publish the letter of the emperor and insert the four councils in the sacred diptychs in both cities. Reaching Caesarea, they were met by the sainted John

162,25

of Choziba, who had been appointed bishop there. After fulfilling their instructions there, they went to Scythopolis, where all the citizens together with the most holy metropolitan Theodosius came out to meet them at the apostolic shrine of Saint Thomas. They

163.

made their entry with psalms, the liturgy was celebrated in the ancient church,[82] the imperial letter was read out, and the four councils were inserted in the sacred diptychs.

There was at Scythopolis a lawyer called John, the son of the collector of tax arrears,[83] a wise man in-

163,5

spired in soul, who came to see Saint Sabas in the bishop's palace and spoke at length about Silvanus the Samaritan,[84] who at that time exercised some authority as an imperial dignitary and was plotting against the Christians, describing his wickedness and war against God. On hearing this, our sainted father Sabas was

163,10

filled with the Holy Spirit and said to the bishop and those present, 'Behold, the days are coming, says the Lord, when the fifty-first Davidic psalm shall be fulfilled in the case of Silvanus by his being consumed by fire in the middle of the city.'[a] This was the prophecy he made about Silvanus.

62. THE WOMAN WITH A HAEMORRHAGE

163,15   There is a monastery there called Enthemaneith, in the district around the church of Saint John,[85] in which there was an anchorite named John, who was inspired in soul and full of the charism of second sight, although he had lost his bodily sight as a result of his all-night vigils, abundant tears, and extreme old age. They say that he had passed his hundredth year and 163,20 spent eighty years in this monastery, during fifty of which he had never gone outside. As the sainted elder was on his way to this holy man and was passing through the middle of the city, by the so-called Apse of Saint John, a woman with a haemorrhage, who had been ill for many years and had become so malodorous 163,25 that no one could bear any longer to go near her, was lying in the western colonnade of the street. She had heard about our sainted father Sabas and, when she saw 164.   him pass accompanied by a crowd, cried out, 'Have mercy on me, servant of God Sabas, and deliver me from the affliction that besets me.' Yielding to her cries and taking pity on her, he came over to her in the colonnade and said, 'I have nothing to supply you with, 164,5   but what I have I give you.[a] This my hand I lend to you: place it on the spot of your pain, and I trust in the God I worship that you will be cured.' Taking the saint's hand, she applied it to the hidden spot and immediately the flux of her blood ceased and the woman was cured from that hour. This miracle, as you know, 164,10   venerable father, is to this day venerated among us.

a. Cf Ps 52:1-7(51:3-9).
a. Cf. Ac 3:6.

63. THE GIRL POSSESSED BY A DEMON

In this metropolis there was a man who had a daughter possessed by a demon. Full of faith, he brought her to the elder in this same monastery of Enthemaneith and recounted to him the outrages inflicted on her by the foul demon. The miracle-working old man had 164,15 compassion on him and asked for oil from the all-holy Cross. Taking the girl and her father into a garden apart and telling her to undress, he anointed her whole body from tip to toe, front and back.[86] Immediately the impure spirit was banished from her and the little girl was 164,20 healed from that hour. My father, called John, was an eyewitness and minister of the miracle and from this day did not leave the holy elder all the time of his stay there. During this time our house was honored by his visits, and my mother enjoyed his prayer and blessing. 164,25 May Your Piety not be surprised if I have included in this composition addressed to you some facts of which you possess accurate knowledge, of which indeed my knowledge may well derive from you. I have done this with a view to a single goal, venerable father: the benefit of my readers.

64. HIS FASTING AND FEASTING

165. On his return from Scythopolis the sanctified Sabas was invited to dinner by Archbishop John, who also invited other superiors of the desert and his brother Antony, bishop of Ascalon.[87] The sanctified Sabas in 165,5 addition to the other charisms had obtained this one: although he was so abstinent as to pass the whole of Lent foodless without getting at all exhausted though often laboring in the burning heat and had learnt to fast on weekdays throughout his whole life, if ever he was entertaining anyone or was found at a festal meal, he

165,10   would eat twice in one day and partake beyond satiety
without harming his stomach. Making him sit at his
side, the archbishop had in front of him rolls and other
things provided, while Bishop Antony of Ascalon, at
his right side, pressed him equally. The godly old man
165,15   ate everything laid before him in a honest and
straightforward way. As the two brother bishops had
him between them and devoted themselves to pressing
food on him, he said to them, if I may record his very
words, 'Leave me, fathers. I shall help myself to as
much as I need.' The great Abba Theodosius, present
165,20   on this occasion, said graciously, 'Lord Sabas is so
hungry that both of you, who after God are feeding
Palestine during the present famine in particular, are
competing in helping him eat.' The archbishop replied,
'Concede, fathers, that, while all of us can bear neither
fasting nor satiety, this man of God possesses the apostolic charism of "knowing how to be abased and how
to abound, in all and any circumstances having learnt
166.   both to feast and to hunger, to abound and to be in
want, and to have strength for everything through
Christ who empowers him."'[a]

65. SABAS AND THEODOSIUS

Our father Sabas was humble of spirit, gentle in conduct and most simple in character, full of complete
166,5   spiritual prudence and discernment. He maintained the
most unfeigned and sincere love towards the above-
mentioned Abba Theodosius, while he in his turn
maintained the same sincerity towards our father
Sabas. Truly both were 'sons of light and sons of day,'[a]
166,10   men of God and faithful servants, 'shining luminaries

a. Phil 4:12-13.
a. 1 Thess 5:5.

in the world, proffering the word of life,'ᵇ 'pillars and
bulwark of the truth,'ᶜ both being men of higher
desires. They led all the monks towards the kingdom of
heaven. The sainted Theodosius was leader and archimandrite of all the cenobitic order subject to th'e
166,15   holy city, as was said above, while the sanctified Sabas
was ruler and lawgiver of all the anchoritic life and of
all those who chose to live in cells. These two archimandrites had been appointed by the sainted Sallustius at the request of the whole monastic order as
being true hermits and men detached, and as having
been strictly trained in the things of God, attained
166,20   monastic strictness and guided many towards the
knowledge of God. They could be seen visiting each
other and conversing together frankly with spiritual
affection. In these conversations the sanctified Sabas
frequently addressed to Theodosius, now among the
saints, the following remark: 'My lord Abba, you are
166,25   the superior of children while I am the superior of superiors, for each of those under me, in his independence, is the superior of his own cell.'⁸⁸ Theodosius
167.   would reply to this, 'I shall take your remark as being
not harsh but utterly charming, for friendship will endure all it experiences or hears.' So much for these
men.

66. THE MIRACLE OF RAIN AT THE CAVE

When already the fourth year of drought was drawing
[AD 520]   to a close,⁸⁹ the disciples of the sanctified father i
167,5   the Cave came to see him at the Great Laura and said,
'Give us permission to leave, father, for we cannot stay

b. Phil 2:15-16.
c. 1 Tim 3:15.

in your monastery since we have no water at all, and
now that May is over the season of rain is closed.' After partly rebuking them and partly admonishing them
167,10   to submit with thanksgiving to whatever was im-
minent, the saint said, 'I have faith in God that in three
days' time all your cisterns will be full. So go and repair the conduits. Get yourselves ready, and you will
behold the gift of God and his speedy visitation.' On
the third day a cloud was seen above the cenobium
167,15   alone, there was heavy rain, and all its cisterns were
filled in accordance with the saint's prophecy.

     In the monasteries either side of the Cave, those of
Castellium to the east and of Scholarius to the west at
roughly five stades' distance, and in the Great Laura to
the south-west no drop of rain fell. The leaders of these
167,20   monasteries came aggrieved to the elder and said,
'What is our sin, venerable father, that you have rejected us in this way by not praying for your other
monasteries?' The saint answered them, 'It is to those
in need that God has sent his blessing. You yourselves
should not be despondent, for you will not lack water
till the Lord sends rain on the earth.'

67. THE MIRACULOUS ENDING OF THE DROUGHT

167,25   At the beginning of the fifth year of famine[90] such
was the lack of water that the poor of the holy city
168.   were begging for water and perishing of thirst. Because
of the long-continued dryness and lack of rain, the
water had disappeared from Siloam and Lucillianae,[91]
and even the springs of Colonia and Nephthous had
diminished. The archbishop, fearing a revolt of the
168,5   people, went round the more humid spots, using a large
work-force to dig ditches in the hope of finding water,
but did not find any. Descending into the gorge of

Siloam near the cave of Saint Cosmas by the road to
the Great Laura, he employed an engineer and a mass
168,10   of workmen to dig down two hundred feet; on not finding water he was distressed, especially since the Feast
of the Dedication was near. Using Summus as his
adviser,[92] a man of considerable experience who had
held various urban magistracies, he expressed his
perplexity as follows: 'What shall I do, with September
having already begun and the city still without water?'
Summus replied, 'I have heard of Abba Sabas that a
168,15   short time ago, when one of his monasteries had run
short of water, heavy rain fell around the monastery in
distress exclusively, filling all its cisterns, on his being
petitioned thirst, weak. Who am I to have the power to
avert the wrath of God, by its inmates and praying.' On
hearing this, the archbishop summoned blessed Sabas
168,20   to his palace as if on some other matter, and taking him
aside exhorted him to entreat God to be reconciled to
his people and have mercy on mankind perishing of
famine and thirst; he added, 'If I have sinned, what has
that to do with the people who are perishing?' Saint
168,25   Sabas replied, 'I am a sinner and weak. Who am I to
have the power to avert the wrath of God, specially
when Scripture says, "If he closes" the sky, "who will
open?"'[a] When the archbishop had uttered many words
169.   of exhortation, the inspired Sabas finally yielded,
saying, 'See, I shall return to my cell and in obedience
to Your Beatitude entreat the face of God. I know that
he is kind and merciful and that "his compassion is on
169,5   all his works."[b] All the same, let this be the sign: if
these three days pass without rain, know that God has
not listened to me. You too must pray, to ensure that
my prayer is heard.' With these words he left his

a. Job 12:14.
b. Ps 145(144):9.

presence, on 3 September. On the following day, in intense heat the mass of workmen worked in the 169,10 above-mentioned ditch and went off in the evening, leaving all their many tools and baskets since they expected to return to the work in the morning. In the first hour of the night a south wind began to blow, there was thunder and lightning, and rain cascaded down, so 169,15 that before dawn the conduits were filled to the brim and torrents poured from all sides. As the water rose at the spot of the ditch, the mounds of earth raised with such expenditure of time, labor, and money were swept in one moment into their ditch, covering ladders, tools, 169,20 and baskets, and have stayed there to this day. Because of the quantity of water and the help of God the spot of the ditch was so leveled and smoothed as not to be recognizable, the cisterns of the holy city were filled to the brim, and the Feast of the Dedication was celebrated with joy and gladness.[93]

68. THE CURE OF THE SISTER OF THE PATRIARCH PETER

170.   In the eighty-sixth year of the life of our father Sabas, Archbishop John, having completed the seventh year and seventh month of his patriarchate, and leaving the most blessed Peter, of Eleutheropolis by birth, as 170,5 his successor in the high-priesthood, died on 20 April [AD 524] of the second indiction. Three years later the Roman emperor Justin, being an old man and oppressed by bodily weakness, by God's decree and the consent of the whole senate, Archbishop Epiphanius of Constantinople laying on hands, elevated to the throne his 170,10 nephew Justinian, our divinely protected emperor, who was a patrician, consul, and commander-in-chief and had a firm grip on the affairs of state.[94] He promoted

170,15   him emperor, as has been said, in the month of April of
the fifth indiction on Holy Thursday. Four months later
on 2 August Justin of pious memory, after completing
nine years on the throne, came to the end of his life.
But we must return to the life of the old man.

170,20   The thrice blessed Peter, having obtained the patriarchal throne of Jerusalem, paid the same honor as the
previous patriarchs to the blessed Sabas and frequently
showed eagerness in descending to the desert to visit
him. This patriarch had a sister in the flesh called
Hesychia, outstanding in godly virtues. When she fell
victim to a dire illness and was despaired of by the
doctors, her brother, overcome by sympathy, sent for
blessed Sabas and begged him to take the trouble to go

171.   to her house and say prayers for her. The saint, not
knowing how to refuse, went to see her and, finding
her despaired of, said prayers for her, sealed her three
times with the sign of the cross, and restored her to

171,5   health. When the miracle was reported throughout the
holy city, all gave glory to God.

69. THE FOUNDATION OF THE MONASTERY
OF THE EUNUCHS

When the patrician Juliana, mentioned above,[95] after
doing many good works in Constantinople reached the
end of her life, her eunuchs came to Jerusalem and,
being acquainted with Abba Sabas since Constan-

171,10   tinople, came to him at the Great Laura, bringing much
money and asking to be enrolled in his community.
The old man had decided not to admit an adolescent or
eunuch into the laura, for he could not bear to see a
feminine face in any of his monasteries and specially
in any laura whatever; nevertheless, since they were

171,15   acquaintances, and after reassuring and edifying them

in every way, he entrusted them to the blessed
Theodosius. They, after receiving a monastic formation
for a short time, asked the archbishop to give them a
place to live on their own. The archbishop, summoning
one Alexander, superior of the monasteries of Arch-
171,20   bishop Elias near Jericho and the successor of Nestabus and Zacharias, asked him to receive them for a
short time as guests. Alexander, whether enslaved by
avarice or possessed by vainglory, setting aside the
injunctions of Archbishop Elias and trampling on his
own conscience, separated his monasteries; and from
then on the separated monastery has received the name
171,25   of the monastery of the Eunuchs.

70. THE SAMARITAN REVOLT

At the beginning of the ninety-first year of the life of
our holy father Sabas, the sainted Abba Theodosius
came to the end of his life on 11 January of the seventh
[AD 529]   indiction, 'an old man and full of days.'[a] Sophronius,
172.   venerable for monastic attainments, succeeded him as
superior. In the fourth month after Abba Theodosius'
death, the Samaritans of Palestine[96] marshalled their
whole race against the Christians and performed many
172,5   lawless acts: pillaging and setting fire to the churches
that fell into their hands, mercilessly killing by various
tortures the Christians who fell into their hands, and
setting fire to whole estates, specially in the region of
Neapolis. Thereupon in usurpation they crowned a king
for themselves, one Julian of their race. Then they
slaughtered Bishop Mamônas of Neapolis and, seizing
172,10   and butchering some priests, roasted them together
with remains of holy martyrs. They performed many

a. Gen 25:8.

such acts, so that the so-called imperial highroads became unusable and impassable for the Christians.
When all this came to the ears of our most pious em-
172,15   peror Justinian, the most glorious counts Theodore and
John received orders to gather an army and march
against the Samaritans; a battle ensued, in which Julian
and a great mass of Samaritans with him were killed.
At this juncture Silvanus, mentioned above, coming as
if peaceably to Scythopolis without an imperial order,
172,20   was seized by the Christians and burnt in the middle of
the city, fulfilling the prophecy concerning him made
in the bishop's palace to John son of the *compulsor* by
our sainted father Sabas. One Arsenius, a son of the
burnt Silvanus and having the rank of *illustris*,[97] who
173.   was at this time living in Constantinople and enjoyed, I
know not how, easy access to our divinely protected
emperor and the empress Theodora, used misinforma-
tion to stir their Piety into anger against the Christians
173,5   of Palestine. At this juncture Archbishop Peter with the
bishops under him asked our father Sabas to go up to
Constantinople and beg the emperor to grant remission
of the taxes of First and Second Palestine on account of
the murders and destruction perpetrated by the
Samaritans. Yielding to the instances of the bishops,
173,10   the old man went up to Constantinople in April of the
[AD 530] eight indiction.

71. SABAS AT THE COURT OF JUSTINIAN

The patriarch having sent letters in advance to the
emperor announcing godly Sabas' arrival, our
divinely protected emperor, overjoyed, sent the imperial galleys to meet him; with them went out to
173,15   meet him the patriarch Epiphanius, father Eusebius and
Bishop Hypatius of Ephesus. Receiving him, they led

him in to the emperor, and God revealed the grace accompanying his servant to the emperor as he had done previously in the time of Anastasius. For as he entered the palace with the said bishops and came within the curtain, God opened the emperor's eyes; he saw the radiance of divine favor in the shape of a crown blazing forth and emitting sunlike beams from the head of the old man. Running up, he greeted him with reverence,[98] kissing his godly head with tears of joy; on obtaining his blessing, he took from his hand the petition from Palestine and pressed him to go in and bless the Augusta Theodora. The elder went in and was received with joy by the Augusta, who greeted him respectfully and made this request: 'Pray for me, father, that God grant me fruit of the womb.' The elder answered, 'God the Master of all will guard your empire.' The Augusta said again, 'Pray, father, that God give me a child.' The elder said in reply, 'The God of glory will maintain your empire in piety and victory.' The Augusta was grieved at his not granting her request. So when he left her presence, the fathers with him expressed their doubts by asking, 'Why did you distress the Augusta by not praying as she requested?' The elder answered them, 'Believe, me, fathers, fruit will never come forth from her womb, lest it suck in the doctrines of Severus and cause worse upheaval to the Church than Anastasius.'[99]

They were invited to lodge in the palace. When the divinely protected emperor received from the godly old man the petition of the churches of Palestine, his anger against the Samaritans returned. He was roused into issuing a decree or law that Samaritan assemblies should cease, that they should be expelled from the whole country, and that they should not have the right of bequeathing to their coreligionists or making transfers to each other in the form of gifts; he also decreed the death penalty against them, specially their leaders guilty of lawlessness. At this juncture, with the em-

174,20   peror ordering his execution, Arsenius disappeared for a time; but later he took refuge with the blessed Sabas, while he was still staying in the imperial city, and was baptized, both himself and his whole household.

72. HE PRESENTS REQUESTS TO THE EMPEROR

A few days later the emperor summoned the sanctified Sabas and said to him, 'I have heard, father,

175.   that you have founded many monasteries in the desert. For whichever of them you wish, ask for a revenue for the needs of the inmates and we shall provide it, so that they may pray for the state entrusted to our care.' Sabas replied, 'Those praying for Your Piety do not

175,5   need such a revenue, for their portion and revenue is the Lord, who in the desert showered bread from heaven and poured forth quails for a disobedient and refractory people.[a] We however, all-pious emperor, for the support of the holy churches of Palestine request a

175,10   remission of taxes, rebuilding of the sacred edifices burnt by the Samaritans, and assistance for the reduced and plundered Christians of Palestine. We also beg you to found a hospital in the holy city for the care of sick

175,15   strangers, and to build and appoint the church of the Mother of God whose foundations were laid some time ago by our archbishop Elias, for this is specially appropriate for Your Piety; and on account of the inroads of the Saracens we beg Your Serenity to order the most glorious Summus to build at public expense a fort in the desert at the foot of the monasteries founded by your humble servant. I believe that God, in return for

a. Cf. Ex 16:4-13.

175,20   these five acts of yours pleasing to him, will add to your empire Africa, Rome and all the rest of the empire of Honorius, which were lost by the emperors who reigned before Your all-pious Serenity, in order that you may extirpate the Arian heresy, together with those of Nestorius and Origen, and free the city and the

176.   Church of God from the bane of the heresies.'

I shall explain why he asked the emperor to expel these three heresies in particular. He mentioned the heresy of Arius, because at this time the Goths, Visi-

176,5   goths, Vandals and Gepids, who were Arians, were ruling all the west, and he knew for certain through the Spirit that the emperor was going to conquer them. He named the heresy of Nestorius, because some of the monks who had accompanied him had been found siding with Theodore of Mopsuestia when disputing with the Aposchists in the basilica.[100] He included the

176,10   destructive heresy of Origen in the rejection of the said heresies, since one of the monks with him, Byzantine by birth and named Leontius,[101] who was one of those admitted with Nonnus into the New Laura after the death of the superior Agapêtus, had been found embracing the doctrines of Origen; though claiming to

176,15   support the Council of Chalcedon, he was detected holding the views of Origen. On hearing this and remembering the words of the blessed Agapêtus, our father Sabas, acting with severity, expelled both Leontius and those with the views of Theodore and excluded them from his company, and asked the emperor

176,20   to expel both heresies.

73. THESE REQUESTS ARE GRANTED

All these requests of our father Sabas were fulfilled without delay by our most pious emperor, and all his prophecies were accomplished by the benevolent God, as we shall discover clearly in what follows. First, im-

176,25   perial orders were sent to Archbishop Peter and the governors of Palestine, decreeing that Bishops Antony of Ascalon and Zacharias of Pella inspect the buildings

177.   burnt by the Samaritans in First and Second Palestine,

AD 530/2 and that thirteen hundred pounds of gold coin be re-remitted from the taxes of the ninth and tenth indictions in proportion to the damage suffered in each place. Next he ordered them to inspect the burnt houses

177,5   of prayer and to determine the sums to be given for the restoration of each sacred edifice, and that these sums be provided out of either public funds or the property of the Samaritans by the eminent count Stephen, who was also ordered to rescue the bishops with whatever

177,10   help they needed. As regards the old man's third request, he ordered a hospital of one hundred beds to be built in the center of the holy city,[102] assigning it a tax-free income for the first year of 1850 *solidi*; he ordered the same hospital to expand subsequently to two hundred beds, adding the same income, regular and

177,15   tax-free. He displayed much zeal in fulfilling the fourth request of the old man, and sent an architect called Theodore to Jerusalem to build the new church of the holy mother of God and ever-virgin Mary, ordering the treasury officials of Palestine to provide money for the building; while assigning the overall authority to Arch-

177,20   bishop Peter, he charged Bishop Barachus of Bacatha with the supervision of the building works. And so through the zealous use of a large work force the new church of the mother of God and ever-virgin Mary, worthy of all praise, was in twelve years built, richly appointed and consecrated.[103] It is superfluous to de-

177,25   scribe the size, dazzling splendor and rich decoration of this venerable edifice, since it stands exposed to our

178.   eyes and surpasses all the ancient sights and accounts

that men marvel at and the Greeks have recorded in their histories. This was the fruit of the fourth request of the godly Sabas. Attending also to the fifth request of the godly Sabas, our most pious emperor sent a decree to Summus, ordering Abba Sabas to be provided with one thousand *solidi* from the revenue of Palestine for the construction of a fort and with a military guard to protect his monasteries, supported from public funds.

178,5

While our divinely protected emperor was engaged in these matters with the quaestor Tribonian,[104] in the so-called Magnaura,[105] the blessed Sabas drew slightly apart and recited Davidic psalms to himself, performing the divine office of the third hour. One of his disciples called Jeremias, deacon of the Great Laura, came up to him and said, 'Revered father, when the emperor is displaying such zeal in fulfilling your requests, why do you yourself keep to one side?' The elder answered him, 'They, my child, are doing their work. Let us in our turn do ours.'

178,10

178,15

74. SABAS RETURNS TO PALESTINE

The emperor, after making all these arrangements and giving his rescripts to the holy old man, sent him on his way in peace. God gave the emperor an infinite recompense by fulfilling the prophecy of the old man. For the emperor erected two trophies a short time later by being crowned with two victories such as had never been achieved by any of his predecessors; he recovered Africa and Rome from the rule of usurpers and saw the two kings, Witigis of Rome and Gelimer of Africa, brought to Constantinople. Thus in a short time he recovered for the Roman empire the half part of the land and sea; and after liberating all the west from

178,20

178,25

179.   slavery to the said usurpers who were Arians, he issued
          imperial decrees that the churches of the Arians should
          everywhere be destroyed, following the orders or at
          least the prophecy of the godly old man. In addition,
179,5   nobly exerting himself, he overthrew and anathe-
          matized the heresies of Nestorius and Origen both by
          the edicts he issued and through the fifth holy ecumeni-
          cal council lately assembled at Constantinople; but this
          we shall treat later.

          The godly old man, after expelling from his com-
          munity, as has been said, both Leontius of Byzantium
          and the adherents of Theodore of Mopsuestia, and
179,10   leaving them in Constantinople, sailed back to Pales-
[AD 530] tine in the month of September of the ninth indiction.
          Arriving at Jerusalem, he published the imperial
          rescripts, and distributed to his monasteries the money
          he had brought from Byzantium. At this the above-
179,15   mentioned deacon Jeremias, upset at the distribution of
          money, left the Great Laura and settled in a desert
          gorge about five stades to the north of the Cave. Our
          father Sabas visited him and was overjoyed on seeing
          the place. Taking suitable men, money and materials,
179,20   he built by great exertion in a few days a small oratory
          there and various cells; he provided brethren to live
          there, entrusting their direction to Jeremias and giving
          them the rules of his own Great Laura. So by the grace
          of God he made the place a laura. This laura still flour-
179,25   ishes, and is named after blessed Jeremias.

               75. SABAS AT SCYTHOPOLIS, AND CYRIL

               When the imperial rescripts had been published at
          Jerusalem, as has been said, our father Sabas, at the
180.   request of our archbishop and the other bishops, pro-
          ceeded to Caesarea and Scythopolis to publish the

same rescripts there as well. As he arrived at Scythopolis, as you know, the metropolitan Theodosius with all the people came out to meet him, including my
180,5   father, who had authority in the episcopal palace at this time as the metropolitan's assessor. When the imperial rescripts had been published, the great old man, taken into the episcopal palace, stayed in the monastery there of the holy martyr Procopius, having my father as constant companion. I myself, a small boy then, on being found with my father and falling at the feet of the
180,10   godly old man, was blessed, raised up and embraced by the holy elder, who said to my father, 'From now on this boy is my disciple and a son of the fathers of the desert.' And he said to the metropolitan, 'My great lord, I commend this boy to you. Attend to him, be-
180,15   cause I need him.' This was announced to my mother, my father telling her, at which she wanted to pay her respects to the saint. When he was on the point of going to the district of Saint Thomas to see Abba Procopius the solitary, my mother, on hearing of it, informed by my father, went with me to this apostle's church. When the old man arrived there, my father
180,20   took him aside and introduced my mother to pay her respects. When the elder learned that she was a servant of God,[106] he gave her his blessing. Looking at me, he said, 'Look, here is my disciple Cyril!' When I prostrated myself, he blessed me and, raising me up, said to my father, 'Teach him the Psalter, because I
180,25   need him. From now on he is my disciple.' Having said this, he blessed her and sent her on her way, while keeping me and my father with him. After going in to see Abba Procopius and eating there, we returned to the episcopal palace. On the following day, just before journeying to Jerusalem, the old man came with my
181.   father to our house, and said a prayer and blessed my father, my mother, and myself. He then left

Scythopolis, accompanied by the fathers with him.

I believe, venerable father, that you told me you knew all this, when you advised me to enter the laura of blessed Sabas.[107] At any rate, when I said that the New Laura was also his foundation, particularly once the supporters of Origen had been expelled, you replied, 'Yes, yes, I am well aware of the fact. But it is better for you to enter the laura that bears his name. And I know that this will happen in any case, in order that our great father Sabas may be shown to be a prophet in this too.' This is what you said to me; as for myself, I am ready, God willing, to build myself a cell in this same Great Laura and make it my dwelling, in order to fulfil both his prophecy, as has been said, and the command of Your Piety.

From that time the metropolitan often said courteously to my father, 'How is the disciple of Abba Sabas?' At the same time he would press him to teach me the Psalter and St Paul. And so he blessed me and gave me the tonsure, placing me in the initial ecclesiastical grade.[108]

After the publishing of the rescripts and the inspection of the devastation that had occurred, a tax remission of twelve hundred pounds was granted to First Palestine, as containing all Samaria. In the territory of Scythopolis, since not much devastation had occurred there, the bishops decided to grant remission of only one hundred pounds. Applying a considerable sum of money on behalf of the churches burnt down, the Palestinian bishops were liberal in rebuilding every church burnt down and embellishing them with appropriate furnishings.

181,5

181,10

181,15

181,20

182.

76. THE DEATH OF SABAS

182,5

182,10

182,15

182,20

183.

On completing his service on behalf of the Christians, the great champion of piety Sabas returned to Jerusalem and was received joyfully by the patriarch. After venerating the holy places and as if saying goodbye to them, he went to his Great Laura, where a short time later he fell ill. On learning this, the most holy bishop Peter came to examine him and, seeing he had no comforts in his cell except a few carobs and old dates, placed him on a litter and brought him to the episcopal palace, where he looked after him and ministered to him with his own hands. After a few days had passed, our father Sabas saw a vision which revealed that his death would occur in a few days' time; announcing this to the archbishop, he asked to be allowed to return to his own laura in order to die in his cell. The archbishop, wishing to serve him in every way, sent him to his own laura with the tending he needed. Once lying in his tower, the old man, at the beginning of December, summoned the fathers of the laura and gave them as superior a monk of Berytus by birth, called Melitas, telling him to guard inviolate the traditions handed down in his monasteries and giving them to him in writing.[109] After continuing for four days without taking any food or conversing with anyone, late on Saturday at the dawning of the next day he requested and received communion. Then, after saying finally, 'Lord, into thy hands I shall commit my spirit,'[a] he gave up his soul.

a. Ps 31:5 (30:6).

77. BURIAL OF SABAS

So it was that our father Sabas, after fighting the good fight, completing the race, and keeping the faith,

183,5   was adorned with the crown of righteousness.[a] His death occurred on 5 December of the tenth indiction, in

[AD 532]   the year 6024 since the creation of the world, when time began to be measured by the course of the sun

183,10   and in the year 524 since the Word of God became man from the Virgin and was born in the flesh, according to the chronologies composed by the holy fathers Hippolytus the Ancient, the disciple of the Apostles, Bishop Epiphanius of Cyprus, and Hero the philosopher and confessor. The chronology of his life in the flesh is as follows. He came to Palestine at the

184.   age of eighteen and lived seventeen years in the cenobium and passed fifty-nine years in the desert and at the Great Laura. He died in the ninety-fourth year of his life, in the second year after the consulship of Lampadius and Orestes and in the sixth year of the present divinely protected reign.[110]

The news of his death circulated through all the surrounding region and brought together an immense crowd of monks and lay people. The most holy arch-

184,5   bishop Peter also arrived with the available bishops and the leading men of the holy city. And so his precious remains were laid to rest in the Great Laura between the two churches, in the spot where he had seen the pillar of fire. This saint did not die, however, but is asleep, having lived an irreproachable life and been pleasing to God, as

184,10   as it is written, 'The souls of the just are in the hand of God and death shall never touch them.'[b] Certainly his body has been kept sound and incorrupt to this day. This I witnessed with my own eyes in the recent tenth indiction.

a. Cf. 2 Tim 4:7-8.
b. Wis 3:1.

78. APPEARANCE OF SABAS TO A SILVERSMITH

184,15

For when the precious tomb was opened in order to lay to rest the remains of blessed Cassianus, I descended in order to venerate the body of the godly old man and found it had remained sound and incorrupt. In my amazement I gave glory to God who had glorified his servant and honored him with incorruption before the general and universal resurrection. So much for the

184,20

holy remains. As for his spirit, it has been privileged with great access to God,[111] the radiance of which I shall try to show by a few examples.

There is in the holy city a silversmith, of Damascus by birth, named Romulus, archdeacon of holy Geth-

185.

semane. This Romulus told me the following story: 'At the time of the death of blessed Sabas, my shop was burgled and I lost nearly one hundred pounds of silver. Going at once (he continued) to the shrine of St Theo-

185,5

dore, I supplied illumination for the church for five days and stayed there day and night weeping on the sanctuary rails. Around midnight of the fifth day I was rapt in sleep when I saw the holy martyr of Christ Theodore, who said to me, "What is the matter? Why are you in such distress, and weeping?" I replied, "I have lost my own property and that of others, and I

185,10

have spent days here without gaining anything." The saint said to me, "Believe me, I was not here, but I was ordered to hasten to meet the holy soul of Abba Sabas and guide it to the place of repose.[112] But now, go to this place and you will find there the thieves and the money." Getting up at this very hour and taking

185,15

some others with me, I went to the place announced by the saint, and we found it just as had been announced in the vision.'

79. APPEARANCE TO THE BROTHERS OF BURIRAI

A certain two blood-brothers, who originated from the village of Burirai in the plain, had faith in Saint Sabas. Consequently, when members of his mon-

185,20 asteries came this way on business, they would receive them in faith and look after them, eagerly contributing their own labor in a manner pleasing to God. As the result of some satanic action both of them became so ill at harvest time that their household despaired of them. Grieved at the loss of the harvest and remember-

185,25 ing Abba Sabas, they called to their aid his intercession. And he appeared to each of them on his own, and said, 'See, I have prayed to God for your health, and he has granted my request. Therefore in the name of Jesus Christ the true God, rise and go to your work.' They

186. recovered their strength at once and went to their work, announcing the miracle to their household. Since then, on the anniversary of the miracle they celebrate a public festival for all on their estate.

80. APPEARANCE TO SOME WEAVERS

A woman who originated from our mother-city, and was called Genárous, had decided to make two

186,5 curtains[113] for Castellium and the Cave. When everything was ready for the work, the women who had agreed to do the weaving reneged on the agreements made, at which Genárous was very upset. The blessed Sabas appeared to her in her sleep, and said, 'Send for the weavers in the morning, and they will come and

186,10 carry out the work. Do not be upset, for your offering will not be hindered.' He also appeared to the weavers likewise, annoyed at the delay in the work. Early next day they all came in joy and eagerness, relating to each

other their visions. And so they carried out the work, giving thanks to God.

81. THE MIRACLE OF THE CAMEL

186,15   A considerable time later, the steward of the Great Laura hired Saracen camels to convey from the Dead Sea the grain bought at Machaerous. When the camels arrived laden at the laura, one of them, straying to the right of the road leading up to the guest-
186,20   house, fell laden from the cliff into the gorge, the cliff having a depth of about ten times a man's height. The master of the camel, a Saracen, cried out, 'Abba Sabas, your prayers must help my camel.' And as the camel rolled down, he shouted, 'Abba Sabas, help!' And he saw an elder of sacred appear-
186,25   ance sitting on the camel as it rolled. Descending by another path at a run and getting near the camel, he did not find the elder sitting on it but the camel safe and sound with its load. Raising the animal and leading it by a gentler path up to the guest-house, he unloaded it. Out of wonder at the extraordinary character of the
187.   miracle, this barbarian comes to the laura each year to venerate the tomb of the old man and provide the steward of the time out of his own labor a small gold coin in thanksgiving.

82. MIRACULOUS ESCAPE OF AUXENTIUS

187,5   At this time a large cistern was built below the tower of our sainted father Sabas in the cave where there was a secret passage from the church built by God to the said tower. In the rock above, the fathers built a reser-

voir at a height in order to strain the water in it first
and then let it down into the cistern. One Mamas of
187,10 Bethlehem, a plasterer by trade, did the work on the
cistern and the reservoir. Mamas, in directing the appointment of the reservoir, had a boy called Auxentius
as his apprentice. There arose a storm, filling the reservoir with water; when the water reached its maximum,
the work on the reservoir collapsed. Mamas, as a full-
187,15 grown man, was able to escape the danger easily, but
the boy was caught by the fall of the stones and of the
mass of water and swept along with them from the cliff
down into the courtyard between the two churches,
where lie the precious remains of our holy father
Sabas; the height of the cliff is about fifty feet. After
187,20 the rain had ceased, the boy was found beneath the fallen stones in front of the church built by God without
any injury at all. I myself was a witness of this miracle,
having come at the time to the Great Laura from the
New Laura, in order to get a spot where I might build
myself a cell.

Of the miracles of the godly old man I have selected
187,25 and recorded these few out of many. But now the time
calls me to give a partial account of what happened to
his successors and disciples.

83. RECRUDESCENCE OF ORIGENISM[114]

Abba Melitas, the successor of the godly old man,
188. had given to Archbishop Peter, whether out of indiffer-
ence or inexperience, the thousand *solidi* given by
Summus for the building of a fort in accordance with
the imperial order, and so the building of the fort was
prevented. The patriarch, on receiving the thousand
solidi, distributed them among various monasteries.
When this Abba Melitas took over the flock of the

188,5 godly old man in flourishing condition, wolves were about to ravage it, had it not been rescued by the oversight of the chief shepherd, Christ our God. I shall say briefly how and in what way this occurred.

While our all-praiseworthy father Sabas was still in the flesh, there was one confession of faith in all the monasteries of the desert, and one could see all the

188,10 children of Jerusalem walking in the house of God in concord, upholding in harmony the inviolable and irrefragable character of the divine doctrines, so as to fulfil the scriptural saying, 'Lift up your eyes round about; and behold, your children are gathered together.'[a] [115] But when the excellent shepherd left this world, his flock, being led by an inexperience

188,15 shepherd, fell into difficulties. Nonnus and his party, taking advantage of the death of our father, I mean Sabas, made public the heresy in the depths of their hearts and instilled in their neighbor a turbulent upheaval. They seduced into their own foul heresy not only all the more educated in the New Laura but also

188,20 those of the monastery of Martyrius and of the laura of Firminus, at a time when its fathers Firminus and Sozomen, the disciples and fellow-combatants of the godly old man, had already died.[116] In addition, they succeeded in a short time in sowing the heresy of Origen in the Great Laura and the other monasteries of

188,25 the desert. At this same time Domitian, superior of the monastery of Martyrius, and Theodore surnamed Ascidas, who ruled over those of the New Laura, both of them partaking to satiety of the plague of Origen,

189. sailed to Constantinople, where they pretended to be battling for the Council of Chalcedon.[117] Through recommendation by the above-mentioned Leontius of Byzantium they attached themselves to father

a. Is 60:4.

Eusebius[118] and through him to our most pious
emperor. Veiling their heresy by abundant hypocrisy
189,5   and enjoying immediate access to the palace, Domitian
received the first see of the province of Galatia,[119]
while Theodore succeeded to the see of Caesarea of
Cappadocia. Nonnus and his party, gaining greater
strength from this, were zealous and tireless in sowing
the seeds of Origenism throughout Palestine.

84. THE ORIGENISTS ASSEMBLE
AT THE NEW LAURA

189,10   After ruling the flock of Abba Sabas for five years,
Abba Melitas died. Since blessed Theodulus, several
times mentioned above, had also died, his brother
Gelasius[120] succeeded to Abba Sabas' post as superior
[AD 537] at the beginning of the fifteenth indiction. When he
189,15 became superior and saw the plague of Origen with
many of his community in its grip, Gelasius, sharing
the views of the inspired John bishop and solitary, and
having as his allies one Eustathius, a scribe of Galatian
birth, Stephen of Jerusalem, and Timothy of Gabala,
189,20 who to this day is resplendent with virtues in Scetis,
had read out in church the work of the sainted Bishop
Antipatrus of Bostra[121] against the doctrines of Origen.
Incensed by this, those who had embraced this soul-
destroying heresy caused a disturbance in the church.
The leader in this perversion was one John, deacon and
189,25 precentor of the laura, Antiochene by birth, who had
been deposed from his sacred office by the fathers because of his heresy and was conspiring with John nicknamed Demon of Thunder, Ptolemy and others; these
190.   men held unauthorized assemblies and tried to pervert
many souls. At this the fathers by common consent
expelled them from the laura individually, their number turning out to be around forty. They went off to the

New Laura to join Nonnus and Leontius of Byzantium
who had at this stage returned from Constantinople and
190,5 was raging against the successors of blessed Sabas, and
inveighed against Abba Gelasius and the fathers of the
Great Laura.

When all the leaders of the hersy had assembled
there, Leontius of Byzantium, who had long been hostile to the blessed Sabas, urged them all to exercise
190,10 self-will to the extent of demolishing the Great Laura
and making it uninhabitable. He gathered at the New
Laura all those from everywhere who adhered to this
heresy; once assembled, these men accompanied Leontius and the expelled monks to the monastery of
blessed Theodosius, hoping to seduce the celebrated
190,15 Sophronius, superior of the monastery, and the fathers,
but their plan was frustrated and they went away
humiliated. Then, enraged with Gelasius and the Great
Laura, Leontius and his party sent to various places
and collected pick-axes, shovels, iron crowbars and
other tools of demolition, together with a work-force of
190,20 peasants; with these they set off in utter fury to
demolish the Great Laura. But the God of Abba Sabas
worked a great miracle. At the second hour of day
there descended on them mist and darkness; after
wandering at a loss for the whole day through rough
and impassable places, as we learnt from some with
precise knowledge, they found themselves with diffi-
190,25 culty on the following day at the monastery of blessed
Marcianus.[122] And so, seeing again the common light,
they returned home humiliated at achieving nothing.
This miracle was worked by the God of marvels, who
opposes the proud and dispenses his grace on the
humble, and who struck the opponents of Lot[a] and
Elisha[b] with blindness.

a. Cf. Gen 19:11.
b. Cf. 2 Kgs 6:18.

85. AN IMPERIAL EDICT AGAINST THE ORIGENISTS

191.   At this time there arrived in Palestine the patriarch of
          Antioch Ephraem and father Eusebius on account of
          the deposition of Bishop Paul of Alexandria.[123] When
          father Eusebius came to Jerusalem after the dissolution
191,5   of the council, Leontius presented to him those ex-
          pelled from the Great Laura, who accused Gelasius of
          dividing the community into two halves and of expell-
          ing them while currying favor with their opponents.
          Father Eusebius, misled by Leontius' words and know-
          ing nothing of their heresy, sent for Abba Gelasius and,
191,10   in an attempt to resolve the dispute, pressed him either
          to receive back those expelled or to expel their op-
          ponents. In the face of such pressure the fathers, after
          deliberation, sent out of the laura Stephen, Timothy,
          and four others of the brethren, who, putting up with
          their voluntary exile, went off to Antioch, where they
191,15   informed Patriarch Ephraem of what had happened and
          showed him the work of blessed Antipatrus. The
          patriarch, reading of the blasphemies of Origen in the
          work given him, and learning from those who gave it
          of the actions of the Origenists at Jerusalem, was
          stirred to courageous action, and by a public anathema
191,20   of synodical authority condemned the doctrines of
          Origen.[124]
          When this became known at Jerusalem to the vexa-
          tion of Nonnus and his party, they, in alliance with
          Leontius of Byzantium, who had sailed back to Con-
          stantinople, Domitian of Galatia, and Theodore of
          Cappadocia, pressed Archbishop Peter to remove
191,25   Ephraem's name from the sacred diptychs. At their
          causing this great discord, the archbishop sent secretly
          for Sophronius and Gelasius and told them to compose
          a petition against the Origenists, adjuring him not to
          remove Patriarch Ephraem's name from the sacred dip-

191,30   tychs. When the fathers had composed this petition and presented it, the archbishop on receiving it sent it to the emperor with a letter telling him of the innovations of the Origenists. On receiving this petition, our most

192.   pious emperor issued an edict against the doctrines of Origen, to which edict Patriarch Menas of Constantinople and the synod under him appended their signatures.[125] Domitian and Theodore were also forced

192,5   to sign, but their hypocrisy became obvious to all. For after signing, Domitian, learning that some of the Origenist heretics had managed to evade signing, fell into distress and anguish and, cutting off his beard, separated himself from the catholic communion, and so died of dropsy in Constantinople excommunicate; to

192,10   the hypocrisy of Theodore bears witness the fierce persecution he initiated against the orthodox after he had given his signature.

86. ASSAULT ON THE GREAT LAURA

The edict against Origen was published in Jerusalem in the month of February of the fifth indiction in the

[AD 543]   eleventh year after the death of our father Sabas. Al

192,15   the bishops of Palestine and superiors of the desert appended their signatures to it, apart from Bishop Alexander of Abila. In indignation Nonnus, Peter, Menas, John, Callistus, Anastasius, and other leaders of the heresy left the catholic communion and,with-

192,20   drawing from the New Laura, settled in the plain. When this news reached Constantinople, where father Eusebius and Leontius had already died, Theodore of Cappadocia, who controlled the palace, summoned the legates of the holy church of the Resurrection[126] and

192,25   said to them in great anger, 'If Patriarch Peter does not satisfy the fathers and receive them back into their own

laura, I shall make him at this very time an ex-bishop.'
At this the party of Nonnus, on the advice of the said
Theodore surnamed Ascidas, wrote to the archbishop
as follows:

193. *We beg Your Piety to satisfy Your minds with a*
      modest assurance by making with all readiness
      a universal proclamation to this effect: 'Every
      anathema not pleasing to God that has been
      made is to be abrogated, and has been abro-
      gated, in the name of the Father and of the Son
      and of the Holy Spirit.' We shall be satisfied
      with this assurance, even though it lacks strict
      precision.

On receiving this letter, the archbishop would not at
first agree to provide the assurance requested as being
harmful and illicit. But fearing the intrigues of Ascidas
193,10 and wishing to make use of the occasion, he summoned Nonnus and his party from the plain, took them
privately aside and gave them the assurance requested.
Reassured thereby, they returned to the New Laura,
and stayed there, bitter in their opposition to the fathers
of the Great Laura.
193,15   Then Ascidas forced Archbishop Peter, who had
gone up to Constantinople, to take as chancellors Peter
of Alexandria and John Strongulus, while he made
John the eunuch, who ruled the monastery of Martyrius, superior of the New Church.[127] This gave Non-
193,20 nus and his party greater confidence in proclaiming
their impiety publicly and from house to house and in
plotting various persecutions against the fathers of the
Great Laura.[128] If they saw an orthodox monk in the
holy city, they would get some persons of the world to
assault him and insult him as 'Sabas's man,' and so
drive him from the holy city. When several of the or-

193,25   thodox fathers had been assaulted and war had started against the pious, the Bessi of the Jordan,[129] incited by godly zeal, came up to the holy city to help the orthodox who were being warred against. Open warfare was waged against the Bessi and the rest of the orthodox

194.   and, when they took refuge in the hospice of the Great Laura, their adversaries descended on them suddenly, wishing in their utter fury to kill the fathers. Finding the hospice secured, they broke open the windows with stones and mercilessly stoned those within. While the fathers were being besieged, a Bessan called Theo-

194,5   dulus, finding a flail and taking it in his hands, slipped out of the hospice and scattered their adversaries unassisted, although they were around three hundred. He took care not to strike anyone at all; but being himself struck by them with a stone, he fell, and died a few

194,10   days afterwards. This quenched the war against the pious, except that the broken metal jamb of the sale room bears witness to this day against the savagery of those adversaries.

87. APPARENT TRIUMPH OF THE ORIGENISTS

At this juncture the fathers of the Great Laura begged Abba Gelasius to go up to Constantinople and make all

194,15   this known to our most pious emperor. Just before he set off, Abba Gelasius assembled the fathers in the church of the Great Laura, greeted them warmly, and made the following announcement; 'See, fathers, at your request I am going up to Constantinople, not knowing what will happen to me on the journey. I therefore beg you not to let settle with you any ad-

194,20   herent of Theodore of Mopsuestia, who was a heretic, since our sainted father Sabas abhorred him along with Origen.[130] I myself regret deeply having appended my

signature to the petition made by the desert at the order
of the patriarch against his being anathematized. God,
194,25   however, out of care for his Church, so disposed that
the petition was rejected and willed that Theodore himself be anathematized.' After this speech to the fathers,
Gelasius took his leave and departed. When he arrived
at Byzantium, Ascidas was informed of his arrival, and
195.   those of the orphanage, the patriarchal residence, and
the palace were told not to receive a monk from
Jerusalem. So Abba Gelasius, unable to gain entrance
anywhere and fearing the intrigues of Ascidas, left
Byzantium for Palestine, making the journey by foot.
195,5   On reaching Amorium he died, in the month of Oc-
[AD 546] tober of the ninth indiction. When the fathers of the
Great Laura learnt of this, they went up in one accord
to the holy city to ask for a superior; but when they had
told this to the patriarch, they were expelled from the
episcopal palace with violence and blows on the orders
of the chancellors. After suffering many trials as a
195,10   result, they returned to the laura without success.

At this time all had gone over to the Origenists,
whether yielding to necessity or seduced by flattery or
misled by ignorance or in fear of the power wielded by
impiety. And so the heretics, in control of everything,
concentrated their forces against the Great Laura alone
195,15   and took great pains to gain control of it. By extensive
intrigue they got an Origenist called George made superior; conveying him to the laura under protection of
an armed guard, they sat him on the throne of our
sainted father Sabas in the month of February of the
[AD 547] ninth indiction. At the coming of the wolf there ensued
195,20   a great persecution that scattered our holy fathers. Our
inspired father John, bishop and solitary, left his hermitage after many years and withdrew to the Mount of
Olives; with him departed all the nurslings of piety, of
195,25   whom many were scattered through the countryside.

196.   But God worked a great prodigy as formerly in the case of Arius. On the very day of the persecution in which they were expelled from the Great Laura, the chief of the enemy and general of impiety Nonnus was snatched from among men and seized by sudden death.

88. CASSIANUS SUPERIOR OF THE GREAT LAURA

The most oppressive wolf George, after ruling the holy flock of the godly Sabas for seven months, was
196,5   expelled from it by his own supporters on the charges of profligacy and foul conduct; I shall gladly pass over these charges in silence, in order not to publish in my account things deserving deep silence and oblivion. At this the fathers left at the Great Laura, on the advice of the patriarch, took as superior Abba Cassianus of
196,10   Scythopolis, who at this time was governing the community of Souka ably and with orthodoxy. He was a man who had made his renunciation at a tender age and been formed by the godly Sabas; he had become a priest of the Great Laura, governed the laura of Souka for eight years and founded the monastery at Scy-
196,15   thopolis called Zougga. After shepherding the holy flock of the godly old man for ten months, Abba Cassianus both fell asleep and rested in peace[a] on the
[AD 548]   twentieth of July of the tenth indiction in the sixteenth year since the death of the great Sabas.

89. SCHISM AMONG THE ORIGENISTS

The fathers of the Great Laura were now inspired by
196,20   God to make Abba Conon superior, a man celebrated

a. Cf. Ps 4:8(9).

for monastic attainments and orthodox doctrines. Of
Lycian birth, he had practised the monastic life in his
fatherland from childhood and had excelled in many
godly combats; going to venerate the holy places after
196,25   the death of blessed Sabas and led by God to enter the
Great Laura, he edified all the fathers by purity of life,
simplicity of character, gentleness of conduct and a
combination of spiritual understanding and discernment. Taking over the flock of blessed Sabas dimin-
197.   ished and reduced, Abba Conon increased it, made it
eminent, and brought back from all parts the fathers
scattered through the countryside.

At this juncture God, who always exercises provi-
197,5   dence on behalf of his Church, dissolved the concord
of the Origenists, just as long ago in the time of Eber
he divided the languages and broke up the alliance
against God.[a] For when Nonnus was out of the way,
the members of the laura of Firminus quarreled with
those of the New Laura over their own doctrines and
were wholly engrossed in warfare against each other.
197,10   The fissiparous impiety of both has been recorded at
the present time in a more detailed and comprehensive
account by some men, dear to God, of our flock, receiving the refutation it deserves.[131] Whoever wishes
may easily discover their impiety from the very names
197,15   they give each other, those of the New Laura calling
those of Firminus' 'Protoktists' or 'Tetradites' and
those of Firminus' naming those of the New Laura
'Isochrists;' for each was allotted a name from the particular doctrines of their impiety.[132] Theodore of Cappadocia, who was in control of the affairs of state and
197,20   belonged to and supported the party of the Isochrists,
had many of them ordained bishops of Palestine and
made Theodore superior of the New Laura be ap-

a. Cf. Gen. 10:25, 11:9.

pointed guardian of the Cross and metropolitan of
Scythopolis. This brought storms and waves against
not only our flock but also that of the adherents of the
most impious doctrine of the Protoktists, whose superior was Isidore. This Isidore, unable to withstand Ascidas and the monks of the New Laura, came over to
the shepherd of our flock Abba Conon and, giving him
his word by holy Sion that he did not hold the doctrine
of preexistence but would oppose the impiety with all
his strength, went up with him to Constantinople at the
beginning of the fifteenth indiction.

90. THE COUNCIL OF CONSTANTINOPLE
AND THE VICTORY OF ORTHODOXY

On arriving at Constantinople, Abba Conon's party
was subjected by Ascidas to a variety of trials, but
through endurance came out victorious. For when a
short time afterwards, at the death of Archbishop Peter,
Macarius was ordained through the wilfulness of the
monks of the New Laura and war resulted in the holy
city, the most pious emperor, fiercely incensed against
Ascidas and the Origenists, gave orders for Macarius to
be ousted from the episcopacy.[133] Abba Conon's party,
seizing the opportune moment, informed the emperor
of their situation and presented him with a petition
revealing all the impiety of the Origenists, Isidore having died. Then, employing complete frankness,[134] they
proposed Eustochius, administrator at Alexandria, who
was at Constantinople, as bishop of Jerusalem. Our
most pious emperor decreed that Eustochius should
become patriarch, and gave orders for there to be an
ecumenical council. Abba Conon, when sending Eustochius on his way to Jerusalem, asked him to send
Eulogius, superior of the monastery of blessed

198,25 Theodosius, so that he too should be present at the council that was assembling. Eustochius, entering onto his patriarchate, sent three bishops to take his place at the council, and also sent Abba Eulogius with two other superiors, Cyriacus of the laura called 'The Spring' and one Pancratius, a stylite.[135]

199.   When the fifth holy ecumenical council had assembled at Constantinople, a common and universal anathema was directed against Origen and Theodore of

199,5   Mopsuestia and against the teaching of Evagrius and Didymus on preexistence and a universal restoration, in the presence and with the approval of the four patriarchs.[136] When our divinely protected emperor sent to Jerusalem the acts of the council, all the bishops of Palestine confirmed and approved them orally and in writing, except Alexander of Abila, who was there-

199,10 fore expelled from the episcopacy and was finally buried by an earthquake in Byzantium. The monks of the New Laura, however, separated themselves from the catholic communion. The patriarch Eustochius treated them with respect and for eight months used advice and exhortation with them; but on failing to persuade

199,15 them to be in communion with the catholic Church, he applied the imperial commands, and got the *dux* Anastasius to expel them from the New Laura and free the whole province from their destructive influence. Not wishing to leave the place uninhabited, he chose one hundred and twenty monks and transplanted them there, sixty from the Great Laura, from whom he or-

199,20 dained a former *scholarius* called John to be superior,[137] and another sixty from the other orthodox monasteries of the desert; I am one of these, summoned from the monastery of Saint Euthymius by the fathers of the Great Laura on the advice and with the leave of the inspired John, bishop and solitary. Assem-

199,25 bled accordingly in the holy city, we set off with the patriarch and the new superior to the village of Thekoa and, when the Origenists had been expelled by the *dux*

200.

AD 554/5

Anastasius, we took over the New Laura on 21 February of the second indiction in the twenty-third year since the death of blessed Sabas.[138] So it was that the war against piety came to an end.

200,5

I myself, on the point of stopping my account of the godly old man, shall utter appropriately the prophetic saying, 'Let the desert rejoice and blossom like the lily,'[a] for God has had mercy on its children, saying of himself, 'Looking, I have beheld the affliction of my people in Jerusalem and heard their groaning, and I

200,10

wish to deliver them.'[b] Having wished, he has visited us; and having visited us, he has rescued and redeemed us from the power of the Origenists. He has driven them from our presence and enabled us to inhabit their habitations. The fruit of their labors he has allotted to us, so that we may observe his commandments and

200,15

study his law. To him be the glory for ever and ever. Amen.

HERE ENDS THE LIFE
OF OUR FATHER SAINT SABAS

a. Is 35:1.
b. Cf. Ex 3:7-8.

NOTES

1. The Prologue is modeled in part on the *Life of Thecla*, Prologue 9-21. To the promise given in the *Life of Thecla* to provide 'details of places, persons and names', Cyril also promises information about 'times'. This addition shows his interest in chronology. For the parallels between the two works, see Flusin 43-86.

2. The Greek manuscripts provide chapter headings only for the *Life of Euthymius*. This, and all subsequent headings have been added by the translator.

3. Compare *Life of Euthymius* 8.25 with note 6. The births of both saints are compared with that of Samuel.

4. John's regiment is a *numerus* or barbarian unit within the imperial army which retained a distinctive national style of dress and combat.

5. Since Sabas arrived in Jerusalem when he was 18 after having spent 10 years at Flavianae, this episode took place when he was 8. See 90,5.

6. Sabas' cousin, Gregory, settled in the Monastery of the Tower (128,16-25). He was a valuable source for Cyril since he could give information about Sabas' early life.

7. Elpidius had been a leader of the Monophysite party but was persuaded by Euthymius to accept the Chalcedonian faith. See 44, 4-5.

8. An 'order' in Jerusalem was a group of ascetics attached to a church who assisted in its liturgical life and ministered to pilgrims and those in need. Theodosius was attached to the 'order' at the church of the Anastasis (236,12).

9. The rank of 'senator' in a regiment was two grades below that of 'tribune', the post held by Sabas' father. It was a generous offer to make to a young man.

10. In the account of Theoctistus' death (at 54,13-24) the date is given as the fifth indiction.

11. Chapters 11, 12, and 14 show Sabas receiving power from God in order to overcome the three main dangers of desert life: thirst, wild beasts, and barbarians.

12. 'Boy elder' translates '*Paidariogerôn*'. The word is almost a proverb and is found in Palladius, *Lausiac History* 42.15 and other places. See A-J. Festugière, 'Lieux Communs' 137-139.

13. The same story is told in the *Life of Euthymius* 56,19-57,12.

14. A quotation from the *Life of Antony* 9 in which devils appear as wild beasts.

15. The Church of the Cathisma is about two miles south of Jerusalem on the way to Bethlehem. Today it is called Ramat Rahel. See Ovadiah 152 and Vailhé 20.

16. Vailhé suggests that this cistern is that built by Eudocia within sight of Euthymius' monastery (53,10) since the Metaphrastic text of the Life of Sabas give the distance of the cistern as 'fifty stades'. But this is too far from Sabas' cave. A closer location is to be preferred. See Vailhé 54.

17. The arrival of the first monks is a significant moment in the development of Sabas' monastery. In describing it, Cyril is influenced by Theodoret's *History of the Monks of Syria* 1.3 and 2.4, Nilus of Ancryra (PG 79:760C), and the

First Greek Life of Pachomius 24.

18. 'Grazer' or *boskos* describe those ascetics who lived off the wild plants they found. The area around the Great Laura contained many wild plants which made this way of life possible. Evagrius (*Ecclesiastical History* 1.21) regards 'grazers' as extreme ascetics, but the frequency of reference to them in the Palestinian sources suggests that this form of the ascetic life was common in the Judaean Desert.

19. Of the monasteries mentioned here only the New Laura was a Sabaite foundation (122,19-123.18). The Laura of the Towers near the Jordan is 'to be distinguished from the Cenobium of the Tower (127.15-128.23). This Laura appears in Vailhé's list as 135. For Caparbaricha, see 22,16 and 124,18 and Vailhé 115. For the monastery of Firminus at Machmas see Vailhé 43 and Ovadiah 48. For the Laura of Neelkeraba see Vailhé 85.

20. Ascetics were often reluctant to accept ordination. Three Nitrian monks cut off their ears in order to prevent themselves being consecrated bishops (*Historia Monachorum* 20.14).

21. The purpose of the towers which were often built in monasteries is debated. Probably they were built for defensive purposes or for the residence of the abbot. See Festugière, 'La vie de Sabas et les tours de Syrie Palestine'.

22. Presumably the rebels hoped that Sallustius would be more sympathetic to them than Martyrius who, as one of Euthymius's monks, would have known of Sabas.

23. In the early Egyptian monastic circles it was a compliment to be called a 'rustic', which implied the peasant virtues of hard work and personal initiative; see *Apophthegmata Patrum*, Arsenius 5. It suggests here that Sabas is unfit to govern. There is some truth in this accusation. The account of Sabas' education suggests that it was limited to learning the monastic discipline and Cyril makes no reference to any education in Sabas' monasteries (87,25-88,1).

24. The fourteenth indiction was 1 September 490 to 31 August 491. Zeno died on 9 April 491, and Anastasius was crowned two days later.

25. There were many Armenians in the Judean Desert. Theodore of Petra (*Life of Theodosius* 45,5-18) tells us that worship in Theodosius' monastery was conducted in Armenian, Greek and Bessan. The Armenian speakers in the Great Laura later introduced Monophysite formulae into their worship. See 117,19-118,5.

26. Cyril wrote his Life of Sabas between 555 and 557. John died in 559. See 222,10-12.

27. For a similar story see *Apophthegmata Patrum*, Bessarion 4, which has close verbal parallels with this chapter.

28. Sabas' lenten practice is different from that of Euthymius, who used to withdraw to remote parts of the Desert. Chorsia was a thriving town on the eastern shore of the sea of Galilee. Heptapegus was an important pilgrim site, the reputed place of the feeding of the Five Thousand, on the shores of the sea of Galilee. Panias or Caesarea Philippi is further north, at the source of the Jordan near Mount Hermon. Journeys such as this would have added to Sabas' reputation throughout Palestine.

29. The provision of a guest-house shows the close connection between monasticism and pilgrimage. The monasteries both ministered to the pilgrims and received offerings from them.

30. The Hill of Castellium, or Khirbet Mird, was the site of the Herodian fortress of Hyrcania. It was an ideal site for a monastery as the rock formation provides large natural water-cisterns.

31. Cyril acknowledges his dependence on the *Life of Antony* in this passage. The description of the contact with the devils echoes the *Life of Antony* 6, 9, 14.

32. Remains of the church with its apse, sacristy, courtyard, and monastery buildings have been found on Castellium. The first structures of the monastery appear to have been built in waste land by unskilled workmen (Sabas' monks?). As well as Sabas' cenobium, the hill also became the site of a laura, which is mentioned by John Moschus, *Spiritual Meadow* 167. See J.T. Milik, 'The Monastery of Kastellion'.

33. Marcianus' earlier career is referred to at 49,11-13;66,24-67,13. During the Patriarchate of Sallustius he was accepted as archimandrite of the monks of Jerusalem. A possible site of his monastery is Khirbet Siyar el Ghanam, a traditional site of the Shepherds' fields two miles east of Bethlehem. The extensive remains include olive and wine presses, grain silos, a bakery and stables, as well as a church and living quarters. It was a thriving agricultural enterprise well able to provide support for monks toiling at Castellium, about ten miles journey distant—Vailhé 71, Ovadiah 126.

34. Amathus was near the Joradan in the province of Palestine 1; and Aila was on the coast of the Red Sea in Palestine 3, at the start of the important road through Arabia to Damascus.

35. Previously, newly-professed monks had been sent to a nearby cenobium. This new cenobium founded close to the Great Laura was dependent on the Laura and served as a place of preparation for novices.

36. Theodosius is shown to be dependent on the Euthymian monastic tradition. For Marinus and Luke, see 16,9-16.

37. The title 'archimandrite' could refer to any monk in a position of authority. Sabas' first monastery of Flavianae, for example, was governed by an archimandrite, see 90,10. In Jerusalem, an archimandrite's authority extended over all the monasteries dependent on the Holy City. As archimandrite, Sabas represented the interests of the monasteries in Jerusalem and at the Imperial Court at Constantinople.

38. This Anastasius is to be distinguished from the Anastasius who succeeded Juvenal as patriarch, 35,1-25 and 52,2.

39. The Tower of David on Mount Sion was a monastic quarter in Jerusalem which included hermits' cells, monasteries (including a large Georgian monastery) and guest-houses of the desert monasteries. See J.T. Milik, 'La topographie de Jerusalemvers la fin de l'époque byzantine', 187.

40. Peter the Fuller was a Monophysite who arranged for himself to be consecrated patriarch of Antioch during the absence of his predecessor Martyrius, in 469. He introduced the phrase 'who was crucified for us' after each of the three phrases of the Trisagion, 'Holy God, Holy Strong, Holy Immortal...'. The use of this form became a test of Monophysite sympathies and was the cause of

violence and rioting, especially in Constantinople. Peter was ejected from his position in 471 but was restored on two occasions, and was patriarch in 475-7 and 484-8. See Frend, *Rise of the Monophysite Movement* 167-70, 181, 190.

41. Gadara is twenty miles north-east of Scythopolis on the east bank of the Jordan.

42. The Feast of Dedication or Encaenia commemorated the dedication of Constantine's Churchof the Resurrection in 335. The celebrations began on 13 September and lasted for a week. The pilgrim Egeria (*The Travels of Egeria* 48-49) reports that forty or fifty bishops were present as well as monks from Egypt, Syria, and Mesopotamia.

43. Souka or the Old Laura was one of Chariton's three foundations. The numerous caves which formed the centre of the monastery can be seen in the valley south of Bethlehem which still bears the name of the founder, Wadi Khureitun. See Vailhé, 21, and Chitty, *The Desert a City* 14-16.

44. It was the site of Romanus' old monastery, mentioned at 49,12 and 67,17. It is located at Kasr el-'Abd. See M. Marcoff and D.J. Chitty, 'Notes on Monastic Research in the Judaean Wilderness 1928-9'; Vailhé 87; Ovadiah 93.

45. The influence of the Patriarch was weaker in the coastal plain. During the life of Euthymius the main centre of Origenism was in the region around Caesarea (39,27-28).

46. 'To make the desert into a city' is a phrase borrowed from the *Life of Antony* 14. It describes the process by which an ordered society is established in the desert, which had previously been occupied by wild animals, robbers and devils.

47. No trace of this monastery remains. A possible location is Bir al'Amara, on the slopes of Jebel Muntar, where there is a large cistern which could be that referred to at 167, 4-16. See Vailhé 123.

48. Zoilus was Patriarch of Alexandria from 540 to 551. He was Palestinian, Chalcedonian and the nominee of Justinian. As such, his hold on the loyalty of the Egyptian people was not strong.

49. Sebaste is the Old Testament Samaria, and Ascalon a sea-port near Gaza. The deacon John later became Patriarch of Jerusalem (150,8).

50. The second union is that under the Patriarch Martyrius (67,15). The first union was Eudocia's reconciliation with Juvenal (47,9).

51. Cyril has taken his doctrinal statements from Justinian's *Confessio Fidei* 92.

52. The *scholarii* were the seven troops of guards at the Imperial Palace.

53. For this cistern, see 98,19-20.

54. Cyril's fondness for calling Sabas an 'old man' (even when a youth, 89,24) is due to *saba* being the Syriac for 'old man', and the general middle eastern term for a monk.

55. No trace of this monastery remains.

56. Choziba is in the Wadi Kelt three miles west of Jericho. The monastery was founded between 420 and 430 by five Syrian hermits who built an oratory there. A laura was established by John of Thebes, who settled at Choziba in the late fifth century. John was later appointed Bishop of Caesarea (162,24). The monastery has always been famous for its hospitality. A new monastery on the

site was built between 1878 and 1901. See Vailhé 24, Ovadiah 37.

57. For other examples of objects blessed by monks being carefully preserved, see Theodoret, *History of the Monks of Syria* 9.15, where Theodoret's mother gives him Peter the Galatian's girdle as a cure for sickness.

58. The monastery of Calamon is five miles southeast of Jericho, at Deir Hajla. The *Life of Chariton* states that Chariton found hermits already living there when he arrived in the fourth century. Cyril stayed at it for six months before entering the monastery of Euthymius (216,24). Its name Kalamonia, or 'good abode', derives from a tradition that Joseph, the Holy Virgin and the child Jesus lodged there on their journey to Egypt. See Vailhé 16.

59. There are several similar stories in the literature of the monasteries, for example Gerasimus' lion, in John Moschus, *Spiritual Meadow* 107.

60. The following brief sketch of ecclesiastical politics points to the problems faced by the Emperor. On one side was Rome, for whom the Council of Chalcedon was an essential definition of the faith. On the other was Alexandria and its territory of Egypt, which revered the memory of Dioscorus and rejected Chalcedon. Anastasius' policy was based on Zeno's Henoticon which sought to re-unite the Eastern Empire by rejecting Chalcedon. But he succeeded only in antagonising Rome and failing to content the hard-line Egyptian Monophysites. A convenient summary of this phase of Imperial policy is in Frend, *Rise of the Monophysite Movement* 184-220.

61. A further problem faced by Anastasius was that the monks and citizens of Constantinople tended to support the Council of Chalcedon. Euphemius (490-496) was also a strong Chalcedonian. Macedonius, on the other hand, although sympathetic to Chalcedon, was prepared to accept the Henoticon.

62. The *silentiarion* is the same room as the consistory--a hall in which the emperor received visitors. On this occasion he seems to have received them only in an inner part of the hall. The *cubicularii* were the guards, and the *silentiarii* were attendants with the task of maintaining order.

63. Cyril's opinion of Anastasius is unclear. The Emperor is both the Monophysite who disturbs the church (139,25 and 141,17), but also the lover of monks who fulfils the requests of Sabas (142,10 and 20). Anastasius, aged 61 at his accession, was both pious and pragmatic. He disliked change and was impatient about disagreements over Chalcedon (Evagrius, *Ecclesiastical History* 3.30).

64. Ariadne was the daughter of Leo I (457-474) and the wife of, first, Zeno and then, at his death, Anastasius. She died in 515.

65. The suburb of Rufinus is presumably the estate often called Rufinianae, near Chalcedon, where the famous monastery of Hypatius was situated. On the obscure phrase translated here 'tenanted by Demostratus' see A. Cameron, 'Cyril of Scythopolis, V. Sabae 53'.

66. Anicia Juliana was the daughter of the Western Emperor Olybrius and Placidia, daughter of Valentinian III (Emperor 425-455). After her death in 527-8 her eunuchs came to Palestine to become monks under Sabas (171,6-25).

67. Anastasia's husband Pompeius was Chalcedonian and supported Patriarch Macedonius of Constantinople in his exile. Anastasia is mentioned below as giving Cyril information about Sabas' life (147,6-9).

68. The request to lighten the tax burden on Jerusalem was an important part of Sabas' mission. The *collatio lustralis* was a tax levied on tradesmen and craftsmen, and also on prostitutes, instituted by Constantine and suppressed by Anastasius in May.

69. *Superflua discriptio* was the redistribution of taxes, in this case the transfer of liability from the insolvent to the Church of the Resurrection.

70. Marinus was an able financier. The Monophysite sympathies which Cyril attributes to him did not prevent him becoming praetorian prefect in the Chalcedonian government of Justin I (518-527).

71. Together with the Emperor's previous donation Sabas received a total of 2000 *solidi*. Theodore of Petra gives the same sum (*Life of Theodosius* 55,1).

72. The cause of this riot was the use of Peter the Fuller's addition to the Trisagion (see n. 41) in the Great Church of Constantinople on Sunday, 4 November 412.

73. The title Acephaloi was originally given to the extreme group of Monophysites in Egypt who would not recognise the authority of the Patriarch Peter Mongus (482-490). Here it emphasises the intransigence of Severus' following.

74. The flattering and diplomatic letters are those referred to at 143,25-144,1, in which Elias stated his rejection of Chalcedon to secure his position. This chapter is an important historical source. For the background see Frend, *Rise of the Monophysite Movement* 201-231.

74a. The *agentes in rebus*, part of the imperial military corps, were used as couriers.

75. The *dux* commanded the army in the three provinces of Palestine.

76. Aila is on the coast of the Red Sea, at a safe distance of 150 miles from Jerusalem. Perhaps Paul of Melitene was still bishop. See 112,25.

77. The Church of St Stephen was founded by Eudocia and was consecrated, still unfinished, in June 460, a few months before her death. It was situated to the north of the city. The huge complex of buildings around the church included a monastery, gardens, porticoes and ancillary buildings.

78. Hypatius was captured at Odessa on the Black Sea in 514 during the second rising of Vitalian against Anastasius. He was released later that year.

79. Theodore of Petra (*Life of Theodosius* 53,13-70,12) gives an alternative account of Anastasius' response to the archimandrites' petition.

80. Mixed drink or *eucraton* is made with pepper, cumin and aniseed, and was popular in the monasteries. See also 135,2; 216,1; 225,7.

81. This is not strictly accurate. The diptychs are a list of names of those persons to be commemorated in the Eucharistic prayer. The Chalcedonians Euphemius and Macedonius of Constantinople and Leo of Rome were inserted in the diptychs and the Council of Chalcedon was thereby formally recognised. This took place on 15-16 July 518.

82. Excavations on the summit of the hill on which Scythopolis was built have revealed a large round church with the centre open to the sky, built, in the opinion of the excavator, in the early fifth century. In spite of its imposing position, it seems that the citizens preferred an older church. See Ovadiah 24.

83. Some have suggested that this John was the father of Cyril, but this does

not seem likely as Cyril does not suggest that his father was in the imperial service (164,20; 180,4-6).

84. There were large Samaritan communities in many towns in Palestine including Scythopolis. Relations with Christians deteriorated during the reign of Justinian because of legislation which discriminated against them. See below 171,26-173,11.

85. St John the Baptist was a popular saint in Scythopolis and it is probable that there was a healing well or fountain dedicated to him. The Piacenza pilgrim who visited Scythopolis in the fifth century describes it as the place where 'St John performs many miracles'. As late as the twelfth century the Russian abbot Daniel was shown 'a remarkable cavern... where a stream flows which spreads out into a miraculous pool' (B. de Khitrovo, *Itineraires russes en Orient*, 59). The monastery of Enthemaneith or En Temane, which can be translated as 'Well of Eight', perhaps the 'Apse of St John', was built over the fountain.

86. For other examples of anointing the body of a sick person with oil, see Macarius the Egyptian in *Historia Monachorum* 21.17, and Aphrahat's anointing the emperor's horse in Theodoret's *History of the Monks of Syria* 8.11.

87. See above, 127,8.

88. In Palestinian monasticism the cenobitic and anchoritic ways of life coexisted peacefully. Holl (*Enthusiasmus und Bussgewalt* 172-8) contrasts this with the predominance of the cenobitic ideal in Cappadocia and of the solitary ideal in parts of Egypt. Cyril is making a claim for the superiority of the anchoritic life. See also 206,8.

89. This is the end of the drought referred to at 158,8. The winter ends in early March in Palestine and there is little prospect of rain after that.

90. This is presumably August 520.

91. The Lucillianae is the pool in Bethesda (John 5:2), which was embellished in the second century by Pompeia Lucilla.

92. See 178,5 for another sign of Summus' support of Sabas.

93. Compare a similar rain miracle in the *Life of Euthymius* at 38,1-39,16, especially the reference to *parresia* at 38,16 and 169,7. In the case of both saints, the effective intercession which provides rain for the city of Jerusalem is a sign that they can be relied on as advocates in the heavenly court. In the case of Sabas, his authority, derived from God, is contrasted with the vain efforts of the Patriarch to dig for water.

94. Justinian had played an important part in Justin's short reign, becoming consul in 521, patrician in 525 and *nobilissimus* in 526, before being enthroned as Emperor in 527.

95. At 145,7.

96. The centre of the Samaritan sect was on mount Gerizim, near Neapolis or Nablus. At the start of Justinian's reign legislation was enacted against them including a prohibition against bequeathing property, and in 528 their synagogues were ordered to be destroyed. This sparked off their uprising.

97. Procopius (*Secret History* 27,6-19) gives an independent account of this Arsenius and his father.

98. Justinian's greeting Cyril with 'reverence' (*proskynesis*) reversed the accustomed relationship by which the emperor would expect to receive *proskynesis*.

99. Theodora came from a humble background and was loyal to the Monophysite faith of the masses. She protected and supported Severus and the Monophysites, and influenced Justinian to relax his opposition in 530. See Frend, *Rise of the Monophysite Movement* 260-263.

100. A series of discussions took place in the capital between Chalcedonians and Monophysites in 530-531. Justinian hoped that these would lead to the acceptance of Chalcedon by Monophysites, but he was disappointed. The discussion continued for over a year (Zacharias, *Ecclesiastical History* 9.15). Because of the fears that Chalcedon promoted a Diphysite Christology, its supporters were vulnerable to the accusation of being Nestorian.

101. A cluster of literary and historical problems surround the figure of Leontius. In addition to Cyril's Leontius, we know of Leontius, a Palestinian monk, present at the 536 Synod of Constantinople, a Leontius the Hermit who wrote several theological books, and a Leontius who associated with John Maxentius. My view is that the first three Leontiuses are one and the same person. This makes Cyril's Leontius a formidable polemical writer and an active participant in the ecclesiastical politics of Constantinople. The fullest account of the thought and historical problems surrounding Leontius is D.B. Evans, *Leontius of Byzantium*, although his findings have been criticised by, among others, B. Daley, 'The Origenism of Leontius of Byzantium'.

102. This was built next to the new church of the Holy Mother of God. It is referred to by Procopius (*Buildings* 5.6.25).

103. The consecration of this church provided Cyril with an excuse to come to Jerusalem. See 71, 17-19.

104. Tribonian was a prominent member of Justinian's court. He assisted in the compiling of Justinian's *Corpus Iuris*.

105. The building in the palace in which foreign ambassadors were customarily received.

106. This may imply that Cyril's mother was living as a nun.

107. That is the Great Laura, to which Cyril moved in 557.

108. He is ordained reader. Compare the *Life of Euthymius* 10,20.

109. The Great Laura had some form of written rule. A document purporting to be this rule handed over by Sabas was discovered in the last century. It is included in a twelfth-century manuscript but contains traditions which go back to Sabas' life. See S. Vailhé, 'Les écrivains de Mar Saba' and E. Kurtz, 'Tupos kai paradosis'.

110. Cyril, in offering this detailed dating, has allowed himself to become confused and has unwittingly initiated much debate. The 10th indiction ran from September 531 to August 532, making the date of Sabas' death 5 December 531. The ninety-fourth year of Sabas' life and the sixth year of Justinian's reign indicate that he died in 532, in which year 5 December fell on a Sunday. 532 is the correct date and so the indiction date needs to be corrected by adding one year. The same mistake is repeated for dates subsequent to 532, and the necessary adjustment is made in the margins of the text. For a review of this complex problem see E. Stein, 'Cyrille de Scythopolis'.

111. 'Access' translates *parresia*. The death of Sabas brings him into greater intimacy with God and makes his intercessory power more effective.

112. See *Historia Monachorum* 11.8 for another example of martyrs welcoming the soul of the departed into heaven.

113. Presumably these were intended to separate the sanctuary from the nave. See *Life of Euthymius*, note 61.

114. These concluding pages of the life of Sabas are our fullest source for the history of the sixth-century conflict over Origenism. For a full history of these events see F. Diekamp, *Die origenistische Streitigkeiten des sechsten Jahrhunderts*.

115. A nostalgic view which overlooks the conflicts which divided the monasteries during Sabas' lifetime.

116. Origenism provided an intellectual framework for the understanding of the ascetic life which attracted the better educated monks. The monasteries of Firminus and Martyrius were to the northeast of Jerusalem, about fifteen miles from the New Laura. So Origenism had gained a foothold in the northern as well as the southern extremities of the monastic desert. For a description of the remains of Firminus' monastery see M. Marcoff and D. Chitty, 'Notes on Monastic Research in the Judaean Wilderness 1928-9'.

117. Domitian and Theodore Ascidas travelled to Constantinople to take part in the Home Synod (536) in which leading monophysites were anathematised.

118. Father Eusebius was priest at the Great Church of the capital and an administrator. He appears at several points in the narrative.

119. The see of Ancyra.

120. Gelasius had been active in the building of the church of the Mother of God in the Laura, 117,3.

121. The same Antipatrus who was an admirer of Euthymius, 52,23.

122. Leontius and his group were a long way off their route. V. Corbo (*Gli Scavi di Kh. Siyar el-Ghanam*, 162-3) suggested that the site of Marcianus' monastery should be located further east, at Khirbet Giohdham, which is more usually identified with Theognius' monastery. It is certainly more likely that Leontius' group might have ended up here—but these remains seem too small and too distant from Bethlehem to be identified with the large cenobium of Marcianus.

123. Paul had been Patriarch of Alexandria from 537. He was implicated in the murder of Psoius, a deacon, and was deposed by the Synod of Gaza (542).

124. Ephraim was patriarch of Antioch from 527 to 545. He was a leader of the Chalcedonian group and opposed both Monophysites and Origenists. See John Moschus, *Spiritual Meadow* 36 for his opposition to Monophysites, and Liberatus, *Breviarium* 23 for his opposition to Origenists.

125. In addition to the petition from Palestine and the Home Synod of bishops under the presidency of the Patriarch of Constantinople, the orthodox had the support of the papal legate, Pelagius.

126. The church of Jerusalem had resident representatives in the capital.

127. The New Church had just been finished and was dedicated in 543. The position of superior of this the newest of Jerusalem's churches was an important post.

128. It was at this point that Cyril arrived at Jerusalem, with a strict warning from his mother to have nothing to do with the Origenists.

129. The Bessi were a Thracian tribe, many members of which had settled in

the Palestinian monasteries. The Bessi of the Jordan could be the same as the community at Soubiba, near the Jordan, which is mentioned by John Moschus (*Spiritual Meadow* 157). One of the four churches at Theodosius' monastery was set aside for them (Theodore of Petra, *Life of Theodosius* 45,13-16).

130. Supporters of Chalcedon were liable to be branded as Nestorian by Monophysites. Since the group at Constantinople was currently campaigning against Theodore of Mopsuestia and Patriarch Peter had made the mistake of dissociating himself from them, Gelasius was concerned to make clear his rejection of Theodore.

131. This work has not survived.

132. In an important study, A. Guillaumont has demonstrated that Origenist thought developed between Justinian's 543 Edict against Origenism and the Council of Constantinople in 553. The anathemas issued on these occasions show the dogmatic views under attack. Those of 543 refer to commonplaces of Origenist thought, drawn from the *First Principles*. The emphasis on the pre-existence of the soul make the title 'Protoktists' or 'first-created' a natural title for a group holding these views. The anathemas of 553 (which have much in common with Cyriacus' remarks at 230,2-17) attack propositions which seem to be drawn from Evagrius' *Kephalaia Gnostica*. These include the idea that the righteous will reign with Christ in the Resurrection, and so to this group the title 'Isochrists' or 'equal with Christ' could apply. The title 'Tetradites' could imply that the reign of the righteous with Christ introduced a fourth element into the Trinity. Guillaumont suggests that after 543 a new militant group emerged within Origenism which was influenced by the thought of Evagrius. The split between the more conservative and radical Origenists led to the movement's disintegration and downfall. See A. Guillaumont, *Les 'Kephalaia Gnostica' d'Evagre le Pontique et l'histoire de l'Origenisme chez les grecs et chez les syriens*, 136-159.

133. Macarius later renounced his Origenist sympathies and was restored to the Patriarchate of Jerusalem in 563, where he remained until his death in 583 (Evagrius, *Ecclesiastical History* 4.39 and 5.16).

134. 'Frankness' translates *parresia*, here used in the secular context of a petitioner approaching a ruler boldly.

135. Pancratius is the only stylite mentioned by Cyril. This Cyriacus is not the one whose life was written by Cyril.

136. The main purpose of the Council was the condemnation of three writers accused of Nestorianism: Theodore of Mopsuestia, Theodoret and Ibas of Edessa. The teachings of Origen, Evagrius and Didymus were also condemned.

137. This John the Scholarius is not the same John as the superior of the monastery of the Tower (128,17). See note 52 for the meaning of *scholarius*.

138. Assuming that the indiction dates after 532 are one year out, then Cyril arrived at the New Laura in 555 (see note 110, above). But, on this occasion, Cyril's date could be right, since if Eustochius allowed eight months to elapse after the Council of Constantinople before acting against the Origenists of the New Laura, then this would point to February 554 as the correct date. But see Stein, 'Cyrille de Scythopolis' 174-6.

THE LIFE OF OUR FATHER SAINT JOHN, BISHOP AND HESYCHAST OF THE LAURA OF OUR FATHER SAINT SABAS

1. BIRTH AND PARENTAGE

201,5 **F**IRST IN MY ACCOUNT,[1] I place Abba John, solitary of the laura of blessed Sabas, as preceding all the others both in birth and in luster of life. Originating from Nicopolis in Armenia, this our illuminated father John was born of parents named Encratius and Euphemia, who were of flourishing wealth and eminent family and had won distinction in
201,10 many public offices, both military and civil, including posts at the imperial court; numerous stories of their achievements are recounted by the people of Byzantium and Armenia. Lest I make my story tedious at the very beginning, I shall willingly omit them, simply
201,15 relating those facts about him that are familiar to virtually all who know of him.

As he himself told me,[2] he was born on 8 January of the seventh indiction in the fourth year of the reign of Marcian, dear to God. Being of Christian parents, he received a Christian upbringing along with his brothers.

2. HE RENOUNCES THE WORLD AND FOUNDS A CENOBIUM

201,20 Some time afterwards, when his parents had died in Christ and their property had been apportioned, this inspired man dedicated himself to God. Building in Nicopolis itself a church to the mother of God, the ever-
202. virgin Mary, worthy of all praise, he renounced the affairs
[AD 471] of this life in his eighteenth year and, taking on ten

220

brethren who wished to be saved, established a cenobium there.

202,5 Throughout the time of his youth he made great efforts to control the stomach and despise vanity, knowing that a full stomach is incapable of vigil or chastity, and that vanity cannot; bear to be at rest, while asceticism cannot be achieved without wakefulness, purity, and humility. Accordingly he strove in his youth to keep his mind undistracted and his conversation blameless, seasoned with 202,10 holy salt. Those under him he formed in the life of asceticism by both word and action, neither weighing them down when neophytes under the yoke of the rule nor letting them stay idle and untrained; instead, leading them little by little and watering them with holy streams, 202,15 he made them bear fruit worthy of their calling.

3. HE IS MADE BISHOP OF COLONIA

[AD 481] When the twenty-eighth year of his life had begun and the grace that shone forth in him was reported everywhere, the metropolitan of Sebaste, won over by his reputation and at the request of the 202,20 inhabitants of the city called Colonia,[3] summoned him as if on some other business, and ordained him bishop of the said city, its bishop having died; John had already passed through the sequence of the ecclesiastical grades. So having against his will attained the episcopacy, he did not change his rule of monastic life but contended in 202,25 the episcopal palace as in a monastery. In particular he abstained from washing, carefully avoiding not only being seen by another but also seeing himself naked; thinking of the nakedness of Adam and what is written in that passage,[a] he judged abstaining from

a. Gen 3:7-11.

203.   washing one of the greatest virtues. In a word, he
strove in every way to be pleasing to God, in fasts,
prayers, chastity of body, and purity of heart, always
vanquishing both thoughts and every proud obstacle to
the knowledge of God.[b4]

203,5   In addition, his brother Pergamius, who enjoyed the
esteem of both emperors Zeno and Anastasius and held
many public offices, was illuminated by his virtues and
made great efforts to be pleasing to God. Also his
nephew Theodore the most glorious chief secretary,

203,10   hearing that his uncle had grown old in virtues, was
thereby illuminated in soul and became greatly
pleasing to God with all his household. This
Theodore is highly regarded at the present time by
the whole senate and our most pious emperor Justinian for understanding, gravity of life, correct
faith, compassion and almsgiving. But this will come

203,15   later; I return to chronological sequence.

4. JOURNEY TO CONSTANTINOPLE AND
WITHDRAWAL TO PALESTINE

When the inspired John had completed nine years in
the episcopate, the husband of his sister Mary, called
Pasinicus, happened to be governing Armenia. As a result of satanic activity, he tried to penalize and harass

203,20   church entrusted to John, preventing its administrators from taking proper care of the affairs of
the church and dragging away by force those who
sought refuge in its sanctuary, thereby breaching the
inviolacy of sanctuary.[5] Although he was repeatedly
entreated and admonished by appeal to the word of
God, he became still worse, John's sister Mary hav-

b. Cf. 2 Cor 10:5.

203,25   ing already died. Suffering terrible affliction as a
          result, the righteous one was forced to go up to Con-
          stantinople. After arriving there and securing the inter-
          ests of his church with the assistance of Archbishop
204.   Euphemius of Constantinople, towards the end of the
          reign of Zeno,[6] he conceived the plan pleasing to God
          of withdrawing to the holy city and living by himself in
204,5   isolation from the affairs of this life. Sending the
          priests and clerics with him on their way with the im-
          perial decrees he had obtained, he gave them all the
          slip, embarking in a ship on his own, and came to
          Jerusalem, where he lodged just outside the holy city in
          the hospice founded by blessed Eudocia, the hospice in
          which there is a chapel of the holy martyr George.[7] On
204,10   entering it and finding there the hubbub of the world,
          he was grieved in spirit and begged God with tears to
          be led to some pleasant and solitary spot conducive to
          salvation.

5. HE ENTERS THE GREAT LAURA

204,15   When our venerable father John had stayed in the
          said almshouse for a considerable time, spending the
          nights in petition to God, one night when he was
          walking alone in the courtyard of the almshouse and
          looked up to the sky, he suddenly beheld approaching
          him a star of light in the shape of a cross, and heard
          out of this light a voice saying, 'If you wish to be
          saved, follow this light.' Believing the voice, he
204,20   set off immediately and followed that light. Under the
          guidance of the light he came to the Great Laura of our
          sainted father Sabas, while Sallustius was presiding
          over the church of Jerusalem, in the fourteenth in-
[AD 491] diction in the thirty-eighth year of his life, in the year
          when the church of the Great Laura, built by God, was

consecrated and when Anastasius succeeded to the
throne on the death of Zeno, as I heard his own tongue
relate. On entering the Great Laura, he found that the
blessed Sabas had built up a community of one hundred
and fifty anchorites, who lived in great poverty as regards the things of the body but were rich in spiritual
charisms. On receiving him, the blessed Sabas
entrusted him to the steward of the laura, to be under
his orders and to serve, as one of the beginners,[8] not
recognizing the treasure in him. May no one be
suprised that the treasure of John's virtues was hidden
from Sabas the elder, but may he rather consider
that when God wished to reveal something to his saints
they are prophets, but when he wishes to conceal
something they see no more than everyone else. To my
statement bears witness the prophet Elisha, when he
says of the Shunammite woman, 'Her soul is in
great affliction and the Lord has hidden it from me.'[a]
The inspired John paid total obedience to the steward
and the fathers, serving with all humility and eagerness, fetching up water from the gorge, cooking for
the builders, and supplying them with stones and
other building materials, when the guest-house was
being built.

6-7. FIRST MONASTIC LABORS

6. In the second year of his stay in the laura, when
Castellium was cleansed from being inhabited by
demons, as I have already recounted in the Life of
Saint Sabas,[9] he performed many labors there with our
father Sabas and certain others, as he himself related to
me; it was time that the holy Abba Marcianus sent

a. 2 Kgs 4:27.

205.
205,5
205,10
205,15
205,20
205,25

them food in accordance with a divine revelation when they were hungry and had no stock of food supplies.

On the occasion of the change of offices in the first indication, the monk appointed steward made this great luminary guest-master and cook. He accepted this ministry with eagerness and joy, and performed tasks for all the fathers, serving each one with all humility and meekness. During his ministry occurred the building of the cenobium outside the laura and to the north, in order that those renouncing this life should first be educated in strict monasticism there in the cenobium, and then live in the laura, once they had been strictly trained in the cenobitic rule; blessed Sabas used to affirm and maintain that, just as the flower precedes the fruit, so the cenobitic life precedes the anchoritic.[10] While this cenobium was being built, this righteous man was compelled as guest-master, in addition to the other tasks of his office, to cook for the workmen and twice a day to lift and carry the cooked dishes and other provisions and convey them to the laborers ten stades away from the guest-house.

7. When he had completed his year in this ministry and all the fathers had been edified by his deportment, gravity and spiritual insight, our father Sabas gave him a cell for the solitary life. Having taken this cell and received permission to live in solitude, the venerable John continued for three years to show himself to no one at all nor communicate with anyone during five days of the week, while on Saturdays and Sundays he would be the first to enter the church and the last to leave, standing solemnly with total fear and reverence for the office of psalmody, in accordance with the saying in the Psalms, 'Serve the Lord with fear and exult in him with trembling'.[a] So great was his com-

AD 492/3
206.

206,5

206,10

206,15

206,20

206,25

a. Ps 2:11.

207.

punction that he wept profusely during the bloodless sacrifice and was unable to control himself, with the result that the fathers who witnessed this gift of tears were astonished and gave glory to God the giver of good things.

When these three years were over, he was appointed steward of the laura. Since God assisted him in everything, the laura was blessed and the community multi-

207,5   plied during his period of service.

8-10. HIS EPISCOPAL RANK REMAINS A SECRET

8. When he had completed his service, blessed Sabas wished to ordain him, as being a virtuous and perfect

AD 497/8   monk. Taking him to the holy city in the sixth indiction he led him to the blessed Elias the archbishop, recounted his virtues, and asked for him to be ordained

207,10   priest. On hearing about him, the archbishop proceeded to the holy church of Calvary with the intention of ordaining him with his own hands. This great father, held fast to prevent escape, said with his natural intelligence, 'Venerable father, since I have committed some sins, I beg to lay them before Your Beatitude in private, and

207,15   then, if you think me worthy, I shall accept ordination.' Taking him to the ascent to holy Golgotha,[11] he said to him privately, ' I beg Your Holiness to spare my life and reveal this secret to nobody, in order not to drive me from this land.' On receiving his assurance,

207,20   he continued, 'I, Father, was ordained bishop of such and such a city, but because wickedness was multi-plied "I fled afar and lodged in the wilderness,"[a] awaiting the visitation of God. And I thought it right, while I am still in bodily vigor, to serve and minister

---

a. Ps 55:7(54:8).

to the fathers, so that, when I become weak, I shall not be blamed for being served by others.' On hearing this, the archbishop in amazement called blessed Sabas and said to him, ' He has told me something in confidence, and it is impossible to ordain him. From today let him practise solitude, troubled by nobody.' Saying only this, the archbishop sent them on their way.

208.   9. The blessed Sabas, distressed in mind, withdrew about thirty stades from his Great laura to a cave west of Castellium, where he later founded a cenobium,[12] and casting himself before God said with tears, 'Why, Lord, have you so despised me as to deceive me into thinking John worthy of the priesthood? And now, Master and Lord, reveal to me the truth about him, since "my soul is desolate even unto death,"[b] if the vessel I thought sanctified, serviceable, and worthy to receive the holy oil has proved unserviceable in the sight of Your Majesty.' While Abba Sabas was uttering with tears these and similar remarks through the night, an angelic form appeared to him and said, 'John is not a useless vessel but a vessel of election. It is because he has already been ordained bishop that he cannot become a priest.' So ran the vision. Our father Sabas, being used to theophanies and angelic visions, was not frightened but made his way full of joy to the cell of the godly John and, embracing him, said, 'Father John, you hid from me God's gift to you, but the Lord has revealed it to me.' The inspired John replied, ' I am desolate, father. I did not wish anyone to know this secret. I shall now no longer be able to live in this land.'

    10. The elder promised by the word of God to tell this to absolutely no one. From then on John lived in solitude in his cell for four years, neither attending church

207,25

208,5

208,10

208,15

208,20

208,25

b. Mt 26:38.

nor conversing with anyone at all apart from the one who served him—save on the day of the dedication of the revered church of the all-holy mother of God and ever-

209.   virgin Mary that took place in the laura in the ninth
[AD 501]   indiction;[13] then alone he was compelled to come out to greet archbishop Elias who had come for the consecration. The patriarch, on meeting him and falling in love with his spiritual wisdom and pleasant conversation

209,5   held him in honor all the time of his episcopacy.

11. HE RETIRES TO THE DESERT OF ROUBÂ

At the end of four years, when blessed Sabas left the laura for the region of Scythopolis because of the anarchy caused by those who later settled in the New Laura, the most venerable John, fleeing this assembly of disor-

209,10   der, retired to the desert of Roubâ in the fiftieth year of
[AD 503]   his life and in the eleventh indiction. There in a cave he lived in solitude for six years, separating himself from all human intercourse, yearning to consort with God in solitude and to purify the eye of the mind by long philosophy so as with unveiled face to behold the

209,15   glory of God, exerting himself wholly to advance from glory to glory in his desire for the things that are more excellent.[a14] Condescending to the physical needs of the body every two or three days, he would set out from the cave and wander in the desert to gather the *melagria* that grow wild there and are the

209,20   food of the anchorites of the desert.

One day at the beginning of his stay here, before he had gained experience of this desert, he set out to gather as described, but lost his way and stumbled onto impassable cliffs. Having failed to find by what

a. Cf. 2 Cor 3:18.

path to return to the cave and being too weak to walk further, he fell down in despair. And behold, suddenly through a visitation of God's power he became airborne in the manner, I suppose, of the prophet

210. Habakkuk,[b15] and found himself in his own cave. When with the passing of time he had gained experience of this utter desert and discovered the place from where he was carried away airborne, he found that the distance was five miles.

12. THE MIRACULOUS PROVISIONS

210,5   A certain brother came to Roubâ and stayed with him for a short time, practising the anchoritic life with him. This brother, becoming utterly surfeited with this philosophy, said to the elder, as the Easter festival was approaching, 'Let us go up to the laura, father, and celebrate the Easter festival with the fathers, since we

210,10   have nothing to eat here except these *melagria*.' The inspired John did not want to go up there since our father Sabas was not there but had left the laura, as I have said. When the brother pressed him, he admonished him, saying, 'Let us stay calm, brother, and have faith that he who nourished six hundred thou-

210,15   sand in the desert for forty years will himself provide us with not only necessary nourishment but a surplus as well. For he said, "I shall not fail thee nor forsake thee."[a] And in the Gospel he says, "Be not anxious, saying, What shall we eat? or, What shall we drink? or, What shall we wear? For your heavenly Father knows

210,20   that you need all these things. But seek the kingdom of heaven and the righteousness of God, and all these

b. Dan 14:36.
a. Dt 31:16.

things will be added to you."[b] Have patience, my
child, and prefer the narrow path to the broad one. For
self-indulgence in this world begets eternal punishment, while present mortification is a preparation for
the enjoyment of good things.' Unconvinced by these
and similar words, the brother departed and made

211.   the journey to the laura. After his departure a man
totally unknown came to the elder with an ass
loaded with many good things, the load consisting
of hot white loaves, wine, oil, fresh cheeses and
eggs, and a jar of honey.[16] He unloaded and went

211,5   away. Our most venerable father John rejoiced in spirit
at this divine visitation, while the brother who had left,
after losing his way and being totally thwarted, returned on the third day hungry and exhausted, having
enjoyed the fruits of his own disobedience. When he
found such good things in the cave, he recognized his

211,10   own lack of faith and stubbornness and prostrated himself shamefacedly before the elder, begging to receive
forgiveness. The elder, sympathizing with human
weakness and having compassion on the brother, raised
him up and admonished him, saying: 'Recognize pre-
cisely that God is able to prepare a table in the desert.'[c]

13. AN INCURSION OF SARACENS

211,15   At this same time Alamundarus the son of Sikika, who
had attained the dignity of being king over the Saracens
subject to Persia, invaded Arabia and Palestine in great
fury against the Romans, carrying off everything as
plunder, taking countless thousands of Romans into captivity, and after the capture of Amida perpetrating many

b. Mt 6:31-33.
c. Cf. Ps 78:19(77:20).

211,20   lawless acts. So with a multitude of barbarians swarm-
ing over the desert and those entrusted as phylarchs with
guarding the desert warning the monasteries to secure
themselves against the incursion of the barbarians,[17] the
fathers of the Great Laura told the venerable father to
abandon his sojourn in Roubâ and return to the laura

211,25   to live in solitude in his own cell. But the inspired John,
having tasted the divine sweetness as a result of his soli-

212.   tude, held onto this keenly and could not bear to abandon
it, reasoning with himself in the following words: 'If God
is not looking after me, why should I live?'[18] Accordingly, he made the Most High his refuge, and remained
undaunted. God, who at all times looks after his own

212,5   servants, commanded his angels, as in the Scripture, to
protect his holy one.[a] Out of a wish to reassure John,
who had felt some slight fear, he sent, as a visible
protector, an enormous and terrifying lion to protect
him day and night from the plots of the wicked barbarians. The first night that he saw the lion lying be-

212,10   side him he naturally felt some slight fear, as he himself
related to me; but when he saw that the lion followed
him day and night as his inseparable companion and
warded off the barbarians, he offered up hymns of
thanksgiving to God for not 'releasing the staff of sinners onto the lot of the righteous'.[b]

14-15. HIS RANK IS REVEALED

212,15   14. Our father the blessed Sabas had returned from
Nicopolis, founded the New Laura and proceeded to the
construction of the Cave, as related in my second account. Remembering the vision that had once come to

a. Cf. Ps 91(90):9-11.
b. Ps 125(124):3.

him concerning the pious John, he went off to see him in
212,20   Roubâ and said to him, 'See, God has protected you
from the plots of the barbarians and reassured you by
sending you a visible protector. But get up, act now
like other men, and flee as the fathers have, in order
not to be thought conceited.' Exhorting him in many
other ways as well, he led him back to the Great
Laura in the second indiction and enclosed him in a
212,25   and enclosed him in a cell in the fifty-sixth year of his
[AD 509] life, no one else in the community knowing that he
213.   was a bishop. But after a long time God ordained that
the hidden treasure of John should be revealed in the
following way.

      15. A man originating from the province of Asia,
called Aetherius, who had been elevated to archbishop[19] and conducted himself worthily of this posi-
213,5   tion, came to Jerusalem and venerated the honored
places together with the life-giving wood of the Cross.
After distributing much money to the poor and to the
monasteries, he left the holy city, eager to return to his
native land. After he had embarked on a ship and sailed
over a small expanse of sea, he was compelled by
213,10   compelled by contrary winds to return in great danger to
Ascalon. As two days later he was planning to set sail
again, an angel of the Lord appeared to him in a dream
and said: 'It is inadmissible for you to sail unless you
return to the holy city, go to the laura of Abba Sabas,
and meet Abba John the solitary, a righteous and vir-
213,15   tuous man, a bishop abounding in worldly wealth, who
out of fear and longing for God has despised all the
things of this life and humbled himself in voluntary
poverty and asceticism.' At this, Aetherius, rising from
sleep and examining the vision, made eager inquiries
and came to the laura of Abba Sabas, where he an-
213,20   nounced his vision to the fathers and was taken to the
solitary. He greeted him warmly and stayed with him for

two days. When their conversation had become expansive, he adjured him to relate and declare his personal history frankly. Compelled in this way, he revealed his family and fatherland and his episcopal rank. On discovering this, Aetherius exclaimed in amazement, 'Truly today also holy stones roll on the land.'[a] And so taking his leave of the righteous one, he returned to the

214.
blessed Sabas and related to him and the fathers the whole truth about the inspired John. From this moment the family and episcopal rank of John were known to the fathers.

16-17. THE DEATH OF SABAS

16. In the seventy-ninth year of the life of holy John

214,5
the twenty-fourth of his reclusion in the cell, our sainted father Sabas both fell asleep and rested in peace[a] on 5

[AD 532]
December of the tenth indiction.[20] This most precious pearl John was then distressed in mind because he had not left his cell and been present at the death of the holy

214,10
father. While he was in this state of despondency, and in tears was lamenting being deprived of the father, our father Sabas appeared in his sleep and said to him, 'Do not be distressed, father John, about my death. Even if I have been separated from you in the flesh, I am with you in spirit.' John exclaimed, 'Entreat the Master to

214,15
take me too.' The blessed Sabas replied, 'It is not possible for this to happen now. For tribulation is about to descend most grievously on the laura, and God wants you to remain in the flesh, so as to console and strengthen those contending manfully on behalf of the faith.' On seeing and hearing all this, the inspired John was overjoyed and cast off his

a. Cf. Zech 9:16.
a. Cf. Ps 4:8(9).

214,20   despondency about the father, except that he was concerned about the tribulation that had been mentioned.

17. He once conceived a desire to see how the soul
separates from the body. While he was entreating God
over this, he was snatched up in spirit to holy Bethlehem, and saw in the narthex of the honored church
there a holy man, unknown to him, stretched out and
on the point of death.[21] He saw the man's soul received
215.   by angels and carried up into heaven with a certain
fragrance and singing of hymns. Wishing to see with
his own eyes if this was so, he rose at the same hour
and went to holy Bethlehem, where he found that the
215,5   man had died at this same hour. Embracing his holy
remains in the narthex, he tended them and placed
them in a holy tomb, and so returned to his cell.

18-19. STORIES TOLD BY HIS DISCIPLES

18. Theodore and John, disciples of this illuminated
elder, told me the following story: 'After the death of
215,10   Saint Sabas, the elder sent us on business to Livias.
After crossing the Jordan we met some people on the
road who said, 'Look out, for there is a lion ahead of
you.' We reflected, 'God is able to protect us through
the prayers of our father. Surely we have not altered
215,15   our intentions? We shall fulfil the commands of our
elder.' With these reflections we walked on and, behold, the lion came to meet us. We were utterly terrified and no strength was left us. Immediately we
saw the elder between us two, taking our fear away
and telling us to have confidence. At this the lion
215,20   fled away from us as if driven by a whip.[22] Completing
our journey safely, we came to the elder. He received us
and said to us, 'Did you see how I was with you in your
peril? But in fact here too I made many petitions to God
on your behalf and, behold, he has shown mercy.'

215,25
216.
216,5

19. The following story was told to me by one of his disciples called Theodore: 'He spent many years taking only broth, which he would mix with ashes from the censer and then eat the result. We caught him doing this in the following way. On one occasion he forgot to push the bolt of his door, and I, wishing to give him some mixed drink, pushed the door and opened it, to find him emptying the censer into his bowl. Since he was very distressed by this, I said, hoping to relieve his distress, "You are not alone in doing this, father, but the majority in this laura do so too, fulfilling the Scripture that says, I ate ashes like bread."[a] By these words I managed with difficulty to satisfy the elder.'

20. THE AUTHOR COMES TO KNOW JOHN

[AD 543]
216,10
216,15
216,20

In the ninetieth year of the life of this holy elder, in the month of November of the sixth indiction, I left the metropolis of Scythopolis, as I have already mentioned in my account of the holy Euthymius,[23] taking with me instructions from my devout mother to accomplish nothing relating to the soul save at the advice and bidding of the inspired John. 'You must not' she said, 'be carried away by the error of the Origenists and so lose your own stability at the very outset.'[a] Accordingly, after coming to Jerusalem and celebrating the consecration of the New Church of the mother of God and ever-virgin Mary, worthy of all praise, I came to the laura of blessed Sabas and paid a visit to this inspired elder, laying my case before him and asking to receive from him advice pleasing to God. He said to me, 'If you want to be saved, enter the monastery of the great Euthymius.' But I being young and foolish,

a. Ps 102:9(101:10).
a. Cf. 2 Pt 3:17.

despised his injunction and went down to the Jordan, wishing to enter one of the monasteries there, where I not only did not prosper but in addition was gravely ill

217.   for six months in the laura of Calamon.[24] While I was in great distress and anguish through being sick and in a foreign land and not being under the yoke of a community, this illuminated elder appeared to me in my sleep and spoke to me as follows: 'You have been sufficiently punished for disobeying my injunction.

217,5   But now rise and go to Jericho, and you will find one Gerontius, a monk, in the hospice of the monastery of Abba Euthymius. Follow him to the monastery and you will be saved.' Rising from sleep, I found my strength immediately restored and, after partaking of the undefiled mysteries and tasting food, ascended on foot

217,10   to Jericho, so that the fathers marveled at such a sudden recovery. Ascending in this way, I settled in the

[AD 544] monastery of Saint Euthymius in the month of July of the sixth indiction. It was from this time onwards that I continually visited him, to lay my whole state before him—except that from my Scythopolis days I had known his disciples, who used to come to our house as

217,15   if it were their own hospice and receive form my parents an annual offering for the community of the laura and for the inspired father. My parents were greatly attached to him and to the fathers of the laura form the time when our house was honored by the presence of our sainted father Sabas. This is why my mother gave

217,20   me on my departure the injunctions I have mentioned. And because of this I too go along with still greater confidence to enjoy his admonition and prayer, especially now that I have been told by him to stop living in the New Laura and to enter the Great Laura—a thing which, with God's approval, I have done.[25] But this I shall treat later.

21-22. HIS MIRACLES OF EXORCISM

217,25   21. A considerable time ago, I visited this holy elder
when oppressed by a satanic thought.[26] On laying it be-
218.   fore him and receiving his blessing, I experienced immediate relief. While I was right by his door and enjoying his godly teaching, one George brought to him
his son who was possessed by a demon, threw him
down in front of his door and went off. With the
218,5   child stretched out and crying, the elder recognized that
he had an unclean spirit and took pity on him. By praying for him and anointing him with the oil of the all-holy
Cross he restored him to health. For the evil spirit immediately departed, and from that hour the child was
cleansed.

218,10   22. Abba Eustathius, who a short time ago succeeded
as superior of the Cave on the death of Sergius,[27] a
man outstanding by the grace of Christ in spiritual discernment, sound doctrine, and continence of life,
recounted to me the following: 'I was once fiercely
attacked by the demon of blasphemy and, going to
218,15   Abba John the solitary, I laid my temptations before
him and asked for his prayers. Rising, the elder prayed
for me and said, "Blessed be the Lord, my child, for the
temptation of blasphemy will never approach you
again." The event corresponded to the word of the
elder, and from that time I no longer felt that evil
218,20   and blasphemous temptation.'

23-24. BASILINA AND HER NEPHEW

23. A woman of Cappadocian stock, called Basilina,
a deaconess of the great Church of Constantinople,
came to Jerusalem accompanied by a nephew of exalted rank, who was devout in other respects but
218,25   was not in communion with the catholic Church, hav-

ing embraced the heresy of Severus. The deaconess
was making great efforts to change his opinions and
unite him to the catholic Church, and so would ask
every righteous man to pray for him. This woman

219.   having heard of the grace of the inspired John, longed
to pay him her respects. But hearing that it is not per-
mitted for a woman to enter the laura, she sent for his
disciple Theodore and begged him to take her nephew
and present him to the holy elder, confident that

219,5   through the latter's prayer God would alter her
nephew's hardness of heart and grant him communion
with the catholic Church. Taking him, the disciple
Theodore went to the elder and knocked on his door as
usual. As the elder was about to open, both of them
prostrated themselves. The disciple said, 'Bless

219,10   us, father,' and the elder opened and said to the disciple, 'I bless you, but he is without a blessing'. The
disciple said, 'Not so, father'. The elder replied, 'Truly
I shall not bless him until he abandons the views of the
Aposchists and agrees to be in communion with the
catholic Church.' On hearing this, the nephew was

219,15   amazed at the elder's gift of second sight and, convert-
ed by this miracle, agreed with conviction to be in
communion with the catholic Church. At this the elder
blessed him and, raising him up, was the first to give
him a share in the spotless mysteries, now that the man
had purged away all doubt from his heart.

24. When Basilina learned of this, she desired all the

219,20   more to see the holy elder with her own eyes, and
planned to put on masculine attire and visit him in the
laura, in order to lay her state before him. This was
revealed to him by an angelic vision, and he sent word
to her: 'Know that, even if you come, you will not see
me. Do not exert yourself but rather wait, and, wher-

219,25   are staying, I shall come to you in your sleep, hear
what you have to say, and declare to you whatever God

inspires me to.' Hearing this and putting faith in it, she received the vision in all clarity. He appeared to her in her sleep, saying, 'See, God has sent me to you. Tell me what you want.' She told of her state and received 220. an appropriate answer. On rising, she gave thanks to God, and described the dress and appearance of the elder to the disciple on his arrival. I have inserted this story in the present text, having heard it from the deaconess Basilina herself.

25-26. THE MIRACLE OF THE FIG TREE

220,5   25. The spot where the holy elder was enclosed has to the west a very high cliff, which the roof of the cell rests against. The rock of the cliff is so dry and moistureless that it does not cause the least damp to the cell.

220,10 One day, taking the seed of a fig, the holy elder said to his disciples Theodore and John, 'Listen to me, my children. If God in his mercy gives grace to this seed and power to this rock to bear fruit, know that he bestows on me as a gift the kingdom of heaven.'[28] Saying this, he pressed the fig against the smooth rock.

220,15 The same God who ordered the rod of Aaron, despite its dryness, to grow and flower[a] ordered this smooth and utterly dry rock to bring forth, so as to show future generations what grace his servant had attained. Seeing the shoot, the elder gave thanks to God with tears.

220,20 The shoot, growing gradually in height and reaching the roof, which it even covered over, proceeded, in brief, with the passing of time to produce, lo and behold, three figs. Taking and kissing these with tears, the elder ate them, rendering thanks to God for this assurance, and giving a little of them to his disciples.

a. Cf. Num 17:8.

Observe how this tree proclaims its witness to the elder's virtue.

220,25   26. From the time of eating the figs, this inspired elder prepared himself for death. When further he reached extreme old age, his disciples opened up his

221.   cell in order to minister to him. I, on coming to him and seeing the awesome sight of the shoot, examined carefully how it had taken root and if the rock had a fissure. I could not find one, and exclaimed in astonishment, 'O the depth of the riches and wisdom and knowledge of God, how unsearchable are his

221,5   judgments and inscrutable his ways.'[b] All those with long experience of the laura of blessed Sabas know that not even in fresh air and a garden do figs or any tree grow, because of the great heat and dryness of the air of the laura. If anyone adduces the trees of the little

221,10   cenobium of the laura that grow along the road,[29] he should know that these were the work of the prayer of blessed Sabas, who found depth of soil and a supply of rain-water from the gorge, and of the fathers of the same little cenobium, who to this day water them throughout the winter with water from the gorge. And

221,15   indeed, although many have tried to plant along the gorge where there is depth of soil and have watered throughout the winter, the plants have scarcely been able to hold their own for a year because, as I have said, of the great dryness of the air and the excessive heat.

27-28. CONCLUSION

27. These few facts I have selected out of many and recorded in writing, omitting to recount the combats on behalf of the faith which he displayed against the doct-

---

b. Rom 11:33.

221,20 rines and champions of Origen and Theodore of Mopsuestia, and the persecutions he endured in accordance
with the Gospel on behalf of the apostolic doctrines. But
I leave his manly deeds to be recounted by other writers.
For I know well that after his death many will doubtless
221,25 be eager to record the combats, persecutions and dangers he endured on behalf of the orthodox faith, and the
victories and glorious habits of this man who has become renowned and celebrated for his life and his dazzling virtues in virtually all our monasteries.

28. As I have heard his holy tongue relate, he was ordained bishop in the twenty-eighth year of his life, as I
222,5 said above, and spent nine years in the episcopacy. He
stayed in the laura first for twelve years, of which he
spent six in ministries and six as a solitary, and then
stayed six years in Roubâ. Immured in the cell in which
he remains a solitary to this day, he has completed with
the help of God forty-seven years. Behold, he has
222,10 reached the hundred-and-fourth year of his life,[30] and is
an extremely old man, radiant in face, zealous in soul
and filled with divine grace. We in our humility pray
that God will give him yet more and more strength and
make his course end in peace, while through John's
222,15 prayers he will have pity on us humble sinners who
have written this, for ever and ever. Amen.

APPENDIX[31]

He continually awaited the time of his departure, and
longed to receive the crown of righteousness which had
been prepared for him, the crown which God has promised to those who love him. When his death was drawing near, the patriarch sent a summons to Abba Conon
the superior, a man who loved God and who was full of
discretion as well as being perfect in the love of God,

and sent him to Ascalon; with him he took a disciple of the holy elder. When the time of his death arrived, the fathers hastened to him, and thought he was already dead; it was Sunday, and he was still in his death-pangs. They brought him out of his cell, and he said to the fathers: 'I beg you, my fathers, not to be sad, for by the will of God our brethren who are away will arrive on Wednesday. In three days' time you will be assembled, and the will of God concerning me will be accomplished.' And so indeed it proved. Those who were away returned on Wednesday before dinner; they all came to him and received his blessing; and he then immediately committed his spirit into the hands of God, on 8 January. And now both for the saint and for ourselves let us pay honor, glory and worship to the Father and the Son and the Holy Spirit, for ever and ever. Amen.

NOTES

1. The *Life of John the Hesychast (or Solitary)* begins a new stage of Cyril's literary work. He has already declared his intention of writing about John (106,1-6).

2. Cyril had known John personally. The events in this Life derive from John himself or from his disciples (205,1; 205,23; 215,8).

3. Colonia was near Sebaste, the capital of the province of Armenia Prima.

4. The description of John's life as a bishop contains several echoes of earlier ascetic writings, for example, Theodoret, *History of the Monks of Syria* 1.7 on James of Nisibis, also the *Life of Anthony* 60 on not being seen naked.

5. Pasinicus was probably enforcing the law. The Emperors had legislated to restrict the right of asylum in certain cases. For example, state debtors and slaves could be removed from church precincts by the authorities (Theodosian Code 9.45.1 and 5).

6. Zeno died in April 491. Euphemius had become patriarch in March 489.

7. These buildings were on the Jaffa road about two miles west of the city. The hospice was called the Patriarchal Hospice to distinguish it from the Royal Hospice founded by Justinian (see 175,11 and 177,9-14). It would have accommodated all pilgrims, not only the old; see Milik, 'La topographie de Jérusalem', 130-140.

8. This does not imply a formal novitiate, but a recognition of the importance of preparation.

9. See 110,3-112,17.

10. See 113,1-23.

11. The rock of Golgotha was in the south-eastern corner of the courtyard adjoining the Basilica of the Resurrection. The Patriarch had taken John out of the church to stand at the foot of the rock.

12. See 126,13-20.

13. The dedication of the church took place on 1 July 501 (117,18-19).

14. John's ascetic life has graduated from the disciplines involved in renouncing the world to the practice of silent and solitary prayer to draw closer to God. See *Life of Euthymius*, notes 24,28. This passage echoes Theodoret, *History of the Monks of Syria* 1.3.

15. The deacon Fidus, who was transported back to Jerusalem in a miraculous manner, was also compared to Habbakuk. See 69,3.

16. A similar story is told in the *Historia Monachorum* 8.40. The 'white' (litterally 'pure') loaves were made of wheat, whereas the usual bread eaten by the poor was of coarsely milled barley.

17. Mundhir III of Hira began to reign in 506, by which time Amida had already fallen to the Persians (503). The phylarchs were the heads of Saracen tribes who were in alliance with the Romans (18,12;75,8). The threat posed to the monasteries by Saracen invaders remained serious, and one of Sabas' requests to Justinian was a fort to protect the monasteries (175,16-19).

18. Abba Daniel of Scetis said the same when threatened by barbarian attack (*Apophthegmata Patrum*, Daniel 1).

19. Aetherius was Metropolitan of Ephesus.

20. In fact Saba died in the eleventh indiction; see *Life of Sabas*, note 110.

21. There are several parallels in Egyptian literature: *Life of Antony* 60.65; Palladius, *Lausiac History* 26.16-17.

22. Hyenas are driven away by Antony's words 'as if by a whip' (*Life of Antony* 52).

23. See 71,20.

24. For the Laura of Calamon, see *Life of Sabas*, Note 58.

25. Cyril entered the Great Laura in 556, after living for two years in the New Laura.

26. Cyril portrays John, but not Euthymius and Sabas, as a spiritual guide offering advice to those who visit him.

27. This statement is at variance with 127,1, where Eustathius is Sergius' predecessor.

28. The gift of the kingdom of heaven is equivalent to the gift of *parresia* in the Lives of Euthymius and Sabas.

29. The approach to the Great Laura from the north-west still passes by a small olive grove which stands outside the monastery gates.

30. John's one hundred and fourth year began on 8 January 557.

31. Several Greek manuscripts contain concluding notes referring to John's death which are generally considered not to be authentic (see Schwartz, 328-9). An eleventh-century Georgian version ends with the paragraph translated here. It has been argued plausibly but not conclusively that this addition comes from the pen of Cyril. See Garitte, 'La mort de S. Jean Hesychaste'.

LIFE OF ABBA CYRIACUS
OF THE LAURA OF SOUKA

1-2. HIS BIRTH AND BOYHOOD

OF THE ANCHORITE, and best of all anchorites, Cyriacus I made repeated mention in the account I gave of the great Euthymius.[1] I have therefore judged it necessary to make him better known to my readers by means of a few particu-

222,25 lars, that is, by narrating some few first-fruits of his virtuous deeds. For if in the text of Scripture the first-fruits are holy,[a] it is clear that the lump of his whole life has been sanctified.

223. This Cyriacus, illuminated in soul, was of Greek family of the city of Corinth. As for his parents, his father was John, priest of the holy catholic Church of God in Corinth, while his mother was Eudoxia. He was

223,5 born of them at the end of the reign of Theodosius the
[AD 449] Younger on 9 January of the second indiction. He was nephew on his mother's side of Bishop Peter of Corinth, under whom he became from childhood lector of the same holy church. Abba Cyriacus, reading the holy Scriptures, as he himself told me, and spending days and nights on them, was struck with

223,10 them, was struck with amazement at the variety of ways in which, generation after generation, God glorified those who strove to be well-pleasing by correct choice and set them up as luminaries in the world, disposing everything from the beginning for the salvation of the human race.

2. He glorified Abel on account of his sacrifice,[b] honored Enoch by translation for being well-pleasing,[c]

a. Cf. Rom 11:16.
b. Cf. Gen 4:4.

245

223,15   guarded Noah as the spark of the race on account of his
            righteousness,[d] made Abraham the father of nations on
            account of his faith,[e] accepted the devout priesthood of
            Melchizedek,[f] raised up Joseph and Job as models, for
            our life, of continence and endurance, made Moses a
            lawgiver, let Joshua son of Nun control the sun and
223,20   moon,[a] appointed David prophet and king and ancestor of
            an awesome mystery, changed the fire of the Babylonian
            furnace into dew,[b] taught the lions of Daniel to fast in
            their den,[c] and made the sea-monster a prophet's cham-
            ber.[d] 2

            In addition to all these wonders, Cyriacus' mind was in
223,25   a whirl as he reflected on what surpasses them, that ex-
            traordinary conception without seed, the Virgin Mother,
            how God the Word became man without change and by
            his precious Cross and Resurrection harrowed hell, and
            how by his triumph he made the deceitful serpent im-
            potent, restored life to Adam who had lost it through his
224.   sins, and led him back into paradise. As he reflected on
            these and similar points, his heart was pierced with the
            fear of God, and he resolved to withdraw to the holy
            city and renounce the affairs of this life.

3-5. HIS FIRST YEARS IN PALESTINE

            3. While he was meditating on such thoughts, he
224,5   heard one Sunday the Gospel that says, 'If anyone

c. Cf. Gen 5:24.
d. Cf. Gen 7:1.
e. Cf. Gen 17:4-5.
f. Cf. Gen 14:18.
a. Cf. Josh 10:12-13.
b. Cf. Dan (LXX) 3:50.
c. Cf. Dan 6:22.
d. Cf. Jon 1:17.

wishes to come after me, let him deny himself and take up his cross and follow me.'[a] Immediately he left the church and, saying nothing to anybody, came to Cenchreae; there he boarded a ship crossing to Palestine and arrived at Jerusalem in the eighteenth year

224,10   salem in the eighteenth year of his life, the eighth year of the episcopacy of Anastasius at Jerusalem, the ninth of the reign of the great emperor Leo, and the begin-

[AD 466]   ning of the fifth indiction. On his arrival at the holy city he was warmly received by the sainted Eustorgius, a saintly man resplendent in all the charisms of the all-holy Spirit, who had already founded a very famous

224,15   monastery near holy Sion.[3] After spending the winter there, the servant of God Cyriacus conceived the desire to settle in the desert. Hearing from virtually everybody about the godly Euthymius, he asked the great father Eustorgius to be sent on his way with his blessing.

4. After receiving this, he came to the laura of the great Euthymius. After spending some days there with

224,20   a certain priest Anatolius and the monk Olympius, two blood-brothers who were Corinthians by birth and acquaintances of his, he made obeisance to the great Euthymius and was clothed by his holy hands in the habit. He was not allowed to stay there because of his

224,25   youth, but was sent to the Jordan to the sainted Gerasimus (the great Theoctistus having already died); the great Euthymius absolutely forbade having an adolescent in his laura. The sainted Gerasimus

225.   accepted him and, noting his youth, told him to stay in the cenobium.[4] There he hewed wood, carried water, cooked, and performed every kind of service with zeal. He spent his days in labor and toil, and his nights in

225,5   nights in prayer to God, adding to his manual work

a. Mt 16:24.

great zeal in the office of psalmody.

5. While serving in the cenobium, he mastered the life of anchorites, taking bread and water every other day and abstaining from oil, wine, and mixed drink, with the result that the great Gerasimus, observing the ascetic mode of life of the young man, was full of admiration and love for him. Consequently, in the

225,10   for him. Consequently, in the season of the holy fasts, he took him with confidence to the utter desert of Roubâ; there they lived in solitude till Palm Sunday, receiving communion each Sunday from the hands of the great Euthymius. A short time later, when the great

225,15   Euthymius died in Christ, the sainted Gerasimus saw his soul conducted by angels and carried up into heaven; taking Abba Cyriacus, he went up to his monastery and returned after burying his body. In the ninth year of Abba Cyriacus' stay in Palestine, our great father Gerasimus died and was adorned with

225,20   the crown of righteousness on 5 March of   [AD 475] the thirteenth indiction. The brothers Basil and Stephen having become the superiors, Abba Cyriacus left the monastery and came to the laura of the great Euthymius. On being accepted by the superior Elias, he

[AD 475]   took a cell and became a solitary in the twenty-
225,25   life, possessing nothing of this age.

6-7. HIS STAY AT THE LAURAS
OF EUTHYMIUS AND OF SOUKA

6. He labored hard at the building of the cenobium; for this was the time when the laura was changed into a cenobium. There was here at this time one called Thomas, a great man in his mode of life. On discovering his virtues and achievements, Abba Cyriacus became attached to him in spiritual affection, and was instructed and trained by him, adopting his mode of

226.   Thomas was sent by Fidus the deacon to Alexandria to
buy altar-cloths from the archbishop because of the
building of the cenobium; for the monasteries of our
fathers Euthymius and Theoctistus were then in harmony, having a common life and one administration

226,5   under a single steward in accordance with the injunction of the great Euthymius.[5] But twelve years after

[AD 485]   his holy death, when Abba Longinus, the superior of
the monastery of Abba Theoctistus had died and Paul
had succeeded as superior, Terebôn the Saracen, who
had earlier been baptized and healed by the great

226,10   Euthymius, left, when about to die, considerable property to both monasteries. When Paul willfully seized
hold of both the remains and the property of Terebôn,
turmoil resulted and a separation of the monasteries.

7. When in consequence the lands round the
monastery of the pious Euthymius were divided, Paul

226,15   built a tower on the lands so divided and gave two hundred *solidi* for the purchase of a hospice, in order to
keep sole possession himself of the shared hospice in
the holy city. It was at this time that the monks of the
monastery of the great Euthymius bought for these two
hundred *solidi* a hospice near the tower of David from

226,20   the fathers of the laura of Souka. Abba Cyriacus, distressed in mind at the separation of the monasteries,
withdrew and made his way to the laura of Souka at the

[AD 485]   end of the eighth indiction. He filled four offices in
different years, those of baker, infirmarian, guest-

226,25   master, and steward, and, having served and edified all
the fathers, was admitted into the clergy; for he had
already been ordained deacon in the monastery of the
great Euthymius. After four years, in the fortieth year

[AD 489]   of his life, he was appointed treasurer and canonarch;[6]
when he had completed thirteen years in this office,
he was made priest, while remaining treasurer and

227.   canonarch for a further eighteen years.

8-10. HE WITHDRAWS TO THE DESERT

8. He stated categorically to me, 'In this long period of thirty-one years in which I was canonarch and treasurer the sun never saw me either eating or in a temper.' He also said to me, 'I would not stop beating the summoning-block for the night psalmody until I had recited the whole of the "Blameless" psalm.'[a]

[AD 525] In the seventy-seventh year of his life, however, he handed over the treasurership, in the third indiction, and retired to the utter desert of Natoupha, accompanied by a disciple. Since *melagria* were not to be found 227,10 in this place, he begged God to enable them on account of bodily necessity to feed on the squills[7] there. And putting his trust in the Creator of all things, who is able to make the bitter sweet, he said to his disciple, 'Go, my child, gather squills and boil them. Blessed be God, 227,15 that we are able to be gladdened by them.' The disciple gathered and boiled them, and served them with salt. The squills became sweet immediately, and they continued to eat of them for a period of four years. At the end of four years, a man who was headman of the village of Thekoa, and had learnt about him from those 227,20 pasturing animals in the desert, made the journey to him with an ass laden with hot loaves and went away after unloading it.

9. They began to eat of this bread. The disciple, however, independently of the wishes of the elder, boiled squills in his accustomed manner; on tasting them, he could not bear their bitterness and lay there unable to speak. The elder, on learning the cause of the 227,25 misfortune, prayed over him and raised him up. Giving him a share of the spotless mysteries, he restored him to health, and admonished him with the words: 'My 228. child, God works miracles at all times, above all in

a. Ps 119 (118).

time of crisis and necessity, especially when the salvation of souls is also involved. So have no fear.' And when the loaves were exhausted and they were again in

228,5   great necessity, the elder blessed the disciple and instructed him to prepare squill for the hour of eating. The disciple was afraid to touch it; and so the elder took it and blessed it, making the sign of the cross, and was the first to begin to eat it. As a result, the disciple took courage and ate of it, and remained unharmed.

At the end of the fifth year of his stay in Natoupha, a

228,10   man of Thekoa, hearing of him, brought him his son who was severely epileptic and begged him to pray over him. Having compassion on him, the elder prayed over him and, anointing him with oil from the holy Cross, restored him to health.

10. On recovering his son in good health, the man of

228,15   Thekoa began to proclaim the miracle. When this story had been bruited through the whole district, many men came to Abba Cyriacus and importuned him. Fleeing from this importuning, he withdrew to the inner desert of Roubâ and stayed there for the space of five years, satisfied with the roots of *melagria* and hearts of reeds.

228,20   On discovering this, some came to him carrying the sick and those troubled by unclean spirits. These he treated by invoking Christ and using the sign of the venerable Cross. Then, vexed at so much importuning, he withdrew from Roubâ and repaired to a place that

228,25   was pure desert and hidden away, where none of the anchorites had settled. The place is called by the natives of the district Sousakim,[8] and it at the point of juncture of the two watercourses, those of the New Laura and of the laura of Souka, which are very deep and very terrifying. Some say that these watercourses are the rivers of Etham, of which David, in addressing praise to God, says, 'Thou didst dry up the rivers of

Etham'.[b] After he had spent seven years at Sousakim,

229.   the fathers of the laura of Souka in the days of the great
and terrifying mortality, out of fear of the impending
terror, came with one accord to supplicate him and,
after long entreaty, brought him back from Sousakim

229,5   to the laura. On returning to the laura, Abba Cyriacus
took up his abode in the anchoretic cell of the sainted
Chariton, where he strove for five years against the
Origenists.

11-15. THE AUTHOR'S FIRST
MEETING WITH CYRIACUS

11. At this time, having come from the monastery of
the great Euthymius to the Great Laura of blessed
Sabas to visit Abba John, bishop and solitary, I was

229,10   sent by him to Abba Cyriacus with letters recounting
the recent civil war in the holy city and entreating him
to strive now in intercession with God to quell the
raging of Nonnus and Leontius and their party at the
New Laura, who were campaigning against Christ by
means of the doctrines of Origen. When I had accord-

229,15   dingly arrived at Souka and gone to see him in the cave
of Saint Chariton with his disciples Zosimus and John,
I made obeisance and gave him the letter, adding a verbal message to him from the mouth of the inspired
Abba John the solitary. Abba Cyriacus replied with

229,20   tears: 'Say to the one who sent you: Let us not be
despondent, father, for we shall soon see the overthrow
of nonnus and Leontius in death and the expulsion of
the rest of them from the New Laura, in order that the
genuine disciples of blessed Sabas may inhabit the
New Laura, once the false ones have been chased out.'

b. Ps 73:15 (LXX).

229,25   12. I asked him, 'Father, what of the views they advocate? They themselves affirm that the doctrines of pre-existence and restoration are indifferent and without danger, citing the words of Saint Gregory, "Philosophize about the world, matter, the soul, the good and the evil rational natures, the Resurrection
229,30   and the Passion of Christ; for in these matters hitting on the truth is not without profit and error is without danger."'[9] The elder replied in the following words: 'The doctrines of pre-existence and restoration are not
230.   indifferent and without danger, but dangerous, harmful and blasphemous. In order to convince you, I shall try to expose their multifarious impiety in a few words. They deny that Christ is one of the Trinity. They say that our resurrection bodies pass to totaldestruction,
230,5   and Christ's first of all. They say that the holy Trinity did not create the world and that at the restoration all rational beings, even demons, will be able to create aeons. They say that our bodies will be raised etherial and spherical at the resurrection, and they assert that even the body of the Lord was raised in this form.
230,10   They say that we shall be equal to Christ at the restoration.[10]

13. 'What hell blurted out these doctrines? They have not learnt them from the God who spoke through the prophets and apostles—perish the thought—but they have revived these abominable and impious doctrines from Pythagoras and Plato, from Origen, Evagrius,
230,15   and Didymus. I am amazed what vain and futile labors they have expended on such harmful and laborious vanities, and how in this way they have armed their tongues against piety. Should they not rather have praised and glorified brotherly love, hospitality, virginity, care of the poor, psalmody, all-night vigils, and tears of compunction? Should they not be disciplin-
230,20   ing the body by fasts, ascending to God in prayer,

making this life a rehearsal for death, rather than meditating such sophistries? But (the elder added) they did not wish to follow the humble path of Christ, but instead "they became futile in their thoughts

230,25   and their senseless heart was darkened; saying they were wise, they became fools."[a] The sower of all these tares and cause of these evils was Nonnus, who, taking advantage of the death of our blessed father Sabas, began to make his neighbor drink of a foul concoction,[b]

230,30   having Leontius of Byzantium as his assistant, champion and fellow-combatant.

14. 'At first he seduced into his abominable heresy the more lettered, or rather the more unlettered, in the

231.   New Laura. He was not satisfied with these monks, but strove to give the other monasteries of the desert a share in his own plague. What strategems did he not use to drag in as well poor lowly me? But God showed to me by revelation the filth of his heresy. What schemes did he not employ to communicate his evil

231,5   teaching to the community of Souka? But he failed, since I by the grace of Christ warned and exhorted each one not to depart from the true faith. When he strove to make a supporter of his heresy—I mean Peter

231,10   the Alexandrian[11]—superior in our laura and thereby to enslave the community, he did not succeed: on the contrary, the community bestirred itself and expelled Peter from being superior. Again, Nonnus shamelessly bestirred himself into setting up another Peter, the Greek,[12] a supporter of the plague of Origen, as our superior, but the community was again stirred by spiri-

231,15   tual zeal into expelling Peter from being superior; going to the laura of blessed Sabas, it took for itself its present superior, Abba Cassianus, who is of

a. Rom 1:21-22.
b. Cf. Hab 2:15.

Scythopolis by birth, orthodox, and adorned both in his life and in his teaching.[13] It was then that we succeeded, with difficulty, in repelling the supporters of Origen.'

231,20   15. When he had told me this, the servant of God Cyriacus, overjoyed at learning that I am of the great monastery of blessed Euthymius, said to me, 'See, you are of the same cenobium as I.' And he proceeded to begin to recount to me many of the facts about Saints Euthymius and Sabas that I have placed in the two

231,25   works I have already written about them. And so, having nourished my soul with these accounts, he sent me on my way in peace.

Some had begun to pester him in the cave of the sainted Chariton. So when with the death of Nonnus, the leader of the Origenists, their control was over-

231,30   thrown and the campaign against the orthodox was shattered, while the heretics were now occupied in fighting each other, the elder felt free of care and with-

[AD 547]   drew again in the ninety-ninth year of his life from

232.   the cave of the sainted Chariton to Sousakim, where he lived as a solitary for eight years. I, out of a desire to pay my respects to him, came to the laura of Souka and, accompanied by his disciple John, went down to

232,5   Sousakim; this place is about ninety stades from the laura of Souka. As we drew near to the place, we met an enormous and terrifying lion. I was panic-stricken, but Abba John said to me, 'Have no fear.' And when the lion saw that we were going to the elder, it let us pass.

16-19. THE AUTHOR'S SECOND MEETING
WITH CYRIACUS

232,10   16. On seeing us, the elder was overjoyed and said, 'Here is Cyril, of the same cenobium as myself!' Abba

John said to him, 'He was utterly terrified, father, on seeing the lion.' The elder said to me, 'Have no fear, my child. This lion is my faithful servant here, guarding my herbs from the wild goats.' After telling me

232,15   many things about Saint Euthymius and the other fathers of this desert, he invited me to eat with him. While we were eating, the lion came and stood in front of us; rising, the elder gave it a piece of bread and sent it to guard the herbs. The elder said to me, 'It not only guards the herbs but also wards off brigands and bar-

232,20   barians.' After I had spent one day there and enjoyed his teaching to the full, on the following day he gave me a gift and, adding his blessing, sent me with his disciple on our way in peace. After leaving him, we found the lion sitting on the road and eating a wild goat. When the lion saw us standing there and not

232,25   daring to advance, it left its prey and withdrew until we had passed.

17. Since the place had no cistern, he devoted his attention to the holes in the rocks, whence he drew water in the winter which served him plentifully for his own needs and to water his herbs the whole summer.[14] When the water ran out in the month of July one year,

232,30   he was reduced to great straits and, raising his eyes to God, made the following petition: 'Lord God, provide me with a little water on account of the necessary needs of this my poor body.' God hearkened to him,

233.   and immediately a small cloud appeared above Sousakim which rained around his cell and filled all his receptacles between the rocks.

18. I think it right to make mention here of an edify-

233,5   ing story that Abba John related to me. While we were journeying in the desert, he showed me a spot which he said was the tomb of blessed Mary. Amazed at this, I asked him to relate her story.[15] He replied as follows: 'A short time ago, when I was going with my co-

233,10   disciple Abba Parammon to Abba Cyriacus, we beheld,
as we gazed from afar, an apparently human form
standing near a tamarisk. Thinking it to be one of the
anchorites there (for there were then many anchorites
in these parts), we hastened to pay our respects to him.
'When we drew near the spot, he had disappeared.
233,15   Seized with fear and dismay, we stood there praying,
thinking that he was an evil spirit. After completing the
Amen, we looked around here and there, and found an
underground cave, into which we presumed the true
servant of God had descended in order to hide from us.
On getting near the cave, we called to him and at the
233,20   same time adjured him, saying, "Do not deprive us,
father, of your prayers and of the benefit of meeting
you." He replied eventually with reluctance, "What do
you want from me? I am a woman." And she asked us,
"Where are you traveling?" We replied, "We are going
to the anchorite Abba Cyriacus. But tell us what is your
233,25   name and how you live and how you came here." She
said, "Be on your way, and I shall tell you on your
return." When we affirmed that we would not depart
before learning her story, she answered, "My name is
Mary. I became cantor of the holy church of the Resurrection of Christ, and the devil made many scandalized
233,30   with me. Fearing lest, in addition to being responsible
for such scandals, I should add sin to sin, I entreated
God to rescue me from being the cause of such scandals.

234.   19. '"One day, pierced to the heart with fear of God,
I went down to holy Siloam and filled this vessel with
water; taking also this basket of soaked pulses,[16] I left
the holy city by night, commending myself to God,
234,5   who led me here. And behold, I have been here for
eighteen years, and by the grace of God the water
has not failed nor has the basket of pulses run short
to this day. And neither have I seen a human being

except for you two today. But be on your way (she said) and fulfil your task, and visit me on your return." After hearing this, we made our jour-
234,10 ney to Abba Cyriacus and told him this story. On hearing it, he said in amazement, "Glory to thee, O God, for having such hidden saints. But go, my children, and do as she told you." So after we had received the holy elder's bless-ing, we went to the cave and knocked in the manner of
234,15 anchorites. On receiving no reply, we went in, and found her dead. Not having the wherewithal to bury and entomb her, we went up to our laura of Souka and brought down everything we needed. After performing her funeral, we buried her in the cave, blocking up the
234,20 door with stones.' This was Abba John's story. As I have said, I have judged it necessary to assign it to writ-ing for the compunction of my hearers and readers and to the glory of Christ, who provides those who love him with endurance to the end. But I must bring my account back to Abba Cyriacus.

20-21. THE DEATH OF CYRIACUS

20. When he had completed his eighth year at
234,25 Sousakim and attained extreme old age, the fathers of the laura of Souka came and brought him to the cave of the sainted Chariton, after the departure of the Origenists from the New Laura. While he was living in this cave, I in my lowliness often visited him and reaped great benefit for my soul. He was
234,30 very advanced in age, having completed his hundred-
[AD 556] his hundred-and-seventh year. For he came to the holy city at the age of eighteen, and stayed nine years with the sainted Gerasimus and ten years in the monastery of the great Euthymius. He spent thirty-three years at the laura of Souka, distinguishing him-

self in various offices, five years in the desert of Natoupha, eating squills, and five years in Roubâ. He lived as a solitary for seven years at Sousakim, for five years in the cave of the sainted Chariton, and for eight years on returning to Sousakim.[17]

21. Two years before his death, the fathers came and after much persuasion, brought him to the cave of blessed Chariton, when he was, as I have said, far advanced in age. But despite being such an old man, he was strong and zealous, standing for the office of psalmody and serving his visitors with his own hands. He was not in the least debilitated but was able to do everything, since Christ gave him strength. He was a kind and approachable man, good at both prophecy and teaching, and utterly orthodox, while in body he was tall and noble and with all his limbs in perfect condition. He was truly full of grace and of the Holy Spirit.

After several days, he was stricken by bodily weakness and summoned all the fathers of the laura. After greeting them, he died in peace, committing his soul to the Lord and receiving from him the crown of righteousness which he promised to those who love him.[a] And now he is enjoying the repose of all the saints and interceding for us, that we, following in his footsteps, may attain the promised good things in Christ Jesus our Lord, to whom be glory and dominion for ever and ever. Amen.

235,5

235,10

235,15

235,20

a. Cf. 2 Tim 4:8.

NOTES

1. Cyriacus was the source of several stories of Euthymius (29,27;30,6; 34,1; 35,10).

2. The Life of James of Nisibis also begins with a summary of the virtues of Old Testament characters (Theodoret, *History of the Monks of Syria* 1.1).

3. Nothing else in known of the monastery of Eustorgius.

4. Gerasimus' cenobium was used by Euthymius as a training ground for young monks, as Theoctistus' had been.

5. In the Georgian translation of the Life, an extra paragraph appears at this point (for arguments as to its authenticity, see Garitte, 'La version Géorgienne de la vie de Cyriaque' pp. 399-403') 'He brought with him a letter from the patriarch Martyrius to the patriarch of Alexandria and went on to complete his mission. When the patriarch saw the saint, the treasure in him did not escape his notice and he consecrated him bishop for the territory of Abyssinia; radiant with the grace within him, he built for Christ a number of churches and he illuminated all Ethiopia by his virtues. He had with him the mantle of St. Euthymius and, as had happened for Elijah and Elisha, the most radiant of the prophets, in the same way the Holy Thomas, with the mantle, accomplished many miracles.'

6. The canonarch was responsible for leading the singing and for summoning the monks to worship by beating the wooden summoning-block (*simandron*) with a mallet. The treasurer (or 'ceimêliarch') had responsibility for the sacred vessels.

7. Squills were probably the leaves of the desert asphodel, a bitter plant not usually used for food. See also 235,4.

8. Sousakim is further to the east and south than the other monasteries described by Cyril. For a description of the site, see Marcoff and Chitty, 'Notes on Monastic Research in the Judaean wilderness 1928-9'.

9. For this passage of Gregoy of Nazianzus, see *Ad Eunomium* 10 (PG 36:25A). It seems that Cyril was at this time sympathetic to the stimulating speculations of the Origenists.

10. These opinions resemble those attacked by the anathemas issued at the second Council of Constantinople, except that they add a detail not found in the anathemas, that souls in the resurrection will be able to create aeons or 'spiritual entities'. The views under attack are those of the Evagrian Isochrists. See *Life of Sabas*, Note 132.

11. For Peter the Alexandrian see 193,16.

12. Peter the Greek is not mentioned elsewhere.

13. Cassianus became superior at Souka in 538 and then moved to the Great Laura in 546. See 196,10-18.

14. Sousakim has a lower rainfall than the monasteries founded by Euthymius and Sabas, being further south. The deep ravine which it overlooks provided shelter from the sun, and the careful collection of the winter rain enabled Cyriacus to maintain a small vegetable garden. For modern experiments in desert agriculture, see Murphy-O'Connor, *The Holy Land* 134-5.

15. Compare John Moschus, *Spiritual Meadow* 170. The episodes are related to

the traditional story of St Mary of Egypt, recorded by Sophronius. She was a prostitute from Alexandria who visited Jerusalem but found herself unable to enter the Church of the Resurrection, an event which led her to live in the desert as an ascetic. See E. Patlagean, 'L'histoire de la femme deguisée en moine'.

16. For soaked pulses compare Theodoret, *History of the Monks of Syria* 24.5 and 30.2.

17. Cyril's calculations are accurate. The dates are as follows:

Birth: January 449
Arrival at Jerusalem: September 466 (18th Year)
At Gerasimus' cenobium: 466-475
At Euthymius' laura: 475-485
At Souka: 485-525
In Roubâ: 525-530
At Sousakim: 530-537
At Chariton's cave: 537-546
At Sousakim: 546-554

LIFE OF SAINT THEODOSIUS

1. HIS EARLY YEARS[1]

236.

236,5

236,10

236,15

236,20

THEODOSIUS, WORTHILY CALLED BLESSED and citizen of heaven, the great glory of Palestine and boast of the desert, the stay of the monastic order, the general and champion of the correct doctrines, the leader and patron of the cenobitic rule, had Cappadocia as his fatherland;[2] he came from the village called Mogariassus, which is subject to the city of Caesarea and lies not far from the city of Comana called the Golden. He was from childhood a most proficient cantor in the holy church of Comana, where he was accurately instructed in the office of the Church and learnt thoroughly the psalter and the other holy Scriptures. Seized as a result with godly desire and compunction, he came to Jerusalem in the reign of Marcian, dear to God, with the intention of settling as an anchorite in the desert nearby. He was welcomed at the Tower of David by Longinus, a Cappadocian elder in the community of ascetics[3] attached to the holy church of the Resurrection of Christ our God. Although Theodosius wished to withdraw to one of the monasteries of the desert, being a lover of solitude and clothed in the fear of God as in a garment, blessed Longinus did not give him permission, on account of the schism of those monks in the desert who were not in communion with the catholic Church but in the sway of the contentious spirit and heresy of Eutyches and Dioscorus. Instead, he took him and entrusted him to blessed and sainted Hicelia, who was then building the church of the Cathisma of the Mother of God,[4] since he would be able to be of use to her in the office of the Church and the other ministries; it was blessed Hicelia who at this time, having practised the whole way of piety, led the way in having the Presentation of God our Saviour celebrated with

236,25 candles. She received the holy youth Theodosius and, finding him a very gifted cantor, enrolled him in the community of pious ascetics under her there. Some time later, when blessed Hicelia had died, he was appointed steward of the place. While he was performing this ministry blamelessly, it happened that the superior of the place died, at which they all unanimously elected Theodosius superior of the church of the Cath-

237. isma. But he, on hearing this, in fear of the danger in wielding authority, departed in flight.

2. HE RETIRES TO THE DESERT

He went first of all to the region of Metopa, to the blessed Marinus the anchorite and Abba Luke of Metopa.[5] He learnt the rule of the desert from them,

237,5 while they had originally been taught monastic discipline by Saint Euthymius. Having stayed with them for some years, Abba Theodosius went to the mountain where, with the help of God, his holy monastery is now established, six miles from the holy city, and settled there in the cave where his revered remains now lie,

237,10 feeding himself on wild plants. Then he received a disciple and taught him this austere mode of life. Having discovered on one occasion that this disciple had acquired a pot and pan, he expelled him with the words, 'If you are determined to eat cooked food, you cannot stay with me, for I lead a more austere life.' The expelled disciple took refuge with the sainted Marcianus,

237,15 mentioned above, who was a cenobitic superior near holy Bethlehem. This great Marcianus summoned Abba Theodosius and said to him, 'You have expelled a brother for acquiring a pan. Lo, the days are coming,

237,20   says the Lord, when the utensils of your monastery will be carried on poles.[a] For "a city set on a hill cannot be hid,"[b] and therefore God will make you, who have hidden yourself, conspicuous and manifest to all.' This prophecy did not err, as has become clear to all; for by the favor of God the Father, the help of Christ, and the inspiration of the Holy Spirit he has founded there a

237,25   great and populous cenobium, that surpasses all and reigns supreme among the cenobia in the whole of Palestine. That it was by the help and favor of God and not as a result of human effort that the cenobium of Abba Theodosius was founded, I shall try to demonstrate by a few proofs.

3. HE FOUNDS A HOSPICE
AND A CENOBIUM

238.   While he was hidden in the cave, as I have said, in great voluntary poverty, subsisting on plants and devoting himself uniquely to prayer, a man coming from Byzantium, called Acacius, a lover of Christ and honored

238,5   with the rank of *illustris*,[6] who had heard of his virtue and was eager to acquire the fine pearls of the Gospel,[a] came to visit him in the said cave and, after making obeisance to him, sat down to hear his exhortation and teaching. Knowing that he could not bear ever to receive anything from anyone, he buried in the cave without his consent a box containing one hundred

238,10   *solidi*, and so embraced him and departed. On his return to Byzantium he continued for a long time to send each year to the blessed Theodosius a large fixed sum

---

a. Cf. Num 4:14.
b. Mt 5:14.
a. Cf. Mt 13:45.

238,15   as a gift. So much for Acacius. The great Theodosius, on the day after the departure of the *illustris*, found the said money hidden in the cave. With it he first of all founded a hospice above the cave, where he welcomed everyone who visited him; he also bought two little asses, and would go on his own to fetch what was needed for the body. Then he commenced the building of his cenobium. From this time many began to hasten

238,20   to him, asking to live with him; and he accepted them and guided them in following the perfect will of God. God helped him in everything, and 'he was a successful man', as we hear of Joseph.[b]

4. HE IS MADE ARCHIMANDRITE. HIS DEATH

It is said of him that he possessed three exceptional

238,25   virtues: strict asceticism, linked to true and orthodox faith, that lasted from youth till old age, lavish charity, without respect of persons, towards strangers and the poor, and, as the third, zeal at performing the divine liturgy, virtually without interruption.[7] Since the great

239.   Theodosius was preeminent in these and similar feats and combats, as soon as the sainted Abba Marcianus had died in Christ, all the monks of the desert, assembling in the presence of Patriarch Sallustius (who was ill) and being of one mind, elected the great Theodosius by un-

239,5   animous vote archimandrite of the cenobia subject to the holy city, in the place of Gerontius of the monasteries of blessed Melania. They appointed as his deputy the sainted Paul, superior of the monastery of Abba Martyrius. In the place of the blessed fathers Passariôn and Elpidius they appointed our father Saint Sabas archi-

239,10   mandrite and lawgiver of all the lauras and anchorites of

b. Gen 39:2.

Palestine[8] and as his deputy the blessed Eugenius, superior of the laura of the sainted Abba Gerasimus.

So the inspired Abba Theodosius, advancing in godly
excellences, became great. Need one say more about
239,15   him? His virtues are sufficiently proclaimed by his
godly life and the spiritual state of his own famous and
holy monastery. In addition, the most venerable Theodore, the most pious bishop of the city of Petra, who
became his disciple and is conspicuous for monastic and
episcopal virtues, has written at length, with both
239,20   clarity and accuracy, about his life pleasing to God.[9]

After combating and competing in this desert for a
period of fifty years and gaining the crown, after ex-
hibiting countless many combatants and victors in piety
and attaining to extreme old age, he was stricken by
bodily illness and, after continuing in this state for some
239,25   time in a spirit of thankfulness, entrusted his soul into
the hands of God as[a] an old man and full of days, having almost reached the hundredth year of his life. His
[AD 529]   death occurred on 11 January in the seventh indiction
in the twenty-second month of the reign of our God-
protected emperor Justinian.

5. HIS SUCCESSOR SOPHRONIUS

240.   One Sophronius, who had shown himself excellent in
monastic virtues, succeeded as superior of the monastery of Abba Theodosius. Sophronius was Armenian
by birth from the village called Zomeri near the metropolis of Sebaste. Leaving his fatherland when he was
240,5   still young, he came to Jerusalem and met many of the
fathers, discovering the virtue and mode of life of each
one and receiving their imprint in his own soul; he also

a. Gen 25:8.

came to the monastery of blessed Theodosius. Having put on the monastic habit, received a monastic formation and acquired the monastic virtues, he made
240,10 humility and obedience the root and foundation of his life. After he had proceeded through all the ascetic virtues, performed many and various offices in this monastery and won approval, he became prior for a period of fifteen years, and then by the vote of the
240,15 great Abba Theodosius when about to die succeeded him as superior of the monastery.

The blessed Sophronius had a relative called Mamas, who, having had an accident in his youth and been castrated by the doctors, went up to Byzantium, where he became a *cubicularius* of the emperor Anastasius and, after a time, advanced to the rank of *prae-*
240,20 *positus.*[10] This man gave a huge and uncountable offering to the monastery. Out of this offering the sainted Sophronius enlarged and expanded the monastery fourfold after the death of blessed Theodosius, and erected from the foundations in this holy monastery a church to the mother of God and ever-virgin Mary, hymned by
240,25 all. But why should I speak at length? The labors and achievements of Sophronius are conspicuous in the monastery of blessed Abba Theodosius. for he not only enriched it with property and annual revenues, but also increased threefold its community in Christ. In a word,
241. having governed the monastery well for fourteen years and two months, he died in joy on 21 March of the fifth
[AD 542] indiction. When about to die, he said to his disciple who was standing by and weeping, 'Do not grieve, my child, for, if I find free access to God, I shall take you on the seventh day, so that you may be with me
241,5 in the place of rest.' And this took place: on the seventh day the disciple died, and Sophronius' free access to God was thereby made known to all.

NOTES

1. He was born c. 430 (see 239,26-30).

2. There were many Cappadocians in the Judaean monasteries, including Sabas, the patriarch Martyrius, and Cosmas Bishop of Scythopolis. In his cenobitic way of life Theodosius was influenced by Saint Basil, another Cappadocian; see Theodore of Petra, *The Life of Theodosius* 50.13.

3. 'Ascetics' translates '*spoudaioi*', who were monks committed to ministering to pilgrims and visitors to the Holy City. Patriarch Elias was later to provide them with a more regulated way of life (116,9-24).

4. The church of the Cathisma of the Mother of God is on the road between Jerusalem and Bethlehem. See Vailhé 20 and Ovadiah 152.

5. See 16,9-14. Theodosius is claimed to belong to the monastic tradition founded by Euthymius.

6. *Illustris* or *illustrissimus* was a general title for the highest imperial officials of senatorial rank.

7. The monastic traditions of Judaea emphasised hospitality for pilgrims and liturgical worship alongside ascetic discipline.

8. See, for a fuller account, 114.25-115,26.

9. Theodore of Petra's *Life* is lengthy, diffuse, and rhetorical. It has been translated into French by A-J Festugière in *Moines d'Orient* 3/3.

10. A *praepositus* was a commanding officer or tribune.

LIFE OF OUR FATHER
THEOGNIUS THE BISHOP

THE WHOLLY RENOWNED THEOGNIUS,[1] the great glory of the whole of Palestine, the dazzling light of the desert and brilliant luminary of the episcopacy, had as his fatherland the province of Cappadocia and the city of Ararathia, where from early youth he was instructed in the monastic life.[2] On coming to Jerusalem in the fifth year of the reign of Marcian, he found the Aposchists in control of the holy city but, since he refused to be seduced by their irrational opposition and love of turmoil, he attached himself to a virtuous lady, protected by the Holy Spirit, called Flavia, who at this time was founding near the Mount of Olives a monastery and church of the saintly martyr Julian. She received him and, having tested him for a considerable time and found him reliable and virtuous, made him administrator of her monastery. She herself migrated from Palestine to the land that had borne her, because of the needs of the church she had built, and died in her fatherland. At this the wholly renowned Theognius was forced by almost the whole community to become superior of the church. In fear of the danger of wielding authority, he fled to the desert.

He came to the thrice blessed Abba Theodosius and stayed with him for a considerable time. He illuminated all the community by the luster of his life and became outstanding in monastic attainments, so that all who saw his fine works glorified the Father in heaven.[a] But although he was praised by all and admired for his blameless conduct and holiness of life, he himself was afraid of the harm his soul would naturally suffer from praise and human glory; at the same time he saw that

241,15

AD 454/5

241,20

242.

242,5

242,10

a. Cf. Mt 5:16.

242,15   the monastery, with the help of God, was growing
gradually in size and wealth, and was worried about
the turmoil that arises from distraction. Consequently
he withdrew to the district around the monastery and,
on finding a cave, settled in it and lived there in
solitude for some time. Becoming a temple of the all-
holy Spirit and being clothed with power from on high,
he worked extraordinary cures of chronic illnesses and
242,20   performed numerous miracles. Becoming famous as a
result, he founded for himself, in gradual stages, a famous cenobium.[3]

After some time had passed, Archbishop Elias heard
about him and ordained him bishop of Betylius, which
is a small seaside town ninety miles distant from the
242,25   holy city; the godly Theognius unwillingly accepted
episcopal office. When he had been some time in the
said town, the adjacent sea overpassed its bounds and
poured towards the town, threatening to uproot it and
destroy it by force, God having doubtless ordained this
242,30   in order to chastise the inhabitants and display the divine grace of Theognius. Seized with terror as they saw
the sea surge upwards, they fled to the righteous one,
and begged him to curb this great onset by prayer.
Yielding to their repeated entreaty, the great champion
of piety Theognius came to the shore and, going into
242,35   the water, stuck in a cross at the original bounds of the
243.   sea, while uttering the scriptural saying addressed to
the sea: 'Thus says the Lord: You will come as far as
this cross and not overpass it, but in yourself shall your
waves be shattered.'[a] Then, having stuck in the cross,
he returned. The sea immediately returned to its own
243,5   bounds; and to his day, however fiercely it rages, when
it touches the cross stuck in by the righteous one, it is
curbed and goes back.

a. Cf. Job 38:11.

But what need have I of further words about the famous Theognius, especially since Abba Paul, solitary of the city of Elusa, a man radiant in monastic virtues and orthodox doctrines who illuminates our godly steps by his life and teaching, has preceded me in writing the life of the same blessed Theognius both accurately and comprehensively? The great Theognius, having bay his own life given luster to the monastic order and mode of life and adorned the episcopal see by spiritual feats and divine charisms, thereby distinguishing himself greatly and brilliantly in both orders, went up to his own monastery in the desert at the end of his life, God having presumably revealed to him the time of his death. After a short illness, he passed to the life without pain or turmoil, the abode of all those who truly rejoice.

NOTES

1. Theognius is not named in Cyril's other lives. A fuller Life was written by Paul of Elousa, which contains many of the details from Cyril's life. See *Acta Sancti Theognii Episcopi Beteliae, AnBoll* 10 (1891) 78-113.

2. He was born in 425, and was probably a near neighbor of Theodosius. See J. Van den Gheyn, 'St. Theognius Evêque de Bételie en Palestine', 566.

3. Theognius' cenobium is to the south of Theodosius' monastery. Corbo suggests that it was at Khirbet Makhrum (see Corbo, *Gli Scavi di Kh. Siyar el-Ghanam*, 159). See also Vailhé 132.

LIFE OF OUR HOLY FATHER
ABRAAMIUS WHO BECAME
BISHOP OF CRATEA

1. HIS EARLY YEARS

THE WHOLLY RENOWNED ELDER Abraamius had parents called Paul and Thecla, whose fatherland and home was Emesa, the famous metropolis of Syria.[1] He was born of them at the beginning of the reign of Zeno, and made his renunciation at an early age in a monastery near the metropolis. After receiving an excellent formation in the monastic life, in the eighteenth year of his life on the occasion of a Saracen attack on this monastery he went up with his abbot to Constantinople. After a short time had elapsed, it so happened that his abbot became superior of one of the monasteries at Constantinople; he kept this luminary as his authentic fellow-combatant, obedient disciple, and most trustworthy steward. As time progressed, Abraamius distinguished himself by a variety of virtues, both in offices inside the monastery and in external business, and became dear to all on account of his friendliness towards everybody, the sweetness of his character, the purity and dignity of his conduct, and the holiness of his spiritual state.

[AD 474]
244.

[AD 491]

244,5

244,10

2. HE BECOMES SUPERIOR AT CRATEA

While he was excelling in these and similar virtues, a distinguished man called John, originating from the city of Cratea in Honorias,[2] who had won a high reputation in many public offices and was *comes largitionum*, having got his brother Plato made bishop of this city, resolved to found a monastery at the tomb of

244,15

his parents. Learning of the pure conduct and unim-
244,20   peachable life of Abraamius, he asked his superior to
release him to take charge of the monastery to be
founded. Released with his abbot's blessing, Abraamius came to Cratea, where he built the monastery
and in the twenty-seventh year of his life was made
[AD 500]   priest and superior of this monastery by the Bishop
244,25   Plato of Cratea just mentioned. During his ten years as
superior, he made the monastery there famous and assembled many brethren, whom he guided according to
the will of God and educated in the life of monks.

3. HE ENTERS THE TOWER NEAR JERUSALEM

244,30   With the report of him circulating everywhere, many
came to him, both monks and laypeople; even bishops
flocked to him, delighted by his conversation. But he,
as a lover of solitude from boyhood, was distressed at
the disturbance this caused him. Becoming quite de-
245.   spondent, he left the city secretly and fled to the holy
city, taking nothing of the things of this world, and in
great poverty and straits arrived at Jerusalem at the
beginning of the fifth indiction, when he had com-
[AD 511]   pleted the thirty-seventh year of his life. It so happened that, when venerating the holy church of the
245,5   Resurrection, he met the sainted John, the former
scholarius who had become a disciple of our sainted
father Sabas and in this period had been entrusted by
him with the tower previously built by blessed
Eudocia, as I have already said in my two accounts of
Euthymius and Sabas.[3] The blessed John, on noting
245,10   Abraamius' composure of character, disciplined gaze
and timely speech, recognized him as a servant of God.
Taking him to the hospice of the Great Laura (he had
not yet acquired his own hospice), he introduced him
to the blessed Sabas and admitted him, with permis-

245,15 sion, to the tower just mentioned. Abraamius found there two inspired elders adorned with godly understanding, whom blessed Sabas had established there together with the Scholarius; they were called John and Gregory, and were of Pontus by birth.[4] He attached himself to them in spirit, showing obedience to them in everything; for he found them competent to guide souls to salvation.

4. HE IS JOINED BY OLYMPIUS

245,20 At this same time the Holy Spirit led to Jerusalem a distinguished man originating from Claudiopolis in Honorias, called Olympius. Having very frequently been replenished by Abraamius' spiritual discourse at Cratea, which is near Claudiopolis, he was in search of him and,

245,25 on discovering where he was living, visited him in the Tower in order to press and urge him to return to Cratea; for Bishop Plato, by urging him repeatedly, had sent him to search out Abraamius and win him back. Abraamius received Olympius with great joy, and ex-

245,30 horted and urged him by the word of God to renounce the things of this life and to devote himself to the fear of God. Olympius responded to Abraamius' exhortation and, on hearing of the virtue and mode of life of the elders John and Gregory and of John the Scholarius

246. and receiving their impress in his soul, became disposed to renounce this transitory life; he was specially illuminated by the dazzling grace of our sainted father Sabas, who was making the Tower into a cenobium at this time and taking great care of these fathers. So

246,5 Olympius devoted himself wholeheartedly to God, and in a short time reached such a height of virtue that he was forcibly ordained deacon and priest and given the second position in the government of the monastery.

5. HE IS FORCED TO RETURN TO CRATEA

246,10   After completing four years in the monastery of the Scholarius, the venerable Abraamius was forced to return to Cratea in the following manner. The above-mentioned Bishop Plato of Cratea, after summoning him frequently and achieving nothing, applied the ecclesiastical canons: first he suspended him and then, when he continued as before, sent him a decree of excommunication. At this, blessed John the Scholarius,

246,15   taking him to the Great Laura, laid his case before our great father Sabas, and our great father, taking them both to the holy city, introduced them to Archbishop Elias and asked him, if it was possible, to remit the excommunication. But the great bishop replied that it was uncanonical to remit an excommunication issued by another, especially while the ordaining and excom-

246,20   municating bishop was still alive and had not been summoned. On hearing this, the blessed fathers Sabas and John told him to go to his bishop and obtain remission from him. Yielding to the advice of the fathers, Abba Abraamius went to Cratea, at the completion of

246,25   the forty-first year of his life. On arriving at Cratea, he
[AD 515]   was graciously received by his bishop and restored to his office as superior with the excommunication

247.   remitted. After remitting this, Bishop Plato lived on a few days and then died.[5] At this the whole people of Cratea, by unanimous vote and a petition to the metropolitan of the province, asked for Abraamius as bishop, and the metropolitan, summoning him as if on

247,5   some other business, ordained him bishop of Cratea.

6. HIS EPISCOPACY AT CRATEA

At this point, out of consideration for brevity, I shall pass over in silence the individual pious acts performed

by him as bishop—his orphanages, hospices, hospitals, his casting out of demons and succour of the needy, his
247,10 building of churches and working of a variety of miracles—, and hasten on to the end of the account of his episcopacy. When he had distinguished himself in the episcopacy for fifteen years and illuminated his city by his life and teaching, it happened that his church had business to transact with certain individuals such
247,15 that he was forced against his will to frequent palaces and go up to the imperial city. Remembering the monastic solitude he had enjoyed when he was an ascetic in the monastery of the Scholarius, he was deeply grieved and vexed at seeing himself in the distraction and turmoil of the cares of life. He entreated God
247,20 earnestly, saying, 'Lord God, if it is thy pleasure that I should withdraw into the desert, ensure that thy will be done.'[6]

7. HIS RETURN TO THE HOLY LAND[7]

An Boll On his arrival at Constantinople, he heard that our
XXIV: father the lord Sabas was there. Burning with desire to
354,7 see him, he began to look for him eagerly and, when he
354,10 could not find the beloved elder, made inquiries about him. He discovered that three days before his own arrival at Constantinople Sabas had left for Jerusalem. While he was keenly grieving at not having found him, the following night in his sleep he saw Sabas, who said to him, 'Do not regret so bitterly having missed me at
354,15 Constantinople. If it is indeed your wish to be relieved of the cares of this life, return to your monastery and there you will find rest.' When he awoke from sleep, he revealed none of this to anyone; he immediately sent off the deacons to whom he entrusted everything he had procured for the use of his church and, taking with him nothing of the things of this world, boarded a
354,20 ship and departed to Jerusalem, from where he went

immediately to the monastery of the Tower. His return brought immense joy to John the Scholarius and the noble Olympius.[8] These three became like one soul, and by sharing abode, food, and good deeds they urged each other on to pious works. They thought of nothing save what accorded with the divine will and, by withdrawing from the activities of this world, they

354,25   drew near to God. Abraamius had spent a whole year since his arrival when our holy father lord Sabas passed from this life on 5 December.[9]

8. THE DEATHS OF OLYMPIUS
AND JOHN THE SCHOLARIUS

During the days of fasting the holy Abraamius used
354,30   to withdraw with John the Scholarius and Olympius into the utter desert of Roubâ. When they saw the silent inhabitants of this wilderness, they imitated their penance by staying in this place, the three of them together, for eight years, zealous at what pertains to
355.   this mode of life. At the end of this time Olympius died, after so surpassing all the monks as to attain the gift of prophecy.

The great Abraamius was a doctor of both souls and bodies. He was visited at the monastery by a vast num-
355,5   ber of men, in search of cures for every kind of disease. Not long afterwards John the Scholarius became unwell and, after being ill for a short period, was informed by the Holy Spirit that he was about to pass from this world. He gave his last instructions and then departed to Christ four days after the beginning of his
355,10   illness, in the month of January, when Abraamius had
[AD 542]   completed the sixty-eighth year of his life. Cyriacus succeeded him in ruling the monastery, until he resigned from being superior.

9. THE MIRACLES OF ABRAAMIUS

God in his great mercy made known the grace that he had given to the famous Abraamius. He had a disciple called Leontius who had settled at a distance from the monastery;[10] this disciple had attached to 355,15 himself a man of the region called Paul. It happened that Paul had a mental seizure, and so Leontius, bringing him with him, led him to the monastery of the Scholarius to see Abraamius. When the demon saw him, it hurled Paul to the ground and began to torment and afflict him. At his cries everyone in the monastery 355,20 rushed up. Meanwhile the demon was blaspheming God and uttering furious slanders against Abraamius. 'Woe is me because of you, Abraamius,' he said; 'Why do you torture me?' Abraamius exclaimed, 'I order you in the name of Jesus Christ to depart from this man and not to return to him afterwards in any way.' The demon came out immediately, and the man was cured instantly.

355,25   In the monastery of the Scholarius was another brother who suffered seriously from a haemorrhage and had applied in vain every kind of treatment and remedy. When he heard what Bishop Abraamius had performed in the case of Paul, he kept his plan secret and, entering the church about midday, took off his 355,30 clothes and with firm faith sat down on the seat which Abraamius customarily used. As the sick man touched the seat on which the elder was wont to sit, the haemorrhage dried up and at once he recovered his former health. The inmates of the cenobium, when they saw this sudden change, asked him the cause of his restored health. He revealed to them his inspired plan. 356,1 Utterly amazed, they gave praise to God, who is the cause of miracles, and admired the grace which God had given to his servant Abraamius.

10. HIS ORTHODOXY AND DEATH

Abraamius was zealous in the cause of the orthodox faith, and opposed to all who had departed from it. He believed the Son of God to be one of the Trinity and that the same is perfect God and perfect man, endowed with a perfect rational soul, perfect in Godhood and perfect in manhood, working the miracles by his Godhood and undergoing the passion in his manhood.

The brilliant deeds of this elder and the spiritual gifts he received from God made him the glory of the monastic order. He died on 6 December,[11] and passed to the place without pain or turmoil, the abode of those who alone truly rejoice, and received a heavenly crown from Christ our God, to whom be glory, praise and dominion for ever and ever. Amen.

356,10

NOTES

1. Emesa, today known as Homs, is on the river Orontes. It was the capital of Phoenicia Libanensis.
2. Honorias included parts of Bithynia and Paphlagonia in Pontus.
3. See 128, 17-18. John is not mentioned in the *Life of Euthymius* and Cyril uses this general title to refer to the two Lives together.
4. John is mentioned in the *Life of Sabas* 128,17-25. He does not appear in the *Life of Euthymius*.
5. Abraamius' monastery at Cratea was also in Pontus.
6. Plato of Cratea had been present at the Home Synod at Constantinople in July 518 (Schwartz, 246). So he was alive for at least three years after Abraamius' return, which means that the 'few days' of 247,1 is inaccurate.
7. There are several small gaps in the manuscript between 247,10 and 247,23. The text has been reconstructed by Schwartz.
8. The Greek manuscript breaks off at this point, but an Arabic text contains the rest of the Life. It has been translated into Latin by P. Peeters as *Historia S. Abramii*, in *Analecta Bollandiana* 24 (1905). The remainder of the translation is from this version.
9. Here and elsewhere the Arabic version calls Olympius 'Albinius'.
10. The Arabic version wrongly gives 25 December, which Peeters corrects to 5 December. The 'a whole year' implies the incorrect dating of Sabas' death to 531 (see *Life of Sabas*, note 110). A much more serious discrepancy is that, while Cyril dates Abraamius' final visit to Constantinople to 530 (the date of Sabas' visit, 173,11: 179,11), the Acts of the Synod of Constantinople of 536 prove that he visited Constantinople, and was still bishop of Cratea, in that year (Schwartz, 248).
11. The phrases 'called Leontius' and 'at a distance from the monastery' are our own supplement; the Arabic manuscript has a brief lacuna at this point.
12. Cyril's usual practice is to add the Indiction number to the day and month. This enables the date to be calculated. Perhaps the Indiction year was present in the Greek original but was omitted by the Arabic translator as a method of dating unknown to his Arabic-speaking readership.

TABLE OF ABBREVIATIONS

ACO	Acta Conciliorum Oecumenicorum
ACW	Ancient Christian Writers (Westminster, Maryland)
An Boll	Analecta Bollandiana
BZ	Byzantinische Zeitschrift
CCL	Corpus Auctorum Christianorum Latinorum (Turnhout)
CS	Cistercian Studies Series (Kalamazoo, Michigan)
CSCO	Corpus Scriptorum Christianorum Orientalium (Paris, Louvain)
GCS	Die Griechischen Christlichen Schriftsteller der ersten drei Jahrhunderte (Berlin)
IEJ	Israel Exploration Journal
LCL	Loeb Classical Library (Harvard University Press)
NPNF	Nicene and Post-Nicene Fathers series (Grand Rapids, Michigan)
PEFQST	Palestine Exploration Fund Quarterly Statement
PG	Patrologia Graeca, ed J.P. Migne (Paris)
PL	Patrologia latina, ed J.P. Migne (Paris)
PO	Patrologia Orientalis (Paris)
RB	Revue Biblique
ROC	Revue de l'Orient Chrétien
SCh	Sources Chrétiennes (Paris)
SH	Subsidia Hagiographica (Brussels)
TU	Texte und Untersuchungen zur Geschichte der altchristlichen Literatur (Leipzig; Berlin)

BIBLIOGRAPHY

1. Primary Sources

Acta Conciliorum Oecumenicorum, Ed E. Schwartz. Berlin, 1914-71.

Antonius Placentinus, *Itinerarium*, CCL 175.

Antony of Choziba, *Life of George of Choziba*, An Boll 7 (1988) 97-144.

Apophthegmata Patrum. Alphabetical Collection. PG 65:71-440. Trans. Benedicta Ward, *The Sayings of the Desert Fathers*, CS 59. Kalamazoo-Oxford, 1975.

Apophthegmata Patrum, Anonymous Collection, partially published by F. Nau, *ROC* 12-14, 17-18 (1907-9, 1912-3); trans. Benedicta Ward, *The Wisdom of the Desert Fathers*, Oxford 1975.

Athanasius, *Life of Antony*, PG 26:835-976; trans. ACW 10 (1950).

Basil, *Letters*. PG 32:220-1112, and LCL. 4 volumes. 1926-1934.

————. *Rules*, PG 31:901-1305; trans. W. Lowther Clarke, *The Ascetic Works of Saint Basil*. London 1925.

Cassian, *Conferences and Institutes*, SC 42, 54, 64, 109 (1955-65); trans. *NPNF* 2nd Series 11 (1894) 201-545, [forthcoming, CS Series].

Cyril of Alexandria, *Letter to Acacius, PG* 77:181-201.

Cyril of Scythopolis, *Lives*, ed E. Schwartz, *Kyrillos von Skythopolis, TU* 49:2. Leipzig 1939.

Egeria, *Itinerarium, SCh* 296 (1982); trans. J. Wilkinson. London 1971.

Eusebius, *Ecclesiastical History, GCS* 9 (3 vols, 1903-9); trans. Lawlor and Oulton. London 1927-8.

Evagrius, *Ecclesiastical History*, ed. Bidez and Parmentier, London 1898; trans. (anon) London 1846.

Gerontius, *Life of Melania*, SCh 90 (1962).

Gregory of Nazianus, *Elogium on Basil*, ed F. Boulenger, *Discours Funèbres en l'honneur de son frère Césaire et de Basile de Césarée*. Paris, 1908.

————. *Theological Orations*, SCh 247 (1978).

Hesychius, *Works*, PG 27:649-1344, 55:711-784, 93:1180-1448.

Hippolytus, *Chronography*, GCS (1955).

Historia Monachorum in Aegypto, SH 34 (1961). Trans. Norman Russell, *The Lives of the Desert Fathers*, CS 34. Oxford-Kalamazoo, 1980.

Jerome, *Commentary on Ezekiel*, PL 25:15-491.

————. *Life of Chariton*, PL 23:29-55.

283

John Malalas, *Chronography,* PG 97:65-718. Trans. M. Spinka and G. Downey. Chicago, 1940.

John Moschus, *The Spiritual Meadow,* PG 87:2851-3112.

John Rufus, *The Life of Peter the Iberian,* ed. R. Raabe, *Petrus Der Iberer.* Leipzig, 1895; trans. D.M. Lang, *Lives and Legends of the Georgian Saints.* London, 1956.

————. *Plerophoria,* PO 8 (1912) 11-183.

Justinian, *Dogmatic Works,* PG 86:945-1146.

Leontius of Byzantium, *Works,* PG 86:1268-2016.

Liberatus, Breviarium, ACO 2:5:98-141.

Life of Chariton, ed G. Garitte, *Bulletin de l'Institut Historique de Belge* 21 (1940) 5-40.

Life of Hypatius, SCh 177 (1971).

Life of Pachomius (First Greek Life), SH 19 (1932); trans. Armand Veilleux, CS 45. Kalamazoo, 1980.

Life and Miracles of Thecla, SH 62 (1978).

Nilus of Ancyra, *De monastica exercitatione,* PG 79:720-809.

Origen, *Homilies on Luke,* GCS 35 (1930).

Palladius, *Lausiac History,* ed C. Butler. Cambridge, 1904. Trans. ACW 34 (1965).

Paul of Elousa, *Life of Theognius,* An Boll 10 (1891) 78-113.

Socrates Scholasticus, *Ecclesiastical History,* PG 67:33-841. Trans. NPNF 2nd Series 2, 1-178.

Sozomen, *Ecclesiastical History,* GCS 50 (1960). Trans. NPNF 2nd Series 2, 236-427.

Strategius, *Capture of Jerusalem,* ed G. Garitte, CSCO Scr Ib 11-12 (1960).

Theodore of Petra, *Life of Theodosius.* ed H. Usener, *Der Heilige Theodosius.* Leipzig, 1890.

Theodoret, *Religious History,* SCh 234, 257 (1977-79). Trans. R.M. Price, *A History of the Monks of Syria,* CS 88. Kalamazoo, 1985.

Theophanes, *Chronography,* ed C. de Boor. Leipzig, 1883-5.

Zacharias of Mitylene, *Ecclesiastical History,* CSCO Scr Syr 3:5-6 (1924). Trans. Hamilton and Brooks, *Syriac Chronicle known as that of Zachariah of Mitylene.* London, 1899.

2. Cyril of Scythopolis

Cameron, A. 'Cyril of Scythopolis, V. Sabae 53; a note on *kata* in late Greek', *Glotta* 56 (1978) 87-94.

Devos, P. 'Cyrille de Scythopolis, Influences littéraires—Vêtement de l'évêque de Jérusalem—Passarion et Pierre l'Ibère', An Boll 98 (1980) 25-38.

Dolger, F. 'E. Schwartz: Kyrillos von Scythopolis', BZ 40 (1940) 474-484.

Draguet, R. 'Réminiscences de Pallade chez Cyrille de Scythopolis', *Revue d'Ascétique et de Mystique* 98-100 (1948) 213-18.

Festugière, A.-J. *Les Moines d'Orient*. Vols 3/1-3. Paris, 1961-4.

Flusin, B. *Miracle et Histoire dans l'Oeuvre de Cyrille de Scythopolis*. Paris, 1983.

Garitte, G. 'La mort de S. Jean l'Hesychaste d'après un text géorgien inédit', An Boll 72 (1954) 75-84.

———. 'La version géorgienne de la Vie de S. Cyriaque par Cyrille de Scythopolis', *Museon* 75 (1962) 399-440.

———. 'La Vie géorgienne de saint Cyriaque et son modêle arabe', *Bedi-Kartlissa* 28 (1971) 92-105.

———. 'Reminiscences de la Vie d'Antoine dans Cyrille de Scythopolis', *Silloge Bizantina in onore di Silvio Giuseppe Mercati*. Rome, 1957: 117-122.

Genier, R.P. *La Vie de Saint Euthyme le Grand*. Paris, 1909.

Graf, G. 'Die arabische Vita des heiligen Abramios' BZ 14 (1905) 509-18.

Hermann, T. 'Zur Chronologie des Kyrill von Skythopolis', *Zeitung des Kirchengeschichtes* (1926) 318-339.

Peeters, P. 'Historia S. Abramii ex apographo arabico', An Boll 24 (1905) 349-356.

Stein, E. 'Cyrille de Scythopolis à propos de la nouvelle édition de ses oeuvres', An Boll 62 (1944) 169-186.

Thomsen, P. 'Kyrillos von Skythopolis', *Orientalische Literaturzeitung* 43 (1940) 457-463.

3. Secondary Works

Abel, F-M. *Géographie de la Palestine*. Paris, 1938.

———. *Histoire de la Palestine*. Paris, 1952.

Avi-Yonah, M. 'Development of the Roman Road System in Palestine', IEJ 1 (1950-1) 54-60.

———. 'The Economics of Byzantine Palestine', IEJ 8 (1958) 39-51.

———. (ed) *Encyclopedia of Archeological Excavations in the Holy Land*. London 1975-8.

————. *The Madaba Mosaic Map*. Jerusalem 1954.

————. 'Scythopolis', IEJ 12 (1962) 123-134.

Bacht, H. 'Die Rolle des orientalischen Mönchtums in der Kirchenpolitischen Auseinandersetzungen um Chalkedon (432-519), in Grillmeier/Bacht, *Das Konzil von Chalkedon*, vol. 2. Würzburg, 1953: 193-314.

Bartelink, G.J.M. 'Quelques observations sur parrêsia dans la littérature paléo-chrétienne', *Graecitas et Latinitas Christianorum Primaeva, Suppl. 3. Nijmegen 1970*.

Beauvery, R. 'La route romaine de Jérusalem Jericho', *RB* 64 (1957) 72-101.

Brown, P.R.L. *The Cult of the Saints*. Chicago 1981.

————. 'The Rise and Function of the Holy Man in Late Antiquity', JRS 61 (1971) 80-101.

————. *The World of Late Antiquity*. London 1971.

Cameron, Averil *Procopius and the Sixth Century*. London 1985.

Canivet, P. *Le Monachisme syrien selon Théodoret de Cyr*. Paris 1977.

Charanis, P. *Church and State in the Later Roman Empire, 2nd edn, Thessaloniki 1974*.

Chitty, D.J. *The Desert A City*. London and Oxford 1966.

————. 'The Monastery of St. Euthymius', *PEFQSt* (1932) 188-203.

————. 'Two monasteries in the wilderness of Judaea', *PEFQSt* (1928) 134-152.

Chitty, D.J. and Jones, A.H.M. 'The Church of St Euthymius at Khan el-Amar near Jerusalem', *PEFQSt* (1928) 175-178.

Corbo, V. 'L'ambiente materiale della Vita dei Monaci di Palestina nel periodo Bizantino', *Orientalia Christiana Analecta* 153 (1958) 235-257.

Corbo, V. *Gli Scavi di Kh. Siyar El-Ghanam (Campo die Pastori) e i Monasteri dei Dintorni*. Jerusalem 1955.

Couret, A. *La Palestine sous les Empereurs Grecs 326-636*, Grenoble 1869.

Diekamp, F. *Die origenistischen Streitigkeiten im sechsten Jahrundert*. Münster 1899.

Evans, D.B. *Leontius of Byzantium*. Washington 1970.

Festugière, A-J. 'La vie de Sabas et les tours de Syrie-Palestine', *RB* 70 (1963) 82-92.

————. 'Lieux communs littéraires et thèmes du folk-lore dans l'hagiographie primitive', *Wiener Studien* 73 (1960) 123-152.

Fitzgerald, G.M. *Beth-Shan Excavations of 1921-1923: The Arab and Byzantine Levels*. Philadelphia, 1931.

————. *A Sixth-Century Monastery in Beth-Shan (Scythopolis)*. Philadelphia, 1939.

'Frend, W.H.C. *The Rise of the Monophysite Movement*. Cambridge, 1972.

Gray, P.T.R. *The Defense of Chalcedon in the East* (451-553). Leiden, 1979.

Grégoire, H. 'La vie anonyme de S. Gerasime', BZ 13 (1904) 114-135.

Grillmeier, A. *Christ in Christian Tradition*, vol. 2/1. London, 1987.

Guillaumont, A. *Aux Origines du monachisme chrétien*. Begrolle-en-Mauges, 1979.

————. *Les 'Kephalaia Gnostica' d'Evagre le Pontique et l'Histoire de l'Origenisme chez les Grecs et chez les Syriens*. Paris 1962.

Heydock, G. *Der heilige Sabas und seine Reliquien*. Geisenheim 1970.

Holl, K. *Enthusiasmus und Bußgewalt beim griechischen Mönchtum*, 2nd edn. Hildesheim 1969.

Honigmann, E. 'Juvenal of Jerusalem', *Dumbarton Oaks Papers* 5 (1950) 211-279.

Hunt, E.D. *Holy Land Pilgrimage in the Later Roman Empire. AD 312-460*. Oxford, 1984.

Israel Exploration Society, 17th Annual Convention, 'The Valley of Beth-Shar', IEJ 11 (1961) 198-201.

Jones, A.H.M. *The Later Roman Empire*. Oxford, 1964.

————. 'Were ancient heresies national or social movements in disguise?' *Journal of Theological Studies* N.S. 10 (1959) 260-298.

Kelly, J.N.D. *Jerome: His Life, Writings, and Controversies*. London, 1975.

Kurtz, E. 'Tupos kai paradosis tes sebasmias lauras tou hagiou Sabba', *BZ* 3 (1894) 167-170.

Lifshitz, B. 'Scythopolis. L'histoire, les instsitutions et les cultes de la ville a l'époque hellénistique et impériale', *Aufstieg und Niedergang der römischen Welt* II.8. Berlin/New York, 1977: 262-294.

Marcoff, M. and Chitty, D.J. 'Notes on monastic research in the Judaean wilderness, 1928-9', *PEFQSt* (1929) 167-178.

Meinardus, O. 'Notes on the Laurae and Monasteries of the Wilderness of Judaea', *Liber Annuus* 15 (1964-5) 220-250; 16 (1965-6) 328-356; 19 (1969) 305-327.

Milik, J.T. 'The monastery of Kastellion', *RB* 42 (1961) 21-27.

————. 'La topographie de Jérusalem vers la fin de l'époque Byzantine', *Melanges de l'Université Saint-Joseph* 37 (1960-1961) 127-189.

Moeller, C. 'Le chalcédonisme et le néo-chalcedonisme en Orient de 451 à la fin du VIe siècle', *Das Konzil von Chalkedon*, Vol I (Würzburg 1951) 637-720.

Moule, C.F.D. *Miracles*. London 1965.

Murphy-O'Connor, J. *The Holy Land*. Oxford-New York, 1980.

Nau, F. 'Deux épisodes de l'histoire juive sous Théodose II', *Revue des Études Juives* 83-4 (1927) 184-206.

Ovadiah, A. *A Corpus of the Byzantine Churches in the Holy Land*, Bonn 1970.

Patlagean, E. 'Ancienne hagiographie byzantine et histoire sociale', *Annales ESC* 1 (1968) 106-126.

———. 'L'histoire de la femme deguisée en moine et l'évolution de la sainteté feminine à Byzance', *Studi Medievali* 17 (1976) 597-623.

———. *Pauvreté economique et pauvreté sociale à Byzance, 4e-7e siécles*. Paris, 1977.

Perrone, L. *La Chiesa di Palestina e le Controversie Christologiche*. Brescia 1980.

Rousseau, P. *Ascetics, Authority and the Church in the Age of Jerome and Cassian*. Oxford 1978.

Rowe, A. *Beth-Shan, Topography and History*. Philadelphia 1930.

Schneider, A.M. 'Das Kloster der Thotokos zu Choziba im Wadi el Kelt', *Romische Quartalshrift* 39 (1931) 297-332.

Sellers, R.V. The Council of Chalcedon, London 1953.

Stein, E. *Histoire du Bas-Empire*, tr. J-R Palanque, 2 vols. Bruges, 1959 and 1949.

Vailhé, S. 'Les écrivains de Mar-Saba', *Echos d'Orient* 2 (1899) 1-11, 33-47.

———. 'Repertoire Alphabétique des Monastéres de Palestine', *ROC* Ie série 4 (1899) 512-542; 5 (1900) 19-48, 272-292.

Van den Gheyn, J. 'St Theognius, Evêque de Bételie en Palestine', *Revue des Questions Historiques* 50 (1891) 559-576.

Ward, B. *Lives of the Desert Fathers (Introduction)*, CS 34 (1980).

Wright, G.E.H. 'The archeological remains of El-Mird', *RB* 42 (1961) 1-21.

INDICES

References are made to the page and line of Schwartz's Greek text. Because of differences between the construction of the sentences in English and in Greek, there may be minor variations in the position of the reference in the English version. If an item occurs more than once in the same chapter, reference is made only to the first occurrence.

1. Index of Persons

Stephen (bishop of Jamnia) 26,9;
32,12; 41,10; 49,20; 52,27.
Stephen (bishop of Tripoli) 68,19.
Stephen (superior of Euthymius'
monastery) 68,7; 68,31; 161,6.
Stephen (superior of Gerasimus'
monastery) 225,21.
Stephen of Jerusalem (monk of
Great Laura) 189,18; 191,13.
Stephen (count in Palestine)
177,7.
Summus 168,11; 175,17; 178,5;
187,29.
Symeon the Stylite 47,23.
Symeonius of Apamea (superior of
Euthymius' monastery) 68,5.
Synodius (bishop of Melitene)
11,15; 26,8; 32,7.

Tarachus (martyr) 66,14.
Tarasius (superior of Gadara)
120,10.
Terebôn 18,12; 35,26; 45,9; 52,19;
226,9.
Terebôn the Younger 18,15.
Thalabas (Saracen) 75,13.
Thalassius (monk of Euthymius'
monastery) 26,11.
Thallelaeus (priest of Great Laura)
39,18; ;56,20.
Thecla (mother of Abraamius)
243,23.
Theoctistus 14,21; 15,10; 19,14;
21,25; 23,21; 38,4; 48,15;
50,7; 54,12; 56,20; 56,22;
91,11; 91,29; 92,19; 93,13;
114,15; 224,25; 226,3.
Theodora (empress) 173,3; 173,27.
Theodore (martyr) 185,8.
Theodore (bishop of Mopsuestia)
176,8; 179,9; 194,19; 199,3;
221,20.

Theodore Ascidas (bishop of
Caesarea Cappadocia) 188,26;
191,23; 192,22; 194,29; 197,19;
198,8.
Theodore (administrator of Cas-
tellium) 112,21; 136,23.
Theodore (architect) 177,16.
Theodore (bishop of Petra) 239,17.
Theodore (general) 172,15.
Theodore (monk; disciple of John
the Hesychast) 215,8; 215,24;
219,3; 220,10.
Theodore (secretary) 203,8.
Theodore (superior of New Laura)
197,22.
Theodosius (Patriarch of Jerusalem)
41,22; 47,5; 63,1.
Theodosius (bishop of Scythopolis)
162,27; 180,3.
Theodosius (archimandrite) 16,14;
97,5; 114,2; 128,16; 132,1;
151,21; 152,18; 165,19; 166,6;
171,16; 171,29; 242,7.
Theodosius I (emperor) 11,3; 60,10.
Theodosius II (emperor) 87,9;
223,5.
Theodotus (monk of Euthymius'
monastery) 69,16.
Theodulus (Bessan) 194,5.
Theodulus (monk of Great Laura)
117,2; 126,16; 135,18; 189,12.
Thomas of Apamea (superior of
Euthymius' monastery) 69,2;
70,12; 225,27.
Thomas 136,21.
Timothy Aelurus (Patriarch of
Alexandria) 50,21.
Timothy (Patriarch of Constan-
tinople) 141,1; 158,3.
Timothy of Gabala (monk of Great
Laura) 189,18.
Tribonian 178,10.

2. Index of Places

Nitria 50,26.

Olives (Mount of Olives) 145,9;
  195,23; 241,20.
  Monastery of Melania 67,16;
    239,16.
Orthosias 68,30.

Panias 108,15.
Parthenian Sea 63,6.
Pella 176,27.
Pelusium (Egypt) 127,3.
Persia 18,20; 211,16.
Peter (Eudocia's Church of Saint
  Peter) 53,9.
Petra 229,17.
Pharan 79,25.
  Laura of Pharan 14,9; 15,10;
    16,8; 16,26; 26,17; 65,22;
    79,24.
Photinus (monastery) 16,4; 114,4.
Pontus 245,17.

Raithou 26,10.
Ramathaim 87,4.
Romanus' monastery—see Thekoa.
Rome 36,13; 47,15; 124,13;
  175,21; 178,25.
Roubâ 21,25; 44,28; 45,6; 48,14;
  51,10; 56,26; 94,20; 95,12;
  96,17; 97,3; 138,19; 139,2;
  209,10; 210,5; 211,24; 212,19;
  222,7; 228,18; 235,4; Life of
  Abraamius 8.

Samaria 154,4; 163, 6; 172,3;
  174,14; 176,27; 181,20.
Scandus (Cappadocia) 87,18.
Scetis 114,12; 189,19.
Scythopolis 26,4; 55,21; 71,20;
  118,30; 119,16; 162,20; 165,1;
  172,19; 180,2; 196,9; 197,23;

209,7; 216,10; 231,16.
Basil (Church of Saint Basil)
  26,13.
Beella (monastery) 5,3; 86,19.
Enthemenaith 163,14; 164,12.
John (Church of Saint John)
  163,14.
Procopius (Monastery of Saint
  Procopius) 180,8.
Thomas (Church of Saint
  Thomas) 162,28; 180,16.
Zougga (monastery) 196,14.
Sebaste 127,11.
Sebasteia (Armenia) 202,18; 240,4.
Sheshan 160,4.
Sidon 141,18; 143,22; 148,10; 150,2.
Souka (laura) 29,27; 123,1; 196,13;
  226,19; 228,27, 229,15; 231,5;
  234,17; 234,25.
Sousakim 228,26; 232,1; 234,25.
Spring (laura) 198,28.
Syria 25,19; 139,1; 243,24.

Thekoa 199,26; 227,19; 228,10.
  Romanus' cenobium 49,12,
    67,17; 123,6.
Theoctistus' cenobium 24;7; 25,13;
  55,7; 91,11; 159,2.
Theodosius' cenobium 97,21; 114,7;
  134,8; 190,13; 237,24; 240,8.

Theognius' cenobium 242,21;
  243,16.
Thrace 9,24.
Tiberias 26,12; 108,13.
Tomessus (Cilicia) 72,10.

Tower (laura) 48,8; 97,24; 127,15;
  158,24; 167,17; 245,7; 245,25;
  246,9; Life of Abraamius 7.
Tripoli 68,18.

THE CITIES OF PALESTINE

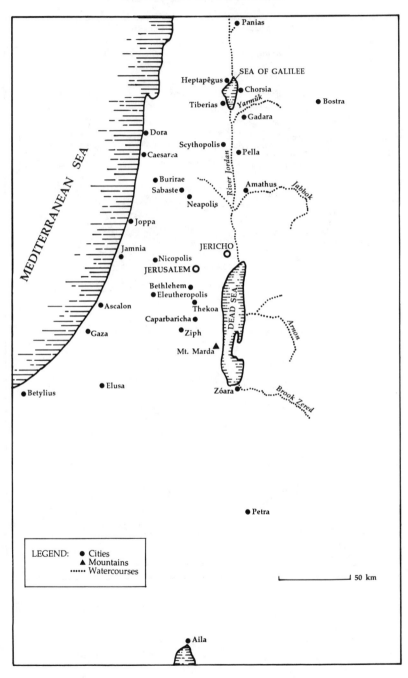

THE MONASTERIES OF THE JUDEAN DESERT

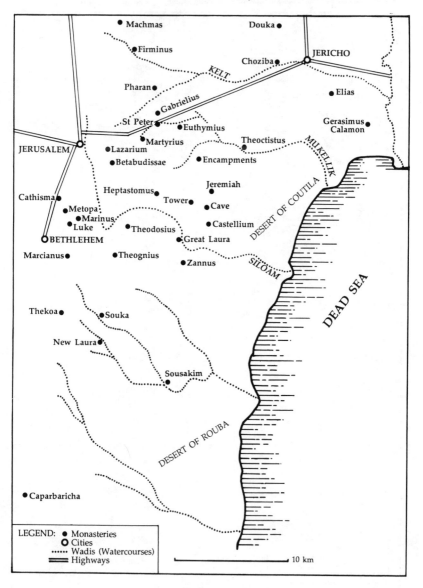

CISTERCIAN PUBLICATIONS INC.
Kalamazoo, Michigan

TITLES LISTING

CISTERCIAN TEXTS

THE WORKS OF BERNARD OF CLAIRVAUX

Apologia to Abbot William
Five Books on Consideration: Advice to a
  Pope
Grace and Free Choice
Homilies in Praise of the Blessed Virgin
  Mary
The Life and Death of Saint Malachy the
  Irishman
Parables
Sermons on the Song of Songs I-IV
Steps of Humility and Pride

THE WORKS OF WILLIAM OF SAINT THIERRY

The Enigma of Faith
Exposition on the Epistle to the Romans
The Golden Epistle
The Mirror of Faith
The Nature and Dignity of Love

THE WORKS OF AELRED OF RIEVAULX

Dialogue on the Soul
The Mirror of Charity
Spiritual Friendship
Treatises I: On Jesus at the Age of Twelve,
  Rule for a Recluse, The Pastoral Prayer

THE WORKS OF JOHN OF FORD

Sermons on the Final Verses of the Song of
Songs I-VII

THE WORKS OF GILBERT OF HOYLAND

Sermons on the Songs of Songs I, II, III
Treatises, Sermons and Epistles

OTHER EARLY CISTERCIAN WRITERS

The Letters of Adam of Perseigne I
Baldwin of Ford: Spiritual Tractates
Guerric of Igny: Liturgical Sermons I-II
Idung of Prüfening: Cistercians and Cluniacs:
  The Case for Cîteaux
Isaac of Stella: Sermons on the Christian Year
Serlo of Wilton & Serlo of Savigny
Stephen of Lexington: Letters from Ireland
Stephen of Sawley: Treatises

MONASTIC TEXTS

EASTERN CHRISTIAN TRADITION

Besa: The Life of Shenoute
Cyril of Scythopolis: Lives of the Monks of
  Palestine
Dorotheos of Gaza: Discourses
Evagrius Ponticus: Praktikos and Chapters
  on Prayer
The Harlots of the Desert
Iosif Volotsky: Monastic Rule
The Lives of the Desert Fathers
Menas of Nikiou: Isaac of Alexandra & St
  Macrobius
Pachomian Koinonia I-III
The Sayings of the Desert Fathers
Spiritual Direction in the Early Christian East
  (I. Hausherr)
The Syriac Fathers on Prayer and the Spiritual
  Life

WESTERN CHRISTIAN TRADITION

Anselm of Canterbury: Letters I-[II]
Bede: Commentary on the even Catholic
  Epistles
Bede: Commentary on Acts
Bede: Gospel Homilies
Gregory the Great: Forty Gospel Homilies
Guigo II the Carthusian: Ladder of Monks
  and Twelve Meditations
Peter of Celle: Selected Works
The Letters of Armand-Jean de Rance I-II
The Rule of the Master

CHRISTIAN SPIRITUALITY

Abba: Guides to Wholeness and Holiness
  East and West
Athirst for God: Spiritual Desire in Bernard
  of Clairvaux's Sermons on the Song of Songs
  (M. Casey)
Cistercian Way (A. Louf)
Fathers Talking (A. Squire)
Friendship and Community (B. McGuire)
From Cloister to Classroom
Herald of Unity: The Life of Maria Gabrielle
  Sagheddu (M. Driscoll)
Life of St Mary Magdalene... (D. Mycoff)
Rancé and the Trappist Legacy (A.J.
  Krailsheimer)
Roots of the Modern Christian Tradition
Russian Mystics (S. Bolshakoff)
Spirituality of Western Christendom
Spirituality of the Christian East
  (T. Spidlék)

MONASTIC STUDIES

Community and Abbot in the Rule of St
  Benedict I-II (Adalbert De Vogüé)
Consider Your Call: A Theology of the
  Monastic Life (Daniel Rees et al.)
The Finances of the Cistercian Order in the
  Fourteenth Century (Peter King)

Fountains Abbey and Its Benefactors
(Joan Wardrop)
The Hermit Monks of Grandmont
(Carole A. Hutchison)
In the Unity of the Holy Spirit
(Sighard Kleiner)
Monastic Practices (Charles Cummings)
The Occupation of Celtic Sites in Ireland by
the Canons Regular of St Augustine and the
Cistercians (Geraldine Carville)
The Rule of St Benedict: A Doctrinal and
Spiritual Commentary (Adalbert de Vogüé)
The Rule of St Benedict (Br. Pinocchio)
St Hugh of Lincoln (D. H. Farmer)
Serving God First (Sighard Kleiner)

CISTERCIAN STUDIES

A Second Look at Saint Bernard (Jean Leclercq)
Bernard of Clairvaux and the Cistercian
Spirit (Jean Leclercq)
Bernard of Clairvaux: Studies Presented to
Dom Jean Leclercq
Christ the Way: The Christology of Guerric
of Igny (John Morson)
Cistercian Sign Language
The Cistercian Spirit
The Cistercians in Denmark (Brian McGuire)
Eleventh-century Background of Citeaux
(Bede K. Lackner)
The Golden Chain: Theological Anthropology of
Isaac of Stella (Bernard McGinn)
Image and Likeness: The Augustinian
Spirituality of William of St Thierry (David
N. Bell)
The Mystical Theology of St Bernard
(Étienne Gilson)
Nicholas Cotheret's Annals of Citeaux
(Louis J. Lekai)
William, Abbot of St Thierry
Women and St Bernard of Clairvaux
(Jean Leclercq)

MEDIEVAL RELIGIOUS WOMEN

Distant Echoes (Shank-Nichols)
Gertrud the Great of Helfta: Spiritual Exercises
(Gertrud J. Lewis-Jack Lewis)
Peace Weavers (Nichols-Shank)

STUDIES IN CISTERCIAN ART AND ARCHITECTURE
Meredith Parsons Lillich, editor

Studies I, II, III now available
Studies IV scheduled for 1991

THOMAS MERTON

The Climate of Monastic Prayer (T. Merton)
The Legacy of Thomas Merton (Patrick Hart)
The Message of Thomas Merton (Patrick Hart)
Solitude in the Writings of Thomas Merton
(Richard Cashen)
Thomas Merton Monk (Patrick Hart)
Thomas Merton Monk and Artist
(Victor Kramer)
Thomas Merton on St Bernard
Toward an Integrated Humanity
(M.Basil Pennington et al.)

CISTERCIAN LITURGICAL DOCUMENTS SERIES
Chrysogonus Waddell, ocso, editor

Cistercian Hymnal: Text & Commentary
(2 volumes)
Hymn Collection of the Abbey of the Paraclete
Molesme Summer-Season Breviary
(4 volumes)
Institutiones nostrae: The Paraclete Statutes
Old French Ordinary and Breviary of the
Abbey of the Paraclete: Text and
Commentary (5 volumes)

STUDIA PATRISTICA

*Papers of the 1983 Oxford Patristics Conference
Edited by Elizabeth A. Livingstone*

XVIII/1 Historica-Gnostica-Biblica
XVIII/2 Critica-Classica-Ascetica-Liturgica
XVIII/3 Second Century-Clement & Origen-
Cappodician Fathers
XVIII/4 *available from Peeters, Leuven*

TEXTS AND STUDIES
IN THE
MONASTIC TRADITION

*North American customers may order these books
through booksellers or directly from the warehouse:*

Cistercian Publications
St Joseph's Abbey
Spencer, Massachusetts 01562
(508) 885-7011

*Editorial queries and advance book information
should be directed to the Editorial Offices:*

Cistercian Publications
Institute of Cistercian Studies
Western Michigan University
Kalamazoo, Michigan 49008
(616) 387-5090

*A complete catalogue of texts in translation and
studies on early, medieval, and modern monasticism
is available at no cost from Cistercian Publications.*